D

a crooked line

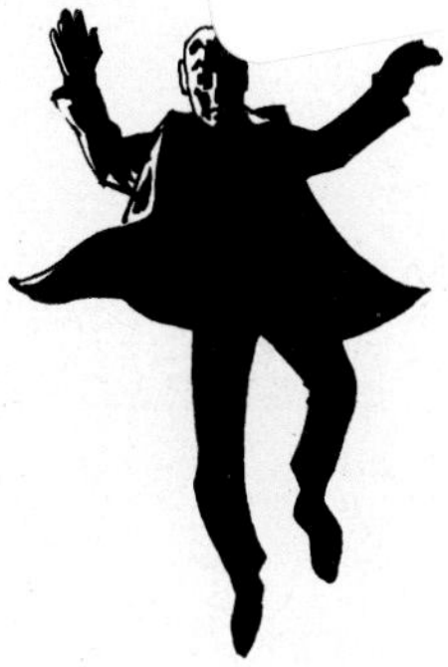

Jim Lee, Editorial Director

John Nee, VP-Business Development

Scott Dunbier, Executive Editor & Editor-Original Series

Alex Sinclair, Editor-Collected Edition

Kristy Quinn, Assistant Editor

Robbin Brosterman, Senior Art Director

Ed Roeder, Art Director

Paul Levitz, President & Publisher

Georg Brewer, VP-Design & Retail Product Development

Richard Bruning, Senior VP-Creative Director

Patrick Caldon, Senior VP-Finance & Operations

Chris Caramalis, VP-Finance

Terri Cunningham, VP-Managing Editor

Alison Gill, VP-Manufacturing

Rich Johnson, VP-Book Trade Sales

Hank Kanalz, VP-General Manager, WildStorm

Lillian Laserson, Senior VP & General Counsel

David McKillips, VP-Advertising & Custom Publishing

Gregory Noveck, Senior VP-Creative Affairs

Cheryl Rubin, VP-Brand Management

Bob Wayne, VP-Sales & Marketing

SLEEPER: A CROOKED LINE, Published by WildStorm Productions. 888 Prospect St. #240, La Jolla, CA 92037. Cover and compilation copyright © 2005 WildStorm Productions, an imprint of DC Comics. All Rights Reserved. Originally published in single magazine form as SLEEPER SEASON 2 #1-6 copyright © 2004, 2005. WildStorm Universe Series, Sleeper, all characters, the distinctive likenesses thereof and all related elements are trademarks of DC Comics. The stories, characters, and incidents mentioned in this magazine are entirely fictional. Printed on recyclable paper. WildStorm does not read or accept unsolicited submissions of ideas, stories or artwork. Printed in Canada.

DC Comics, a Warner Bros. Entertainment Company. ⓦⒷ

Cover illustration & publication design by Sean Phillips

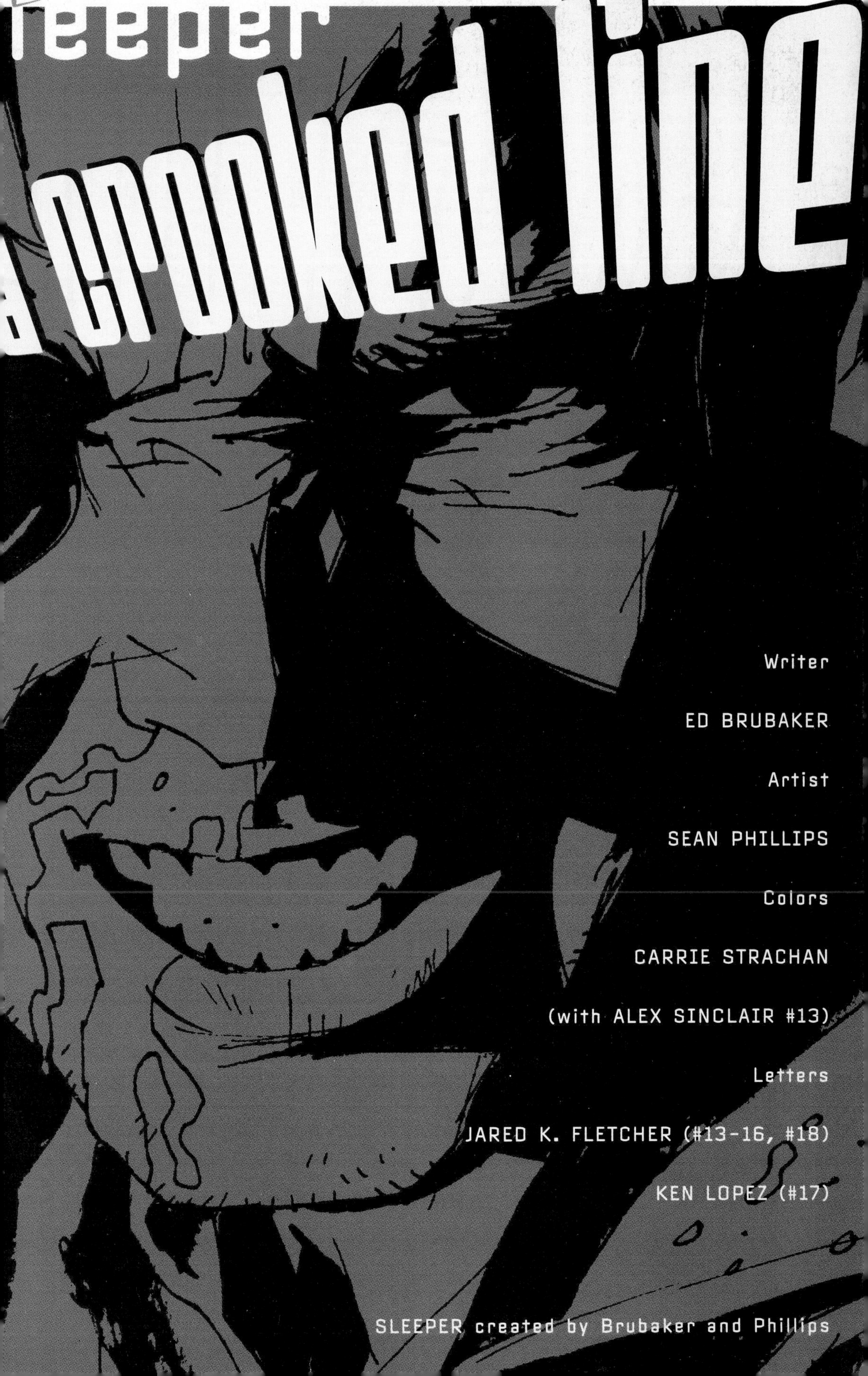

sleeper

a crooked line

Writer

ED BRUBAKER

Artist

SEAN PHILLIPS

Colors

CARRIE STRACHAN

(with ALEX SINCLAIR #13)

Letters

JARED K. FLETCHER (#13-16, #18)

KEN LOPEZ (#17)

SLEEPER created by Brubaker and Phillips

a crooked line

WHAT HAS COME BEFORE

HOLDEN CARVER was once a special agent for the government, a skilled Black Ops leader, and one of the most deadly men alive. But he lost everything the day his squad died while trying to recover a bizarre alien artifact. When Holden awoke, weeks had passed, and the alien artifact had melded with his nervous system. Now he can't feel anything, but his body stores pain that he can pass onto others.

Because of Holden's condition, his boss, JOHN LYNCH, a top government spy-master, decided to force him to become a double agent. He altered the official record so that it appeared Holden had gone rogue and killed his own men on purpose, leaving him no other choice but to do as Lynch wanted.

So Holden was recruited by TAO, a criminal mastermind with the ability to read and manipulate the minds of others. Tao runs a shadowy criminal organization that Holden infiltrated four years ago, slowly working his way up the ladder until he became part of the inner circle.

But then Lynch was shot, and put into what appeared to be an irreversible coma, and Holden was left on his own among the enemy. Because Lynch was the only one who knew Holden was actually undercover. And after a year on his own, Holden had lost his way, he feared he'd become what he pretended to be.

But after the death of his friend GENOCIDE JONES, and the capture and torture of his girlfriend, MISS MISERY, Holden made a desperate run away from both the good and the bad guys, not knowing who to trust anymore. After a few months on the run, though, he was tracked down by Tao and his right hand man, PETER GRIMM. Tao explained to Holden that the differences between good and evil were only a point of view, and that since he'd done so many evil things to keep his cover, why not just come back to the organization?

Left with no other choice than a life on the run, Holden reluctantly agreed.. But what he didn't know was that Lynch was about to awaken from his long slumber, and that his life was about to get even more complicated.

chapter thirteen

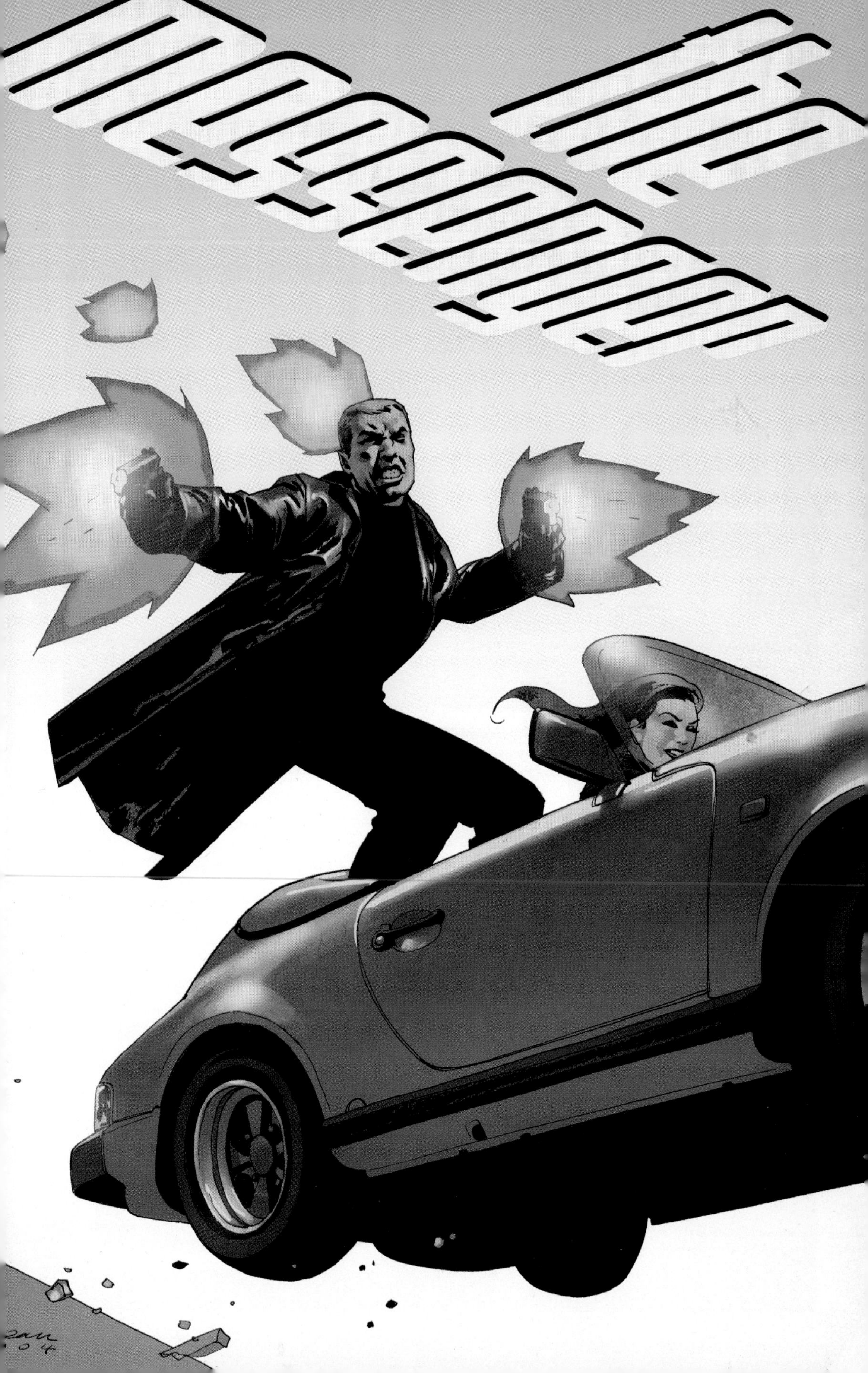

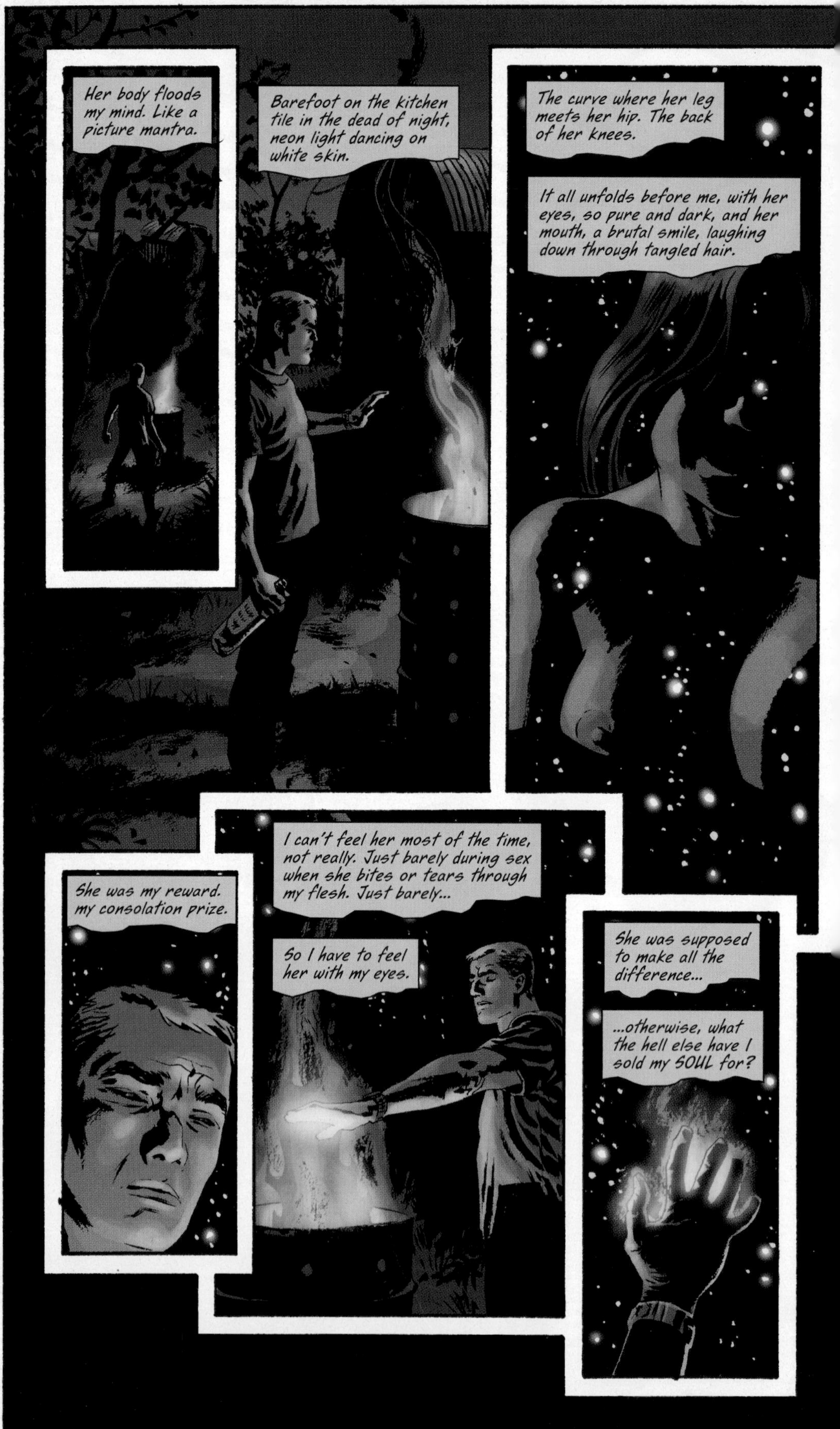
Her body floods my mind. Like a picture mantra.
Barefoot on the kitchen tile in the dead of night, neon light dancing on white skin.
The curve where her leg meets her hip. The back of her knees.
It all unfolds before me, with her eyes, so pure and dark, and her mouth, a brutal smile, laughing down through tangled hair.
She was my reward. my consolation prize.
I can't feel her most of the time, not really. Just barely during sex when she bites or tears through my flesh. Just barely...
So I have to feel her with my eyes.
She was supposed to make all the difference...
...otherwise, what the hell else have I sold my SOUL for?

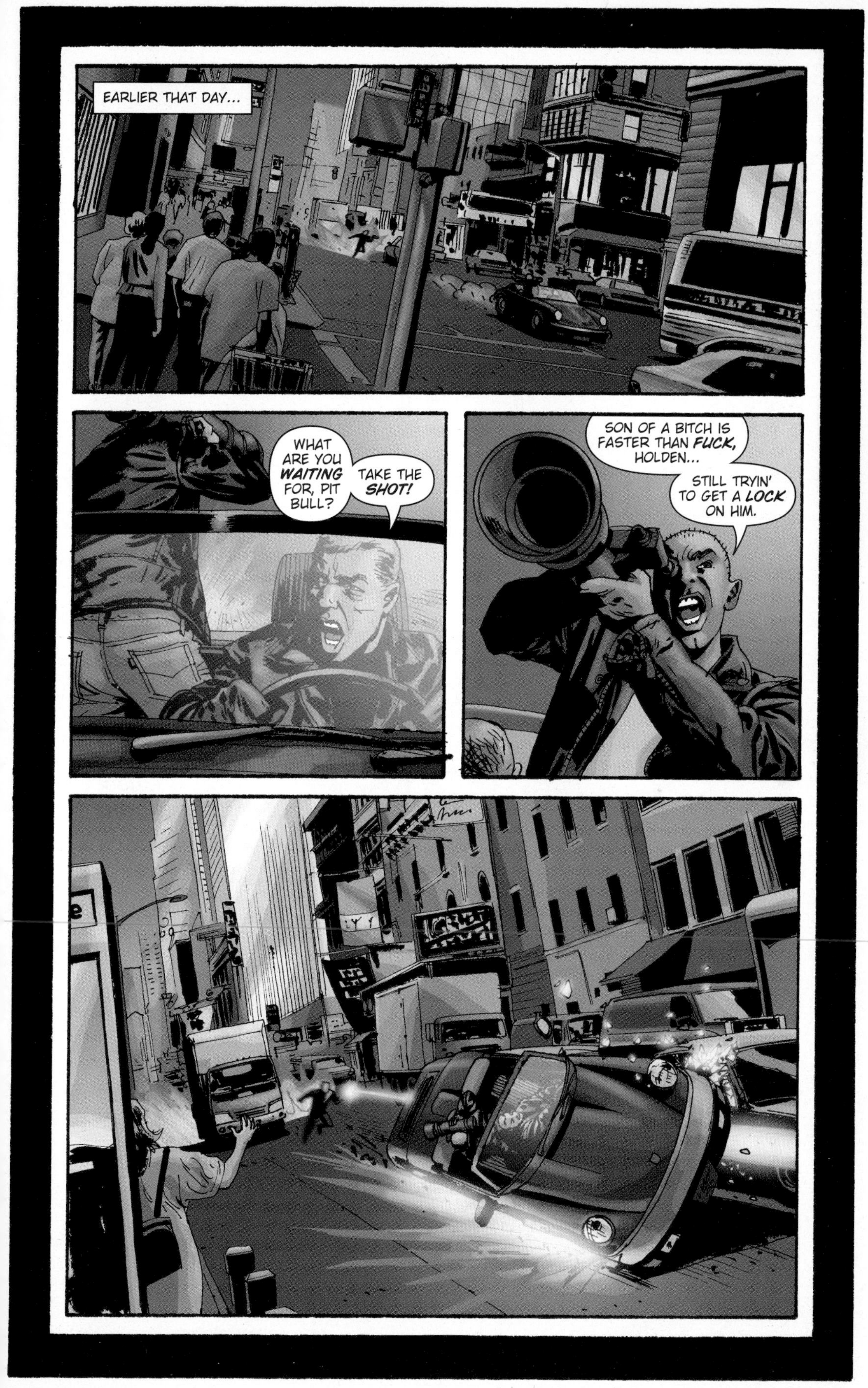
EARLIER THAT DAY...
WHAT ARE YOU WAITING FOR, PIT BULL?
TAKE THE SHOT!
SON OF A BITCH IS FASTER THAN FUCK, HOLDEN...
STILL TRYIN' TO GET A LOCK ON HIM.

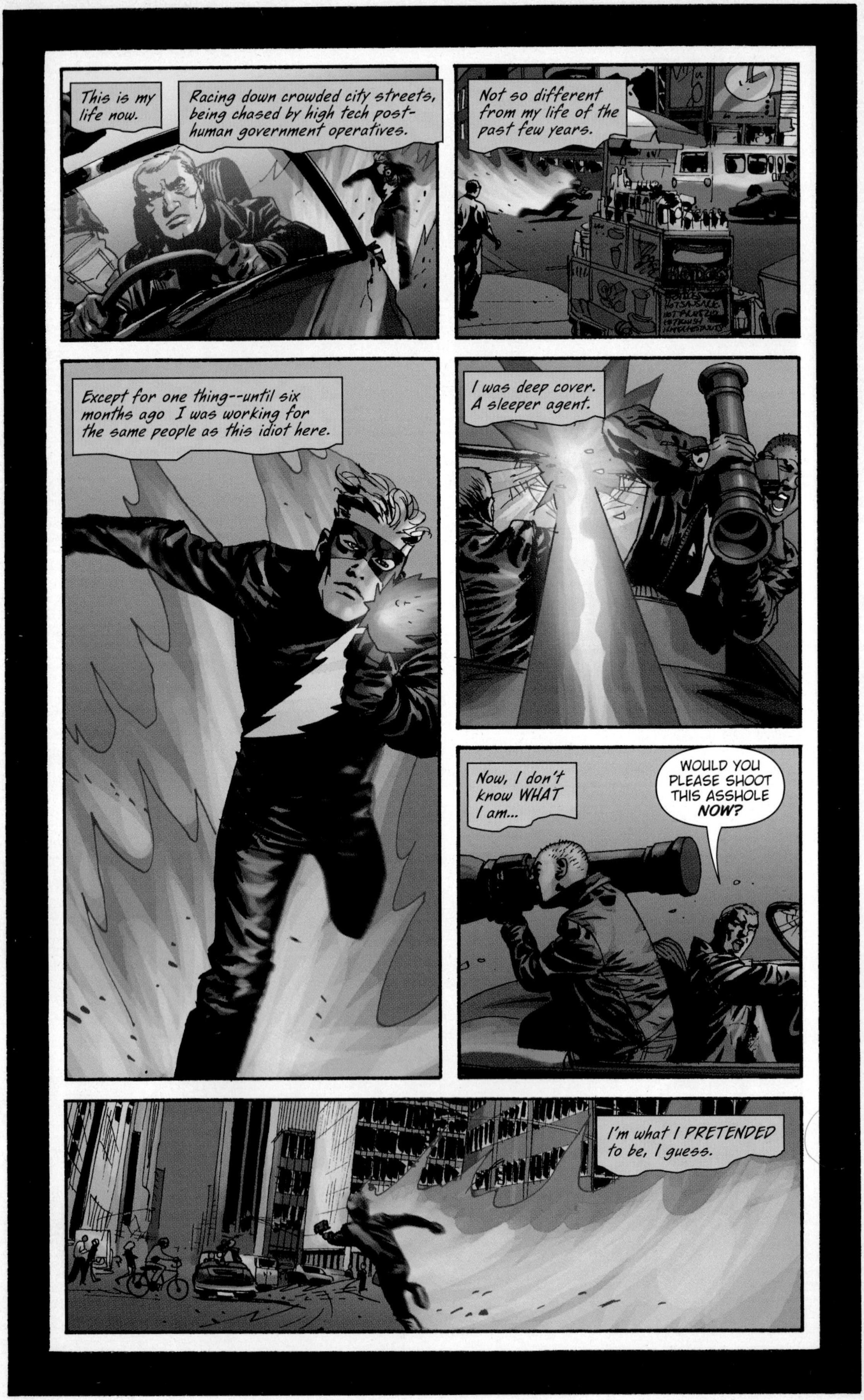

This is my life now.
Racing down crowded city streets, being chased by high tech post-human government operatives.
Not so different from my life of the past few years.
Except for one thing--until six months ago I was working for the same people as this idiot here.
I was deep cover. A sleeper agent.
Now, I don't know WHAT I am...
WOULD YOU PLEASE SHOOT THIS ASSHOLE NOW?
I'm what I PRETENDED to be, I guess.

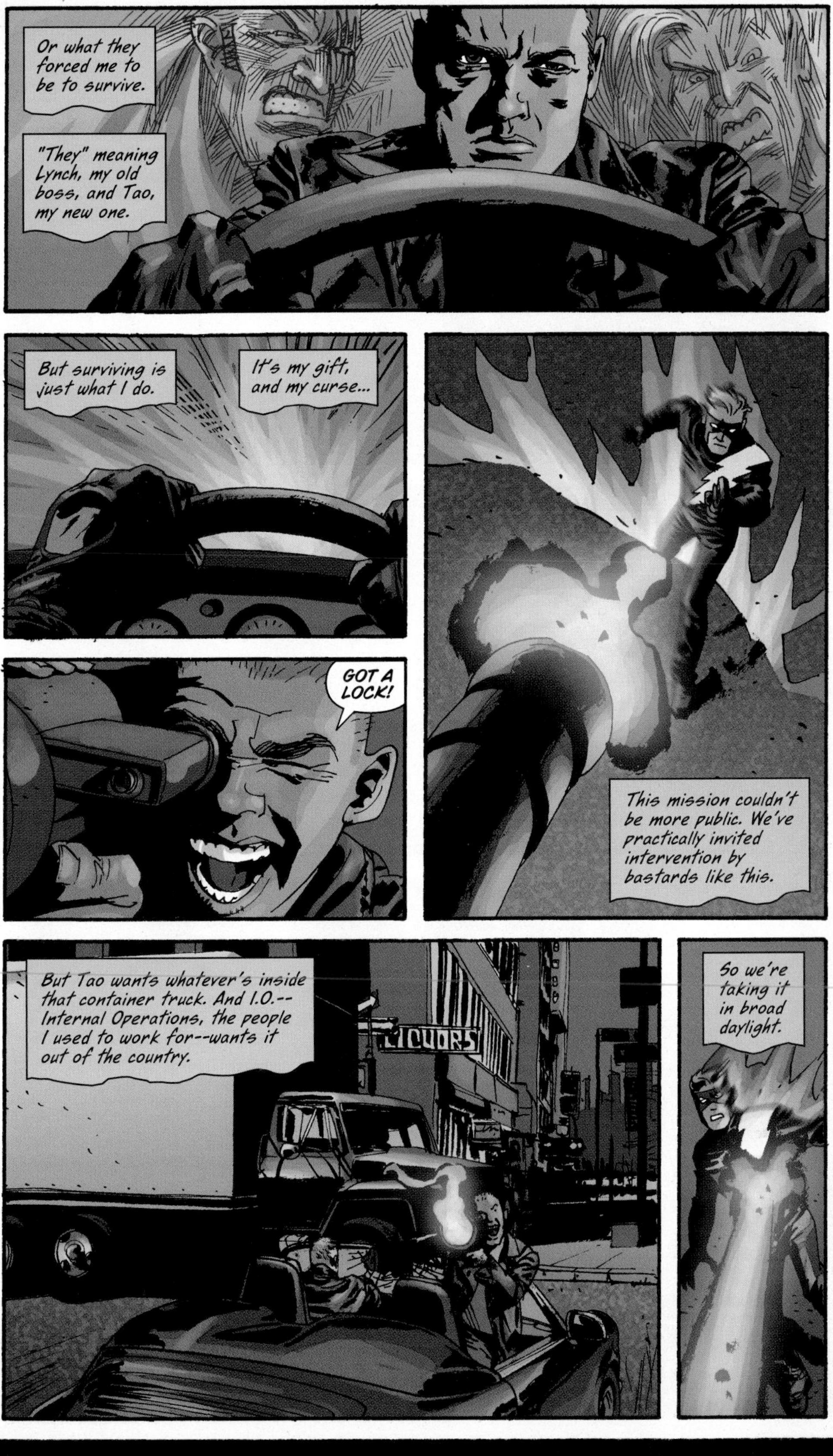
Or what they forced me to be to survive.
"They" meaning Lynch, my old boss, and Tao, my new one.
But surviving is just what I do.
It's my gift, and my curse...
GOT A LOCK!
This mission couldn't be more public. We've practically invited intervention by bastards like this.
But Tao wants whatever's inside that container truck. And I.O.-- Internal Operations, the people I used to work for--wants it out of the country.
LIQUORS
So we're taking it in broad daylight.

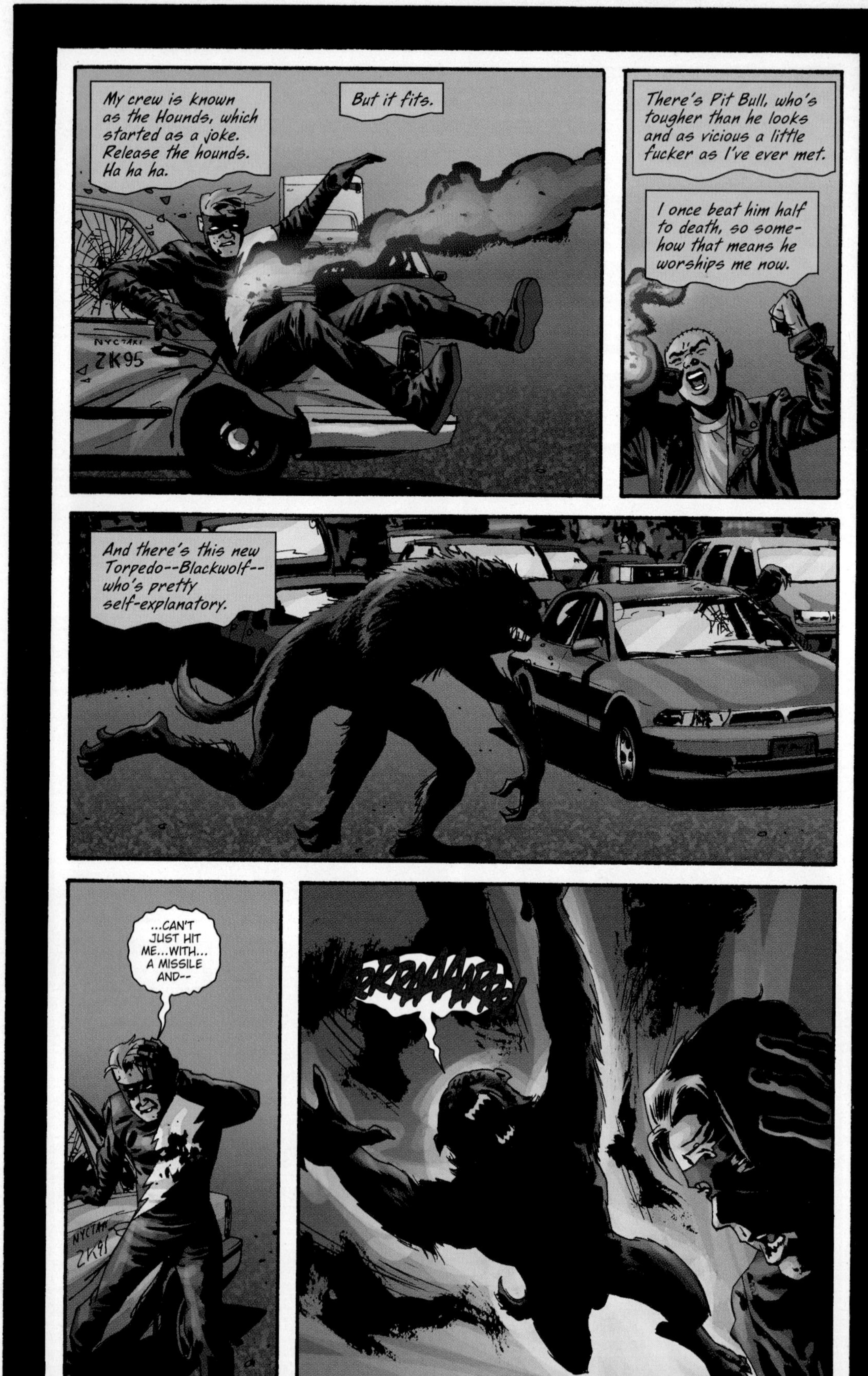

My crew is known as the Hounds, which started as a joke. Release the hounds. Ha ha ha.
But it fits.
NYC TAXI
2K95
There's Pit Bull, who's tougher than he looks and as vicious a little fucker as I've ever met.
I once beat him half to death, so somehow that means he worships me now.
And there's this new Torpedo--Blackwolf--who's pretty self-explanatory.
...CAN'T JUST HIT ME...WITH... A MISSILE AND--

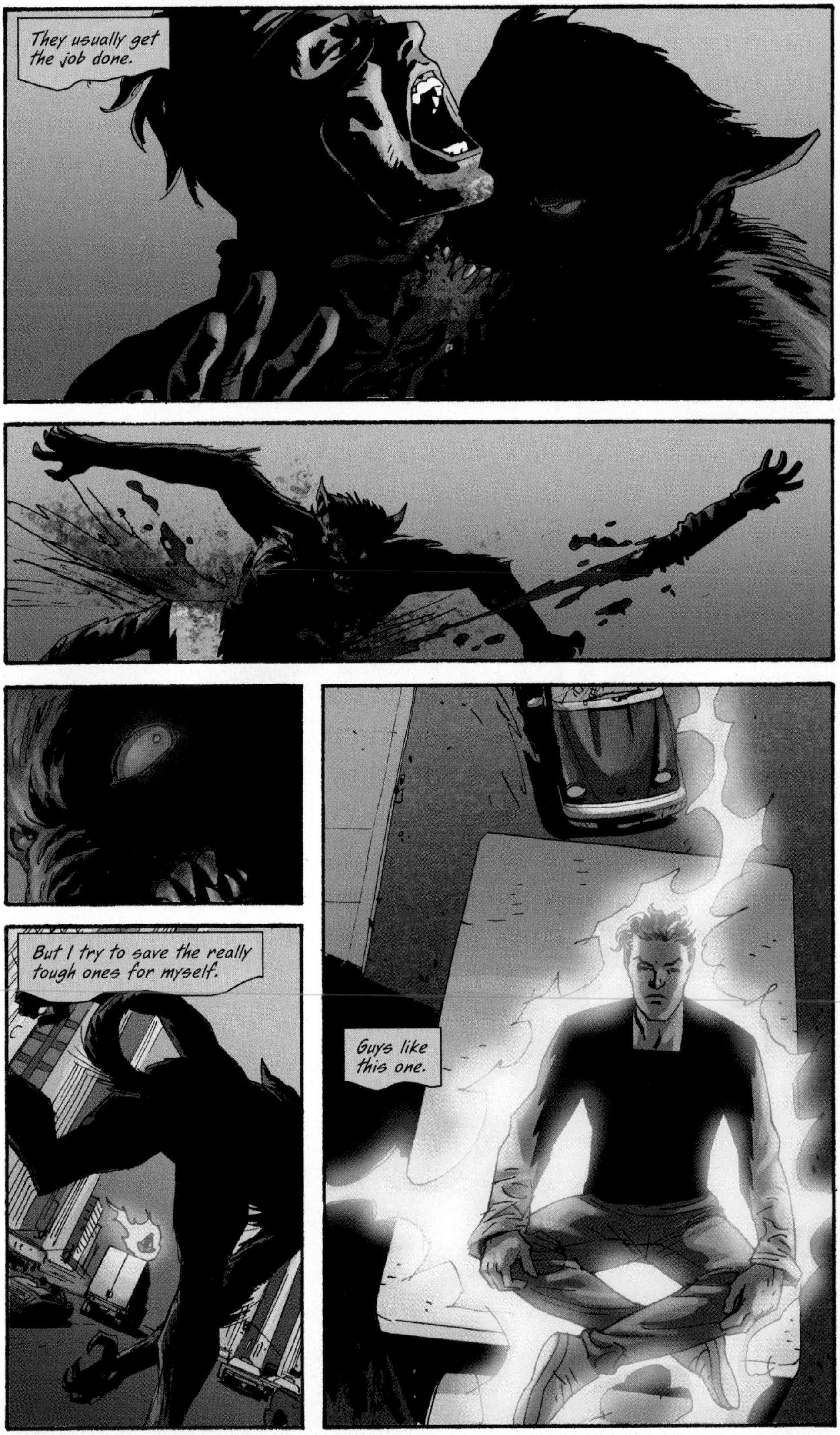
They usually get the job done.
But I try to save the really tough ones for myself.
Guys like this one.

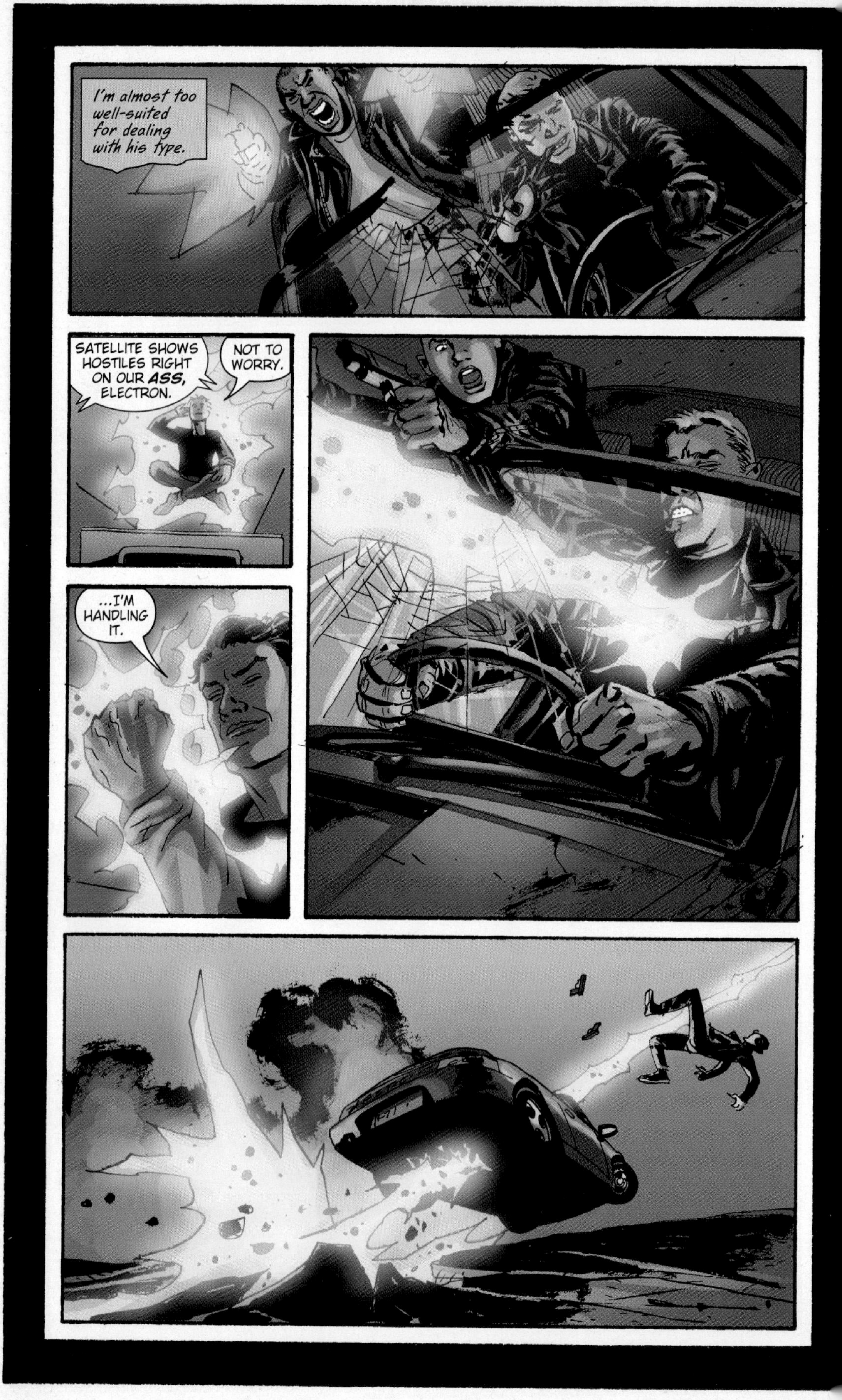
I'm almost too well-suited for dealing with his type.
SATELLITE SHOWS HOSTILES RIGHT ON OUR ASS, ELECTRON.
NOT TO WORRY.
...I'M HANDLING IT.

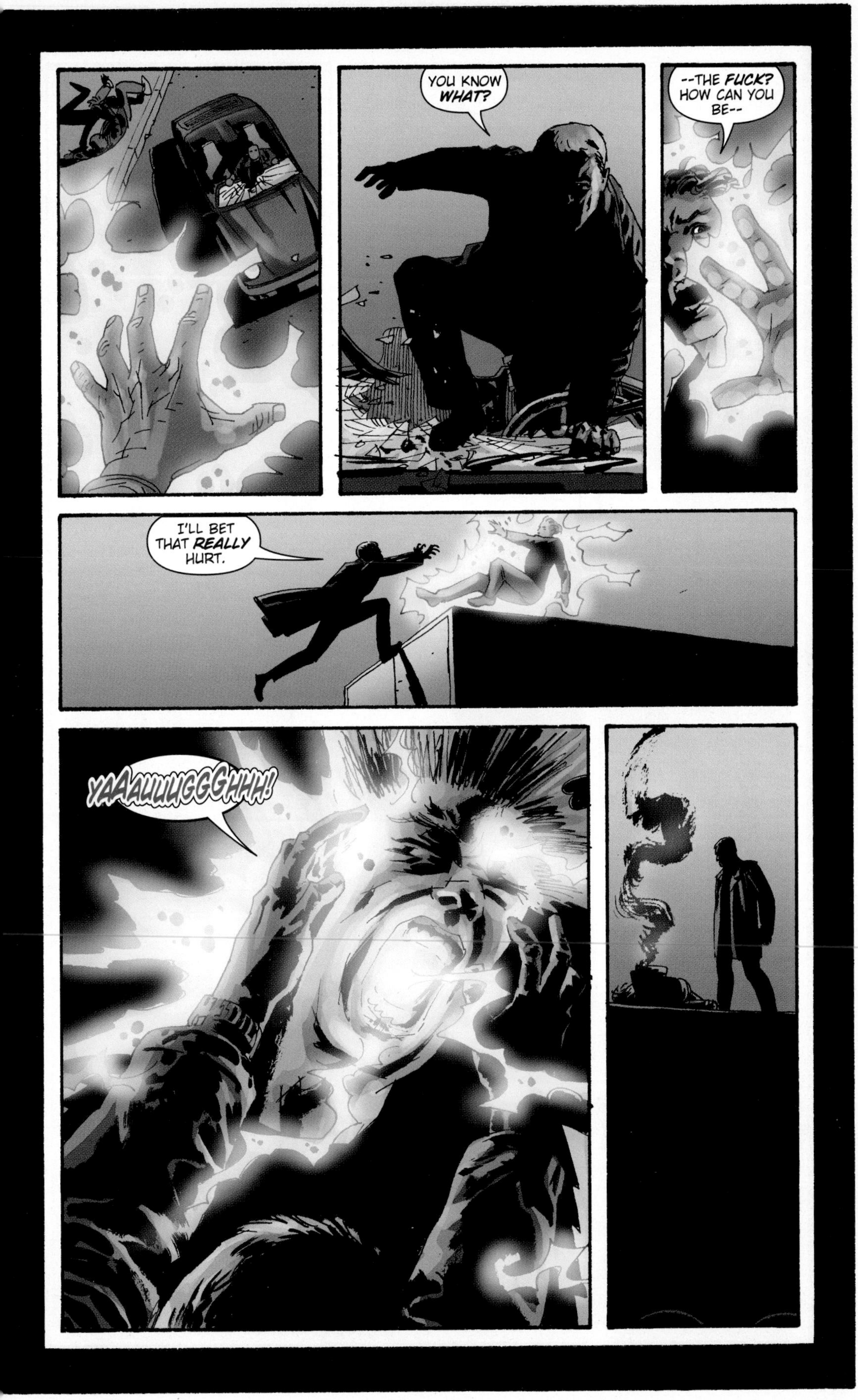
YOU KNOW WHAT?
--THE FUCK? HOW CAN YOU BE--
I'LL BET THAT REALLY HURT.
YAAAUUUUGGGHHH!

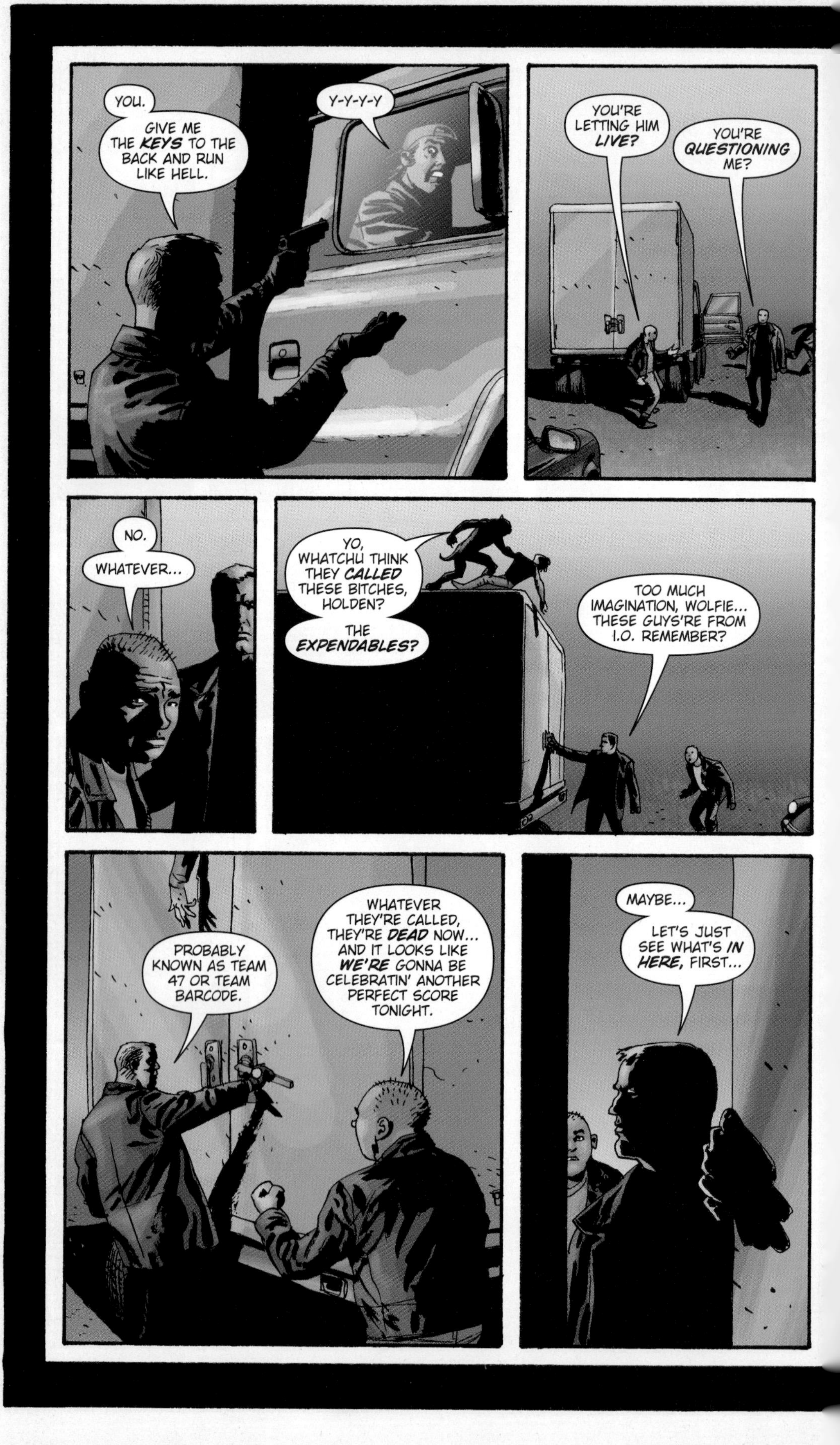
YOU.
GIVE ME THE KEYS TO THE BACK AND RUN LIKE HELL.
Y-Y-Y-Y
YOU'RE LETTING HIM LIVE?
YOU'RE QUESTIONING ME?
NO.
WHATEVER...
YO, WHATCHU THINK THEY CALLED THESE BITCHES, HOLDEN?
THE EXPENDABLES?
TOO MUCH IMAGINATION, WOLFIE... THESE GUYS'RE FROM I.O. REMEMBER?
PROBABLY KNOWN AS TEAM 47 OR TEAM BARCODE.
WHATEVER THEY'RE CALLED, THEY'RE DEAD NOW... AND IT LOOKS LIKE WE'RE GONNA BE CELEBRATIN' ANOTHER PERFECT SCORE TONIGHT.
MAYBE...
LET'S JUST SEE WHAT'S IN HERE, FIRST...

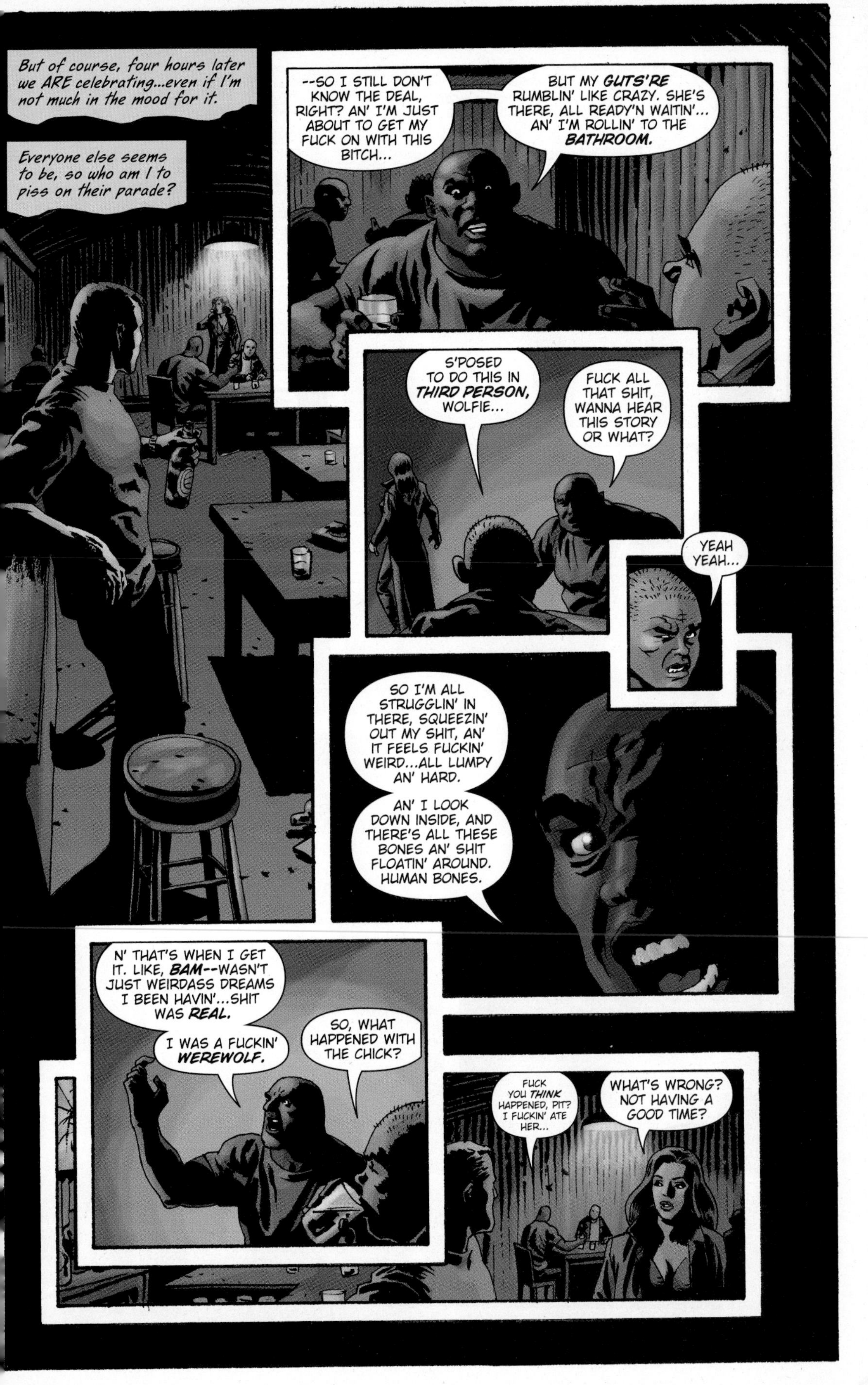

But of course, four hours later we ARE celebrating...even if I'm not much in the mood for it.
Everyone else seems to be, so who am I to piss on their parade?
--SO I STILL DON'T KNOW THE DEAL, RIGHT? AN' I'M JUST ABOUT TO GET MY FUCK ON WITH THIS BITCH...
BUT MY GUTS'RE RUMBLIN' LIKE CRAZY. SHE'S THERE, ALL READY'N WAITIN'... AN' I'M ROLLIN' TO THE BATHROOM.
S'POSED TO DO THIS IN THIRD PERSON, WOLFIE...
FUCK ALL THAT SHIT, WANNA HEAR THIS STORY OR WHAT?
YEAH YEAH...
SO I'M ALL STRUGGLIN' IN THERE, SQUEEZIN' OUT MY SHIT, AN' IT FEELS FUCKIN' WEIRD...ALL LUMPY AN' HARD.
AN' I LOOK DOWN INSIDE, AND THERE'S ALL THESE BONES AN' SHIT FLOATIN' AROUND. HUMAN BONES.
N' THAT'S WHEN I GET IT. LIKE, BAM--WASN'T JUST WEIRDASS DREAMS I BEEN HAVIN'...SHIT WAS REAL.
I WAS A FUCKIN' WEREWOLF.
SO, WHAT HAPPENED WITH THE CHICK?
FUCK YOU THINK HAPPENED, PIT? I FUCKIN' ATE HER...
WHAT'S WRONG? NOT HAVING A GOOD TIME?

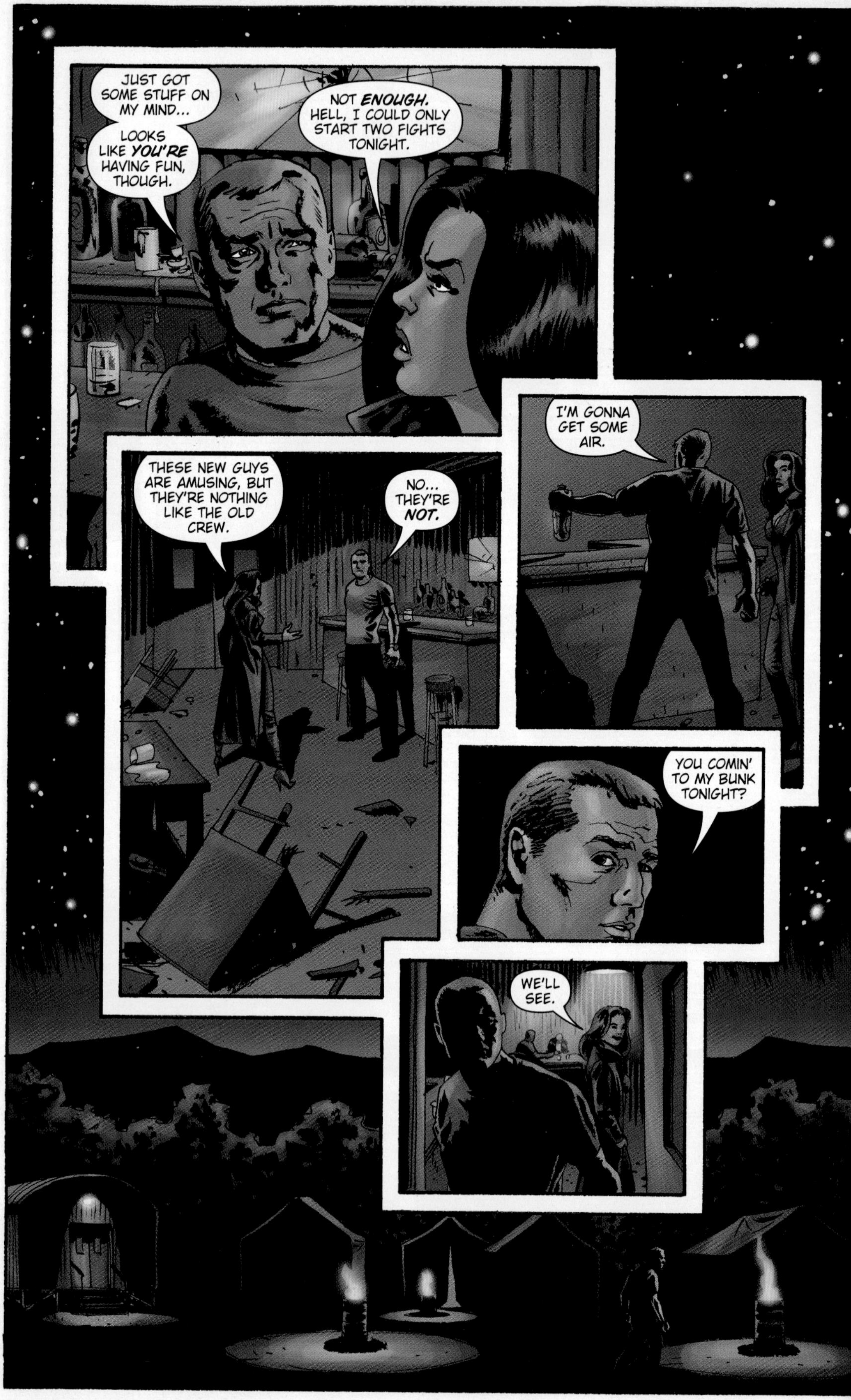
JUST GOT SOME STUFF ON MY MIND...
LOOKS LIKE YOU'RE HAVING FUN, THOUGH.
NOT ENOUGH. HELL, I COULD ONLY START TWO FIGHTS TONIGHT.
THESE NEW GUYS ARE AMUSING, BUT THEY'RE NOTHING LIKE THE OLD CREW.
NO... THEY'RE NOT.
I'M GONNA GET SOME AIR.
YOU COMIN' TO MY BUNK TONIGHT?
WE'LL SEE.

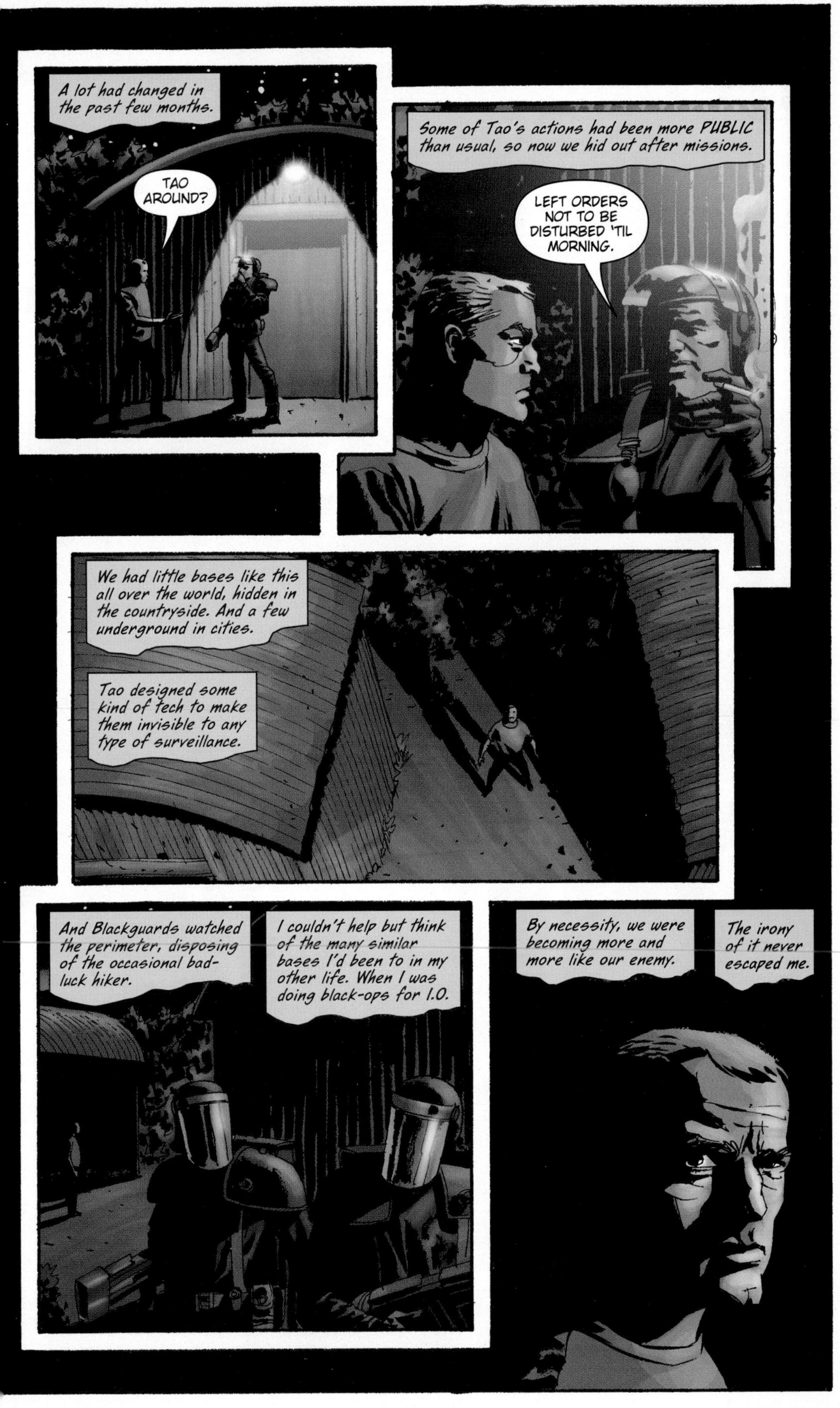

A lot had changed in the past few months.
TAO AROUND?
Some of Tao's actions had been more PUBLIC than usual, so now we hid out after missions.
LEFT ORDERS NOT TO BE DISTURBED 'TIL MORNING.
We had little bases like this all over the world, hidden in the countryside. And a few underground in cities.
Tao designed some kind of tech to make them invisible to any type of surveillance.
And Blackguards watched the perimeter, disposing of the occasional bad-luck hiker.
I couldn't help but think of the many similar bases I'd been to in my other life. When I was doing black-ops for I.O.
By necessity, we were becoming more and more like our enemy.
The irony of it never escaped me.

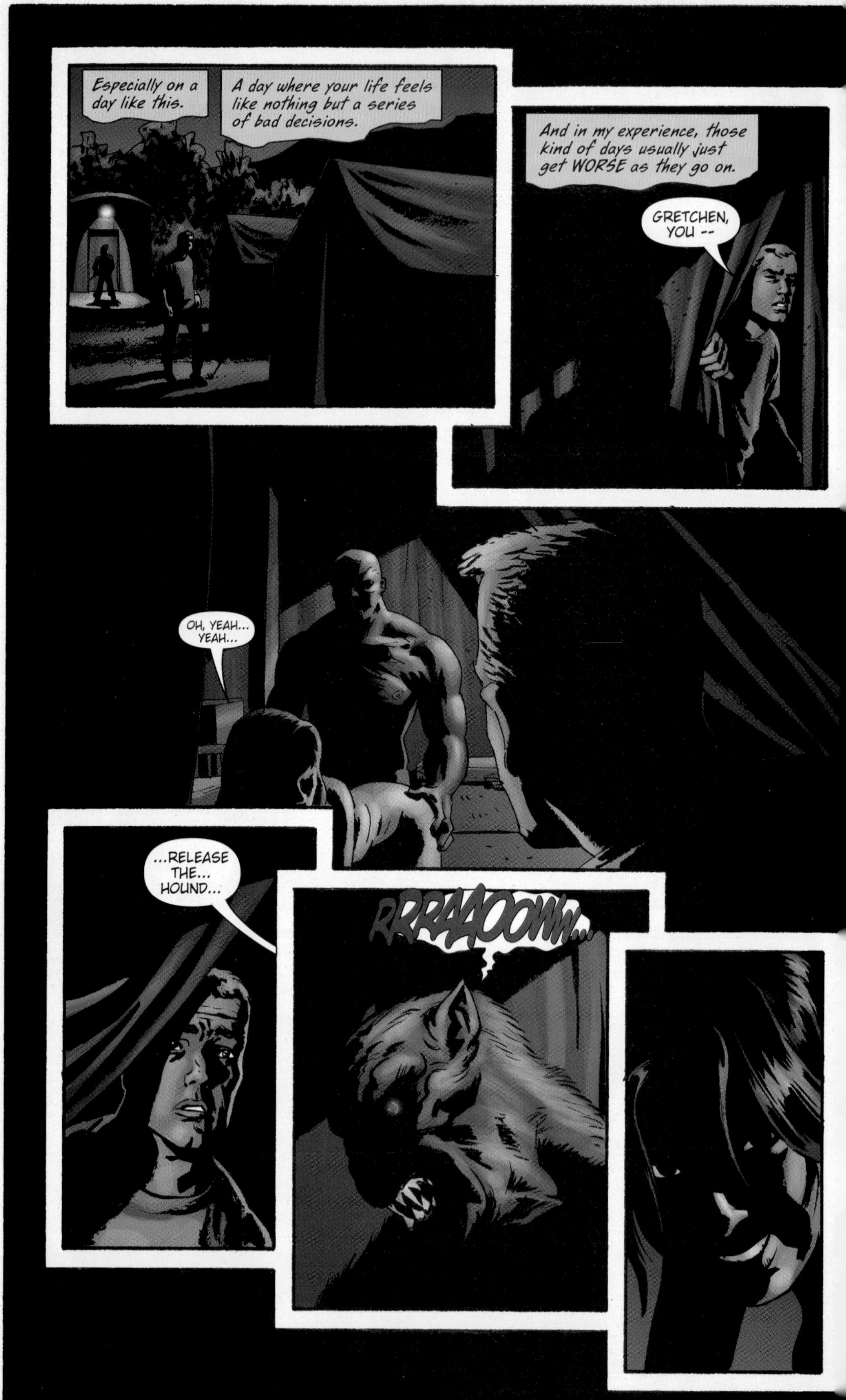
Especially on a day like this.
A day where your life feels like nothing but a series of bad decisions.
And in my experience, those kind of days usually just get WORSE as they go on.
GRETCHEN, YOU --
OH, YEAH... YEAH...
...RELEASE THE... HOUND...
RRRAAAOOWW...

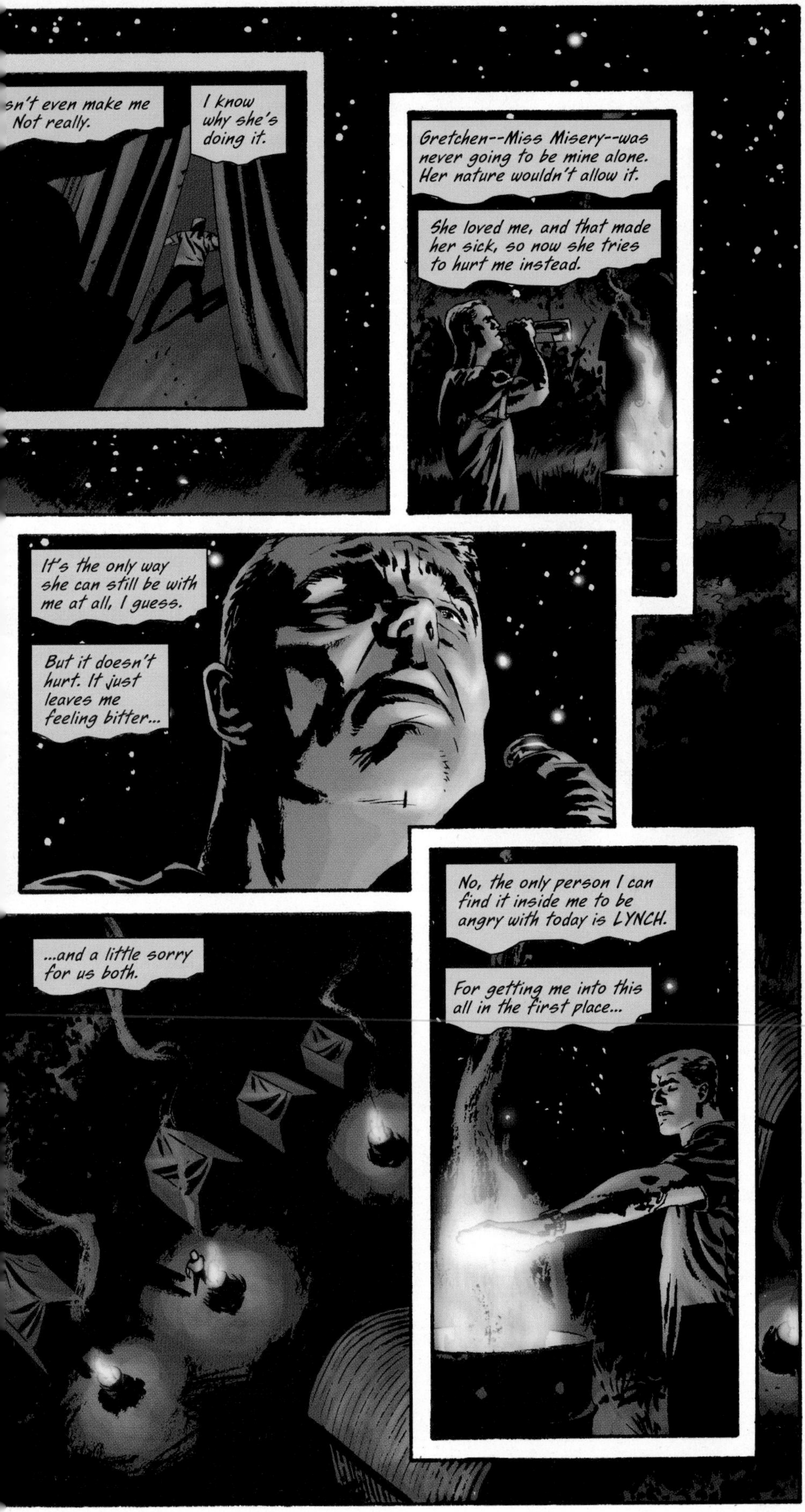

sn't even make me Not really.
I know why she's doing it.
Gretchen--Miss Misery--was never going to be mine alone. Her nature wouldn't allow it.
She loved me, and that made her sick, so now she tries to hurt me instead.
It's the only way she can still be with me at all, I guess.
But it doesn't hurt. It just leaves me feeling bitter...
...and a little sorry for us both.
No, the only person I can find it inside me to be angry with today is LYNCH.
For getting me into this all in the first place...

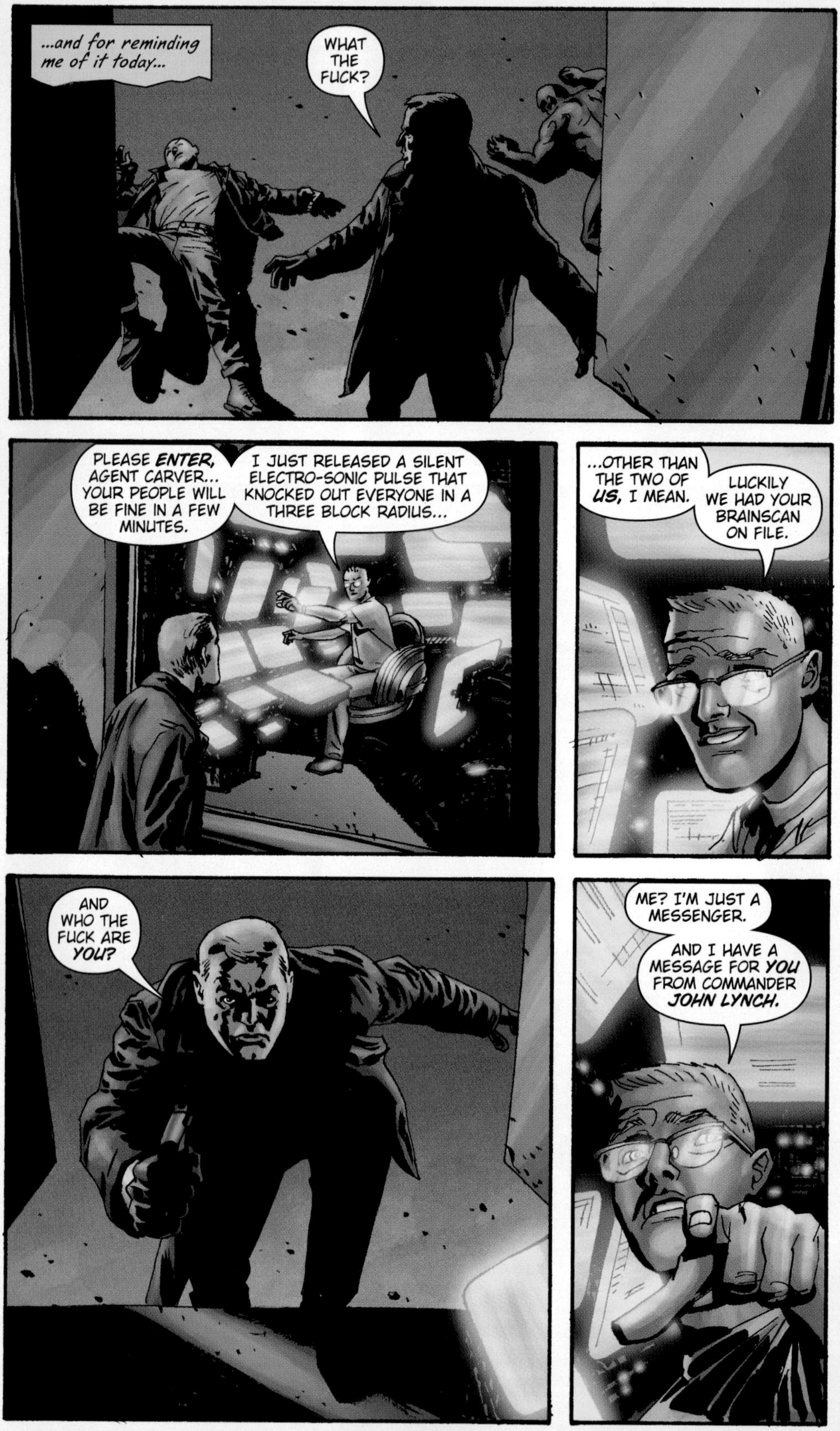
...and for reminding me of it today...
WHAT THE FUCK?
PLEASE ENTER, AGENT CARVER... YOUR PEOPLE WILL BE FINE IN A FEW MINUTES.
I JUST RELEASED A SILENT ELECTRO-SONIC PULSE THAT KNOCKED OUT EVERYONE IN A THREE BLOCK RADIUS...
...OTHER THAN THE TWO OF US, I MEAN.
LUCKILY WE HAD YOUR BRAINSCAN ON FILE.
AND WHO THE FUCK ARE YOU?
ME? I'M JUST A MESSENGER.
AND I HAVE A MESSAGE FOR YOU FROM COMMANDER JOHN LYNCH.

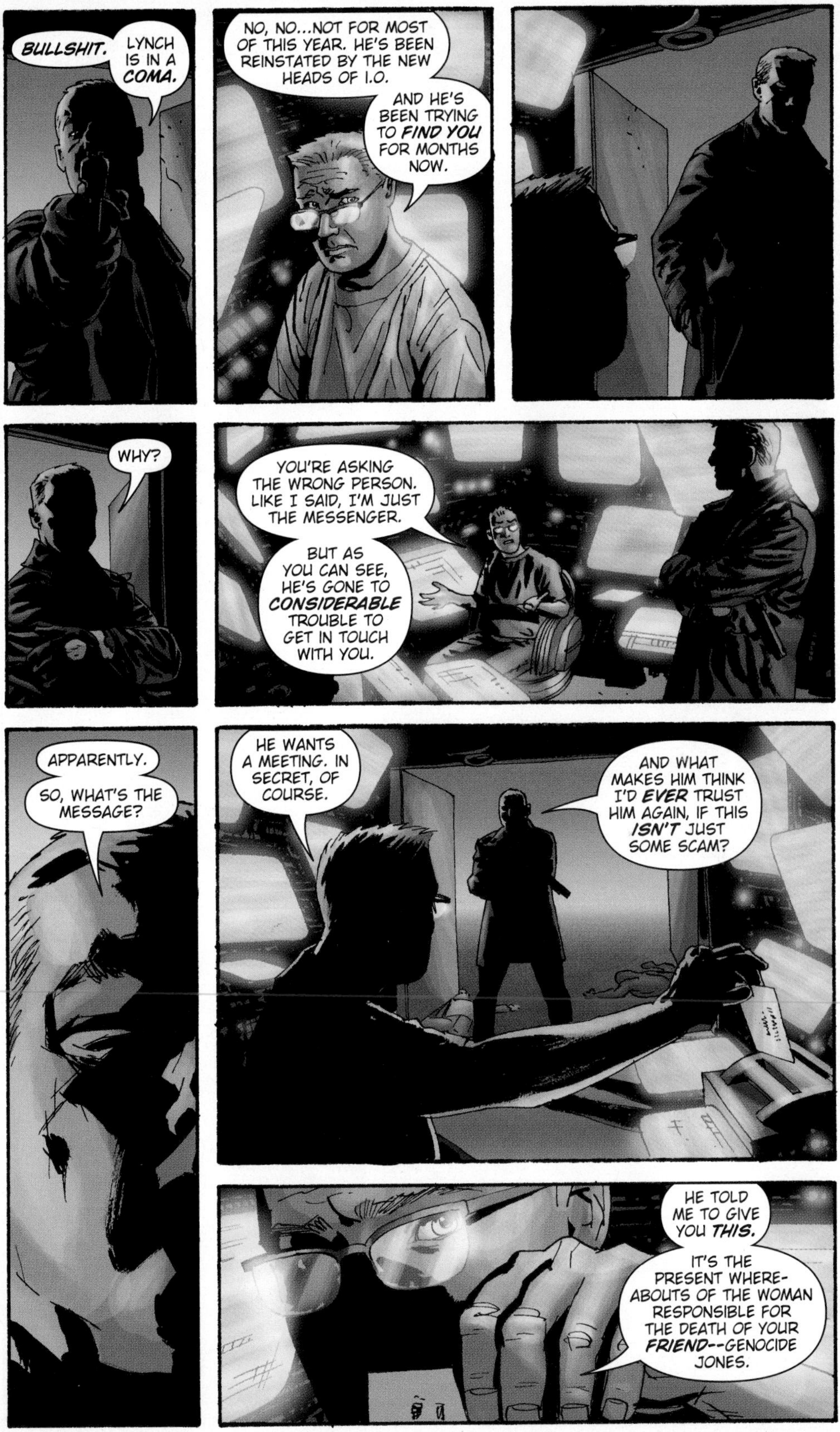
BULLSHIT.
LYNCH IS IN A COMA.
NO, NO...NOT FOR MOST OF THIS YEAR. HE'S BEEN REINSTATED BY THE NEW HEADS OF I.O.
AND HE'S BEEN TRYING TO FIND YOU FOR MONTHS NOW.
WHY?
YOU'RE ASKING THE WRONG PERSON. LIKE I SAID, I'M JUST THE MESSENGER.
BUT AS YOU CAN SEE, HE'S GONE TO CONSIDERABLE TROUBLE TO GET IN TOUCH WITH YOU.
APPARENTLY.
SO, WHAT'S THE MESSAGE?
HE WANTS A MEETING. IN SECRET, OF COURSE.
AND WHAT MAKES HIM THINK I'D EVER TRUST HIM AGAIN, IF THIS ISN'T JUST SOME SCAM?
HE TOLD ME TO GIVE YOU THIS.
IT'S THE PRESENT WHERE-ABOUTS OF THE WOMAN RESPONSIBLE FOR THE DEATH OF YOUR FRIEND--GENOCIDE JONES.

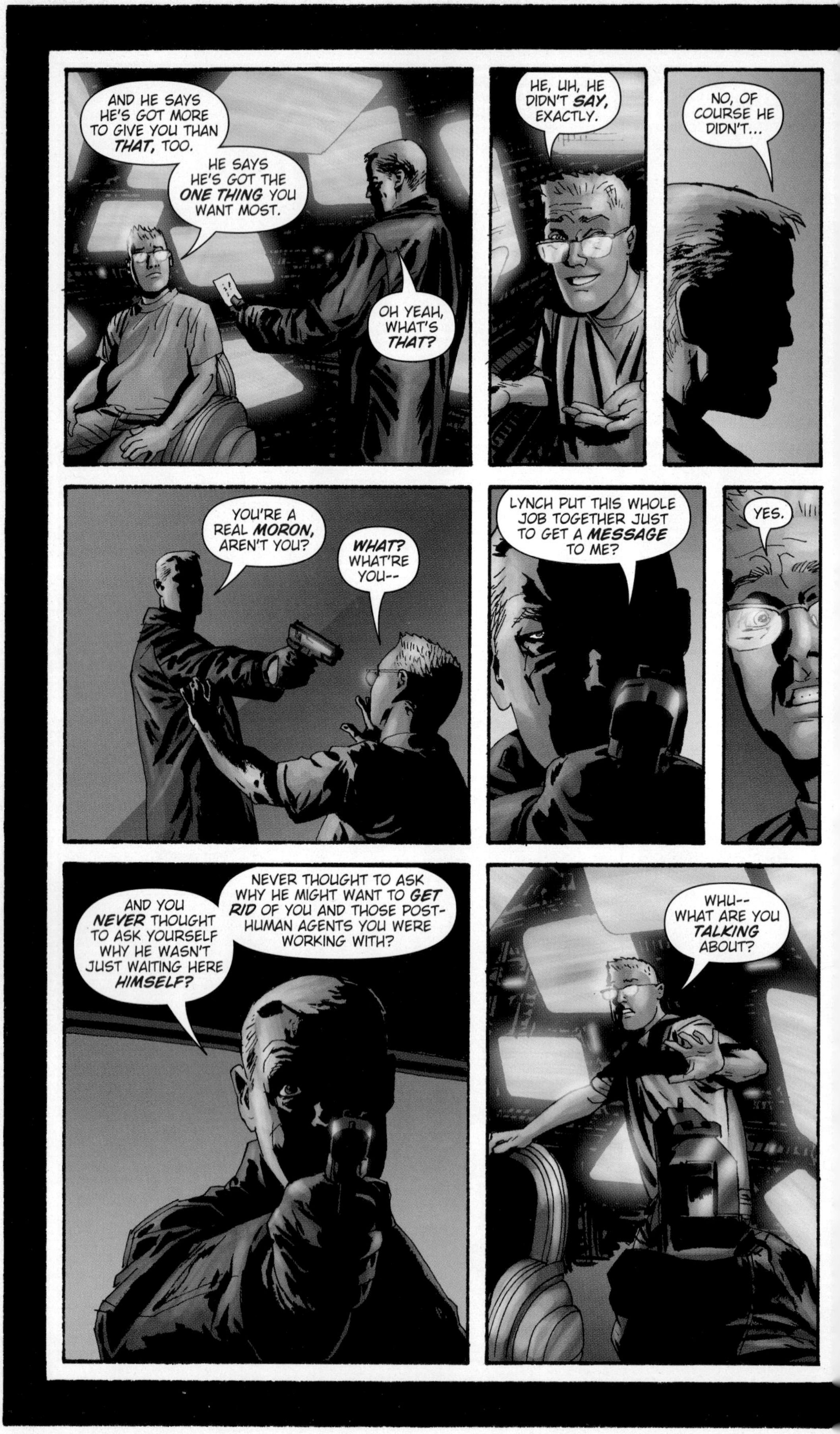
AND HE SAYS HE'S GOT MORE TO GIVE YOU THAN THAT, TOO.
HE SAYS HE'S GOT THE ONE THING YOU WANT MOST.
OH YEAH, WHAT'S THAT?
HE, UH, HE DIDN'T SAY, EXACTLY.
NO, OF COURSE HE DIDN'T...
YOU'RE A REAL MORON, AREN'T YOU?
WHAT? WHAT'RE YOU--
LYNCH PUT THIS WHOLE JOB TOGETHER JUST TO GET A MESSAGE TO ME?
YES.
AND YOU NEVER THOUGHT TO ASK YOURSELF WHY HE WASN'T JUST WAITING HERE HIMSELF?
NEVER THOUGHT TO ASK WHY HE MIGHT WANT TO GET RID OF YOU AND THOSE POST-HUMAN AGENTS YOU WERE WORKING WITH?
WHU-- WHAT ARE YOU TALKING ABOUT?

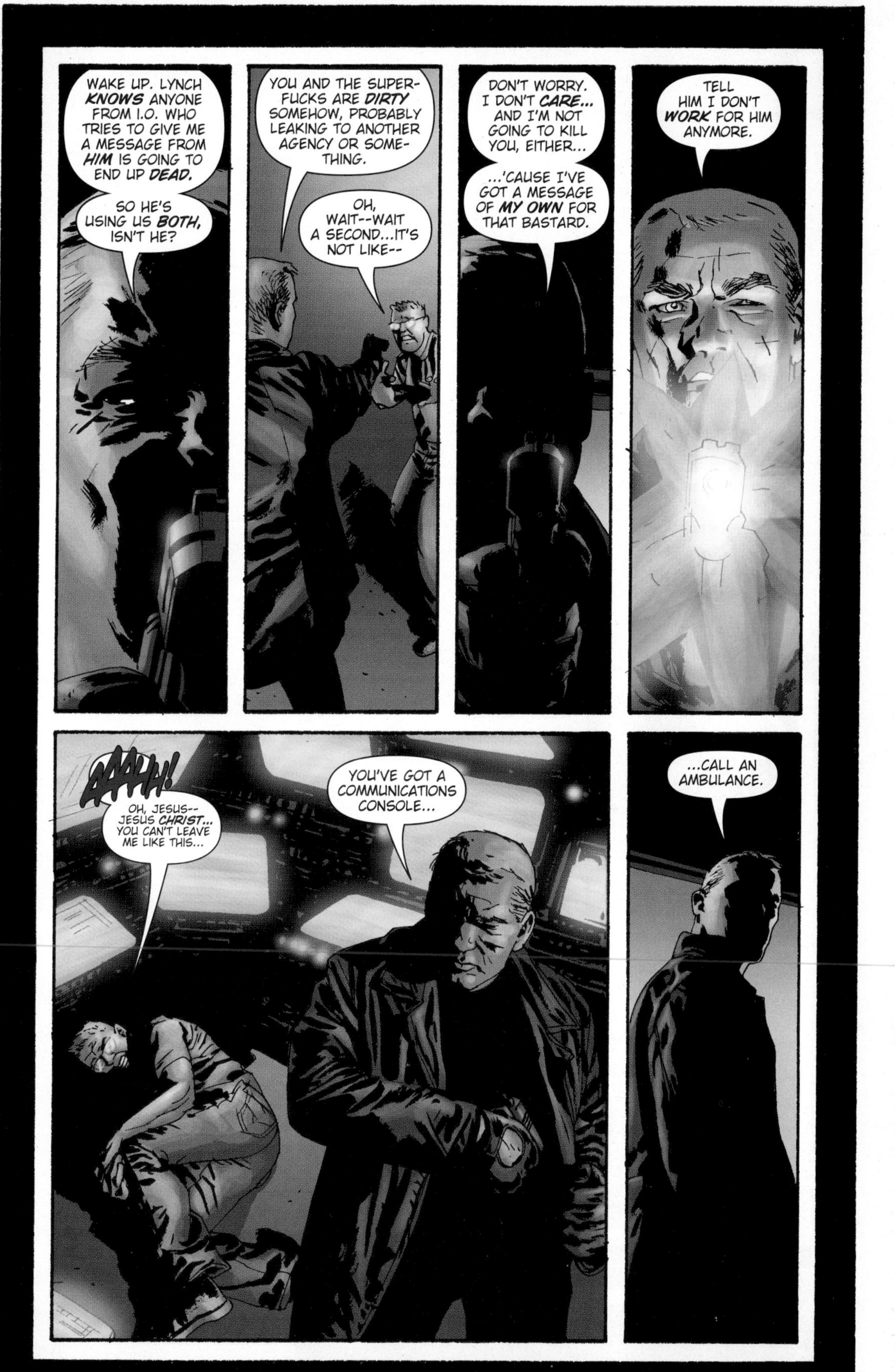
WAKE UP. LYNCH KNOWS ANYONE FROM I.O. WHO TRIES TO GIVE ME A MESSAGE FROM HIM IS GOING TO END UP DEAD.
SO HE'S USING US BOTH, ISN'T HE?
YOU AND THE SUPER-FUCKS ARE DIRTY SOMEHOW, PROBABLY LEAKING TO ANOTHER AGENCY OR SOME-THING.
OH, WAIT--WAIT A SECOND...IT'S NOT LIKE--
DON'T WORRY. I DON'T CARE... AND I'M NOT GOING TO KILL YOU, EITHER...
...'CAUSE I'VE GOT A MESSAGE OF MY OWN FOR THAT BASTARD.
TELL HIM I DON'T WORK FOR HIM ANYMORE.
AAAHH!
OH, JESUS-- JESUS CHRIST... YOU CAN'T LEAVE ME LIKE THIS...
YOU'VE GOT A COMMUNICATIONS CONSOLE...
...CALL AN AMBULANCE.

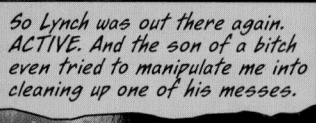

So Lynch was out there again. ACTIVE. And the son of a bitch even tried to manipulate me into cleaning up one of his messes.

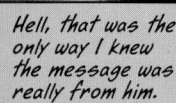

Hell, that was the only way I knew the message was really from him.

But it's far too late for Lynch.

He can't save me anymore...if he ever could have.

HOLDEN?

PUT SOME *CLOTHES* ON, GRETCHEN, IT'S PROBABLY *COLD* OUT HERE. NOT THAT I'D KNOW.

I DON'T GIVE A SHIT ABOUT THE COLD, AND EVERYONE'S PASSED-OUT EXCEPT THE PERIMETER GUARDS.

ARE YOU *MAD?*

NO.

HURT?

NAH...YOU CAN FUCK WHO OR *WHATEVER* YOU WANT. YOU USUALLY *DO.*

GOD *DAMN* YOU.

WHY DO YOU HAVE TO RUIN EVERYTHING?

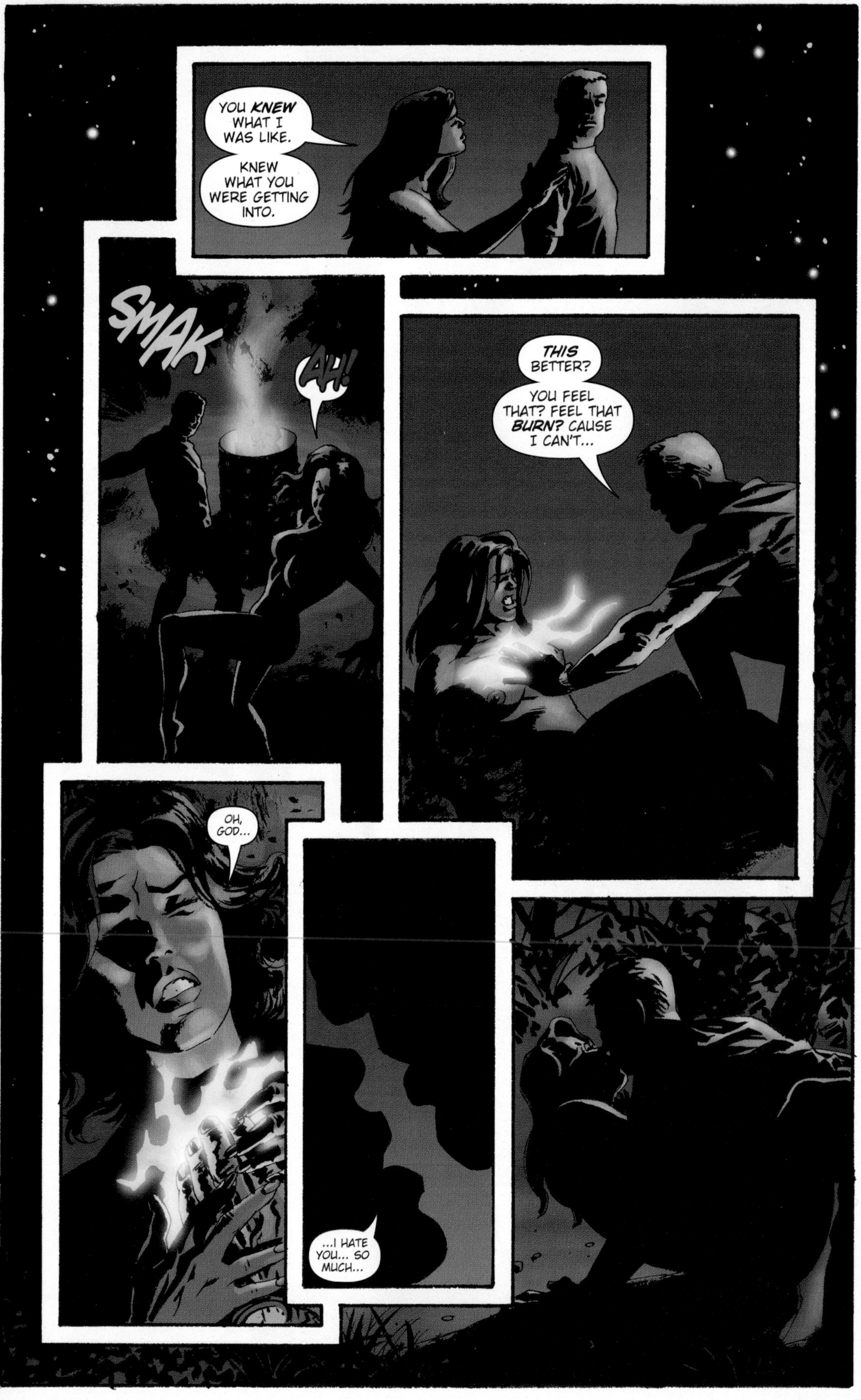

YOU *KNEW* WHAT I WAS LIKE.
KNEW WHAT YOU WERE GETTING INTO.
SMAK
AH!
THIS BETTER?
YOU FEEL THAT? FEEL THAT *BURN?* CAUSE I CAN'T...
OH, GOD...
...I HATE YOU... SO MUCH...

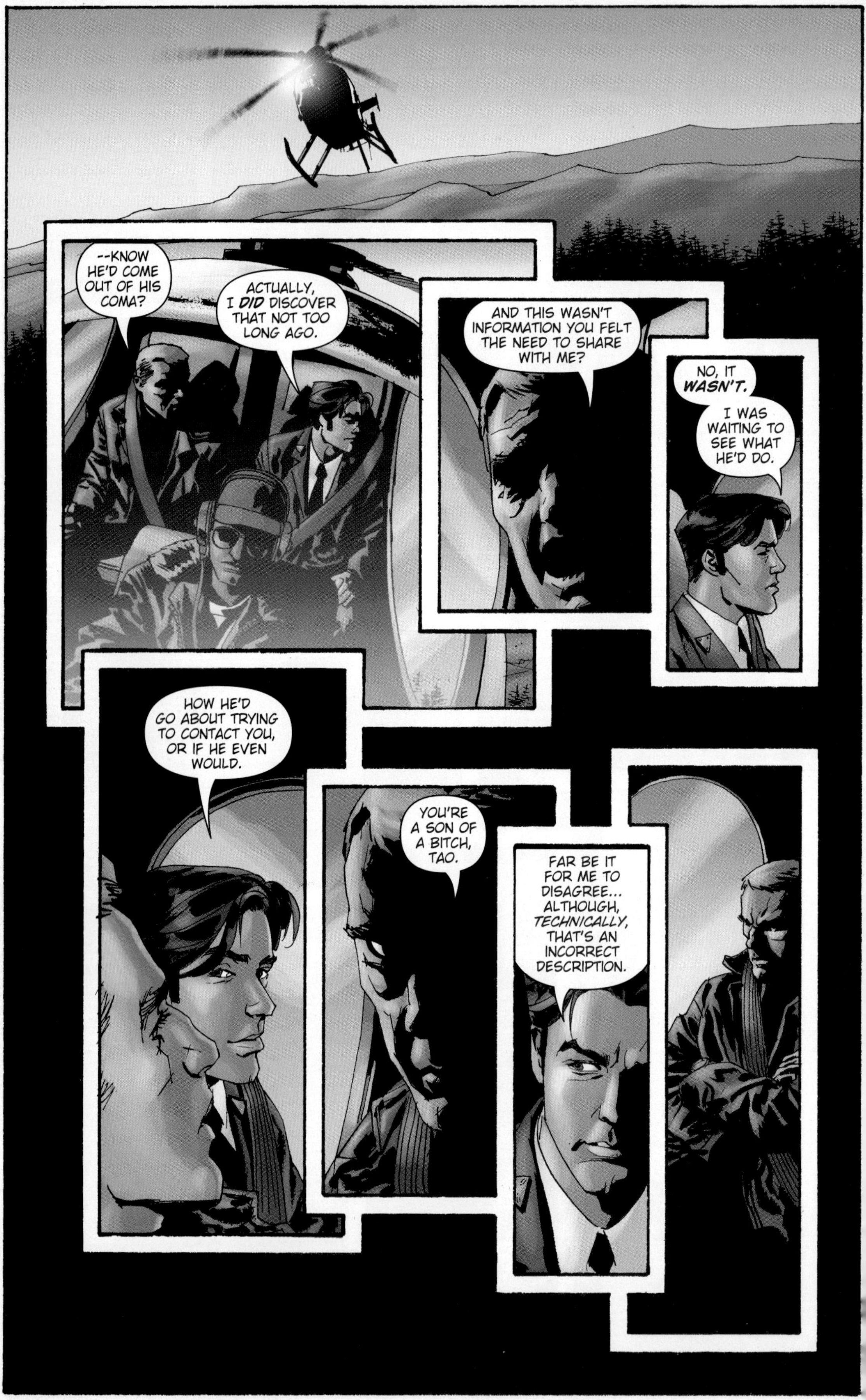
--KNOW HE'D COME OUT OF HIS COMA?
ACTUALLY, I *DID* DISCOVER THAT NOT TOO LONG AGO.
AND THIS WASN'T INFORMATION YOU FELT THE NEED TO SHARE WITH ME?
NO, IT *WASN'T.*
I WAS WAITING TO SEE WHAT HE'D DO.
HOW HE'D GO ABOUT TRYING TO CONTACT YOU, OR IF HE EVEN WOULD.
YOU'RE A SON OF A BITCH, TAO.
FAR BE IT FOR ME TO DISAGREE... ALTHOUGH, *TECHNICALLY,* THAT'S AN INCORRECT DESCRIPTION.

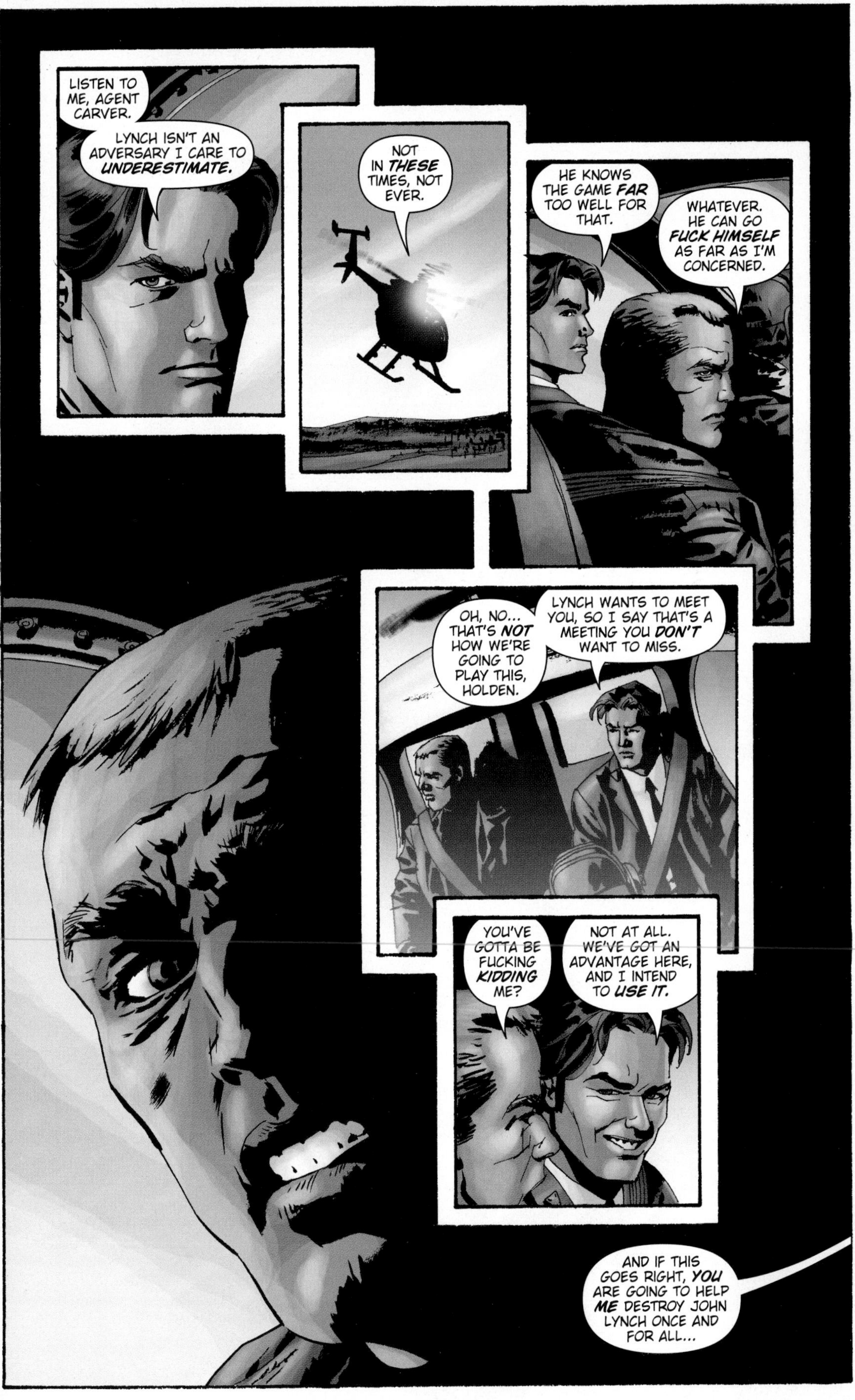
LISTEN TO ME, AGENT CARVER.
LYNCH ISN'T AN ADVERSARY I CARE TO UNDERESTIMATE.
NOT IN THESE TIMES, NOT EVER.
HE KNOWS THE GAME FAR TOO WELL FOR THAT.
WHATEVER. HE CAN GO FUCK HIMSELF AS FAR AS I'M CONCERNED.
LYNCH WANTS TO MEET YOU, SO I SAY THAT'S A MEETING YOU DON'T WANT TO MISS.
OH, NO... THAT'S NOT HOW WE'RE GOING TO PLAY THIS, HOLDEN.
YOU'VE GOTTA BE FUCKING KIDDING ME?
NOT AT ALL. WE'VE GOT AN ADVANTAGE HERE, AND I INTEND TO USE IT.
AND IF THIS GOES RIGHT, YOU ARE GOING TO HELP ME DESTROY JOHN LYNCH ONCE AND FOR ALL...

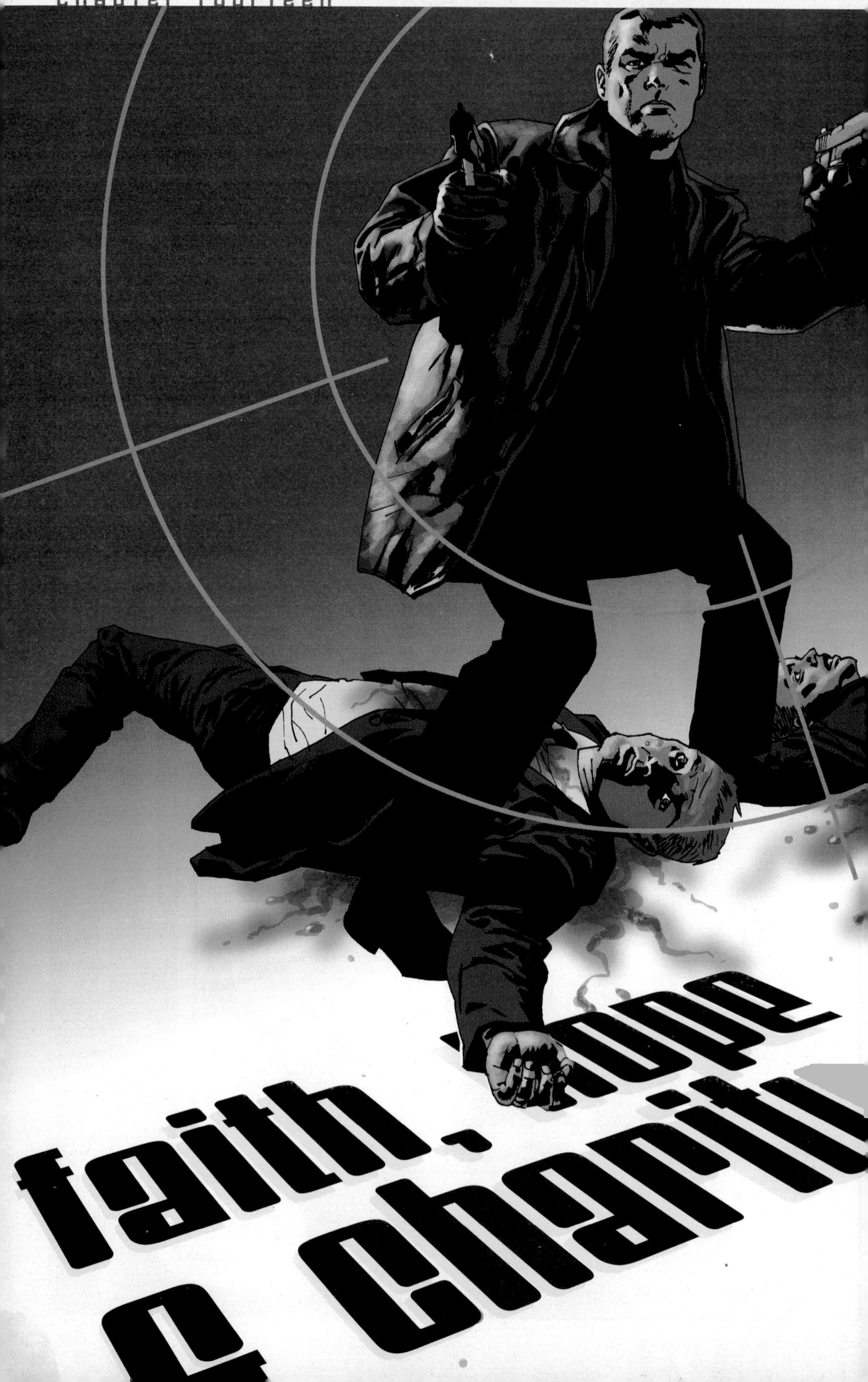
faith, hope
& charity

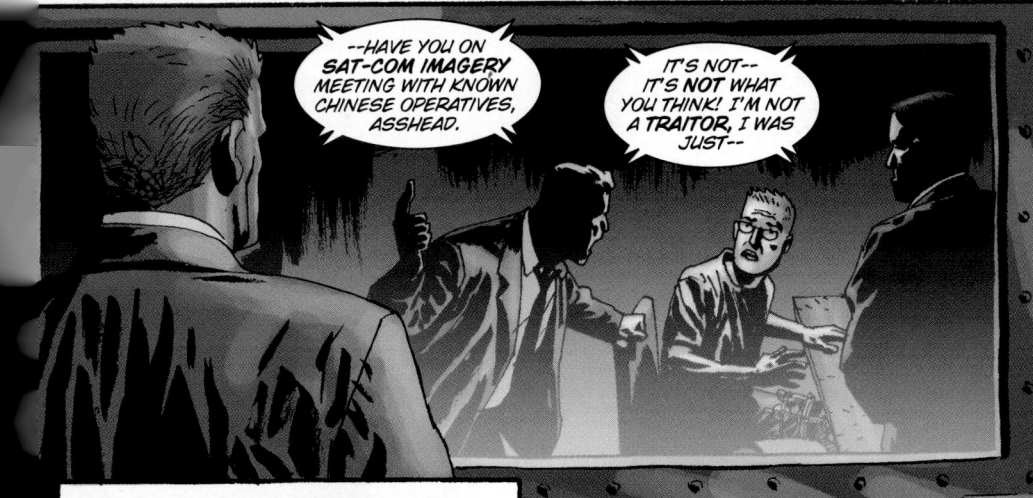

--HAVE YOU ON **SAT-COM IMAGERY** MEETING WITH KNOWN CHINESE OPERATIVES, ASSHEAD.

IT'S NOT-- IT'S **NOT** WHAT YOU THINK! I'M NOT A **TRAITOR**, I WAS JUST--

LOOKS LIKE YOUR LITTLE SCHEME DIDN'T WORK OUT SO WELL, DID IT?

YOU'RE **KIDDING**, RIGHT, SLAYTON?

I GOT RID OF **TWO** CORRUPT POST-HUMAN AGENTS AND THIS IDIOT IS ABOUT TO CONFESS TO LEAKING INFORMATION ABOUT OUR NEW **ADMINISTRATION** TO THE ENEMY.

WHICH IS **EXACTLY** THE KIND OF SCANDAL WE WERE HOPING TO AVOID.

WE'RE ON A TIGHTER LEASH THAN WE USED TO BE, LYNCH, **REMEMBER** THAT. I'M STILL AMAZED THE NEW **POWERS THAT BE** DIDN'T SHUT US DOWN FIRST THING.

IF YOU THINK I CAN'T SWEEP OUR LITTLE FRIEND HERE UNDER THE CARPET, THEN YOU HAVEN'T BEEN PAYING ATTENTION.

HE'S ABOUT TO GET A **RESEARCH ASSIGNMENT** TO ANTARCTICA, WHERE HE'LL BE KEPT UNDER HOUSE ARREST UNTIL HE'S GIVEN US EVERYTHING ON HIS CONTACTS.

THEN HE'LL BE ERASED.

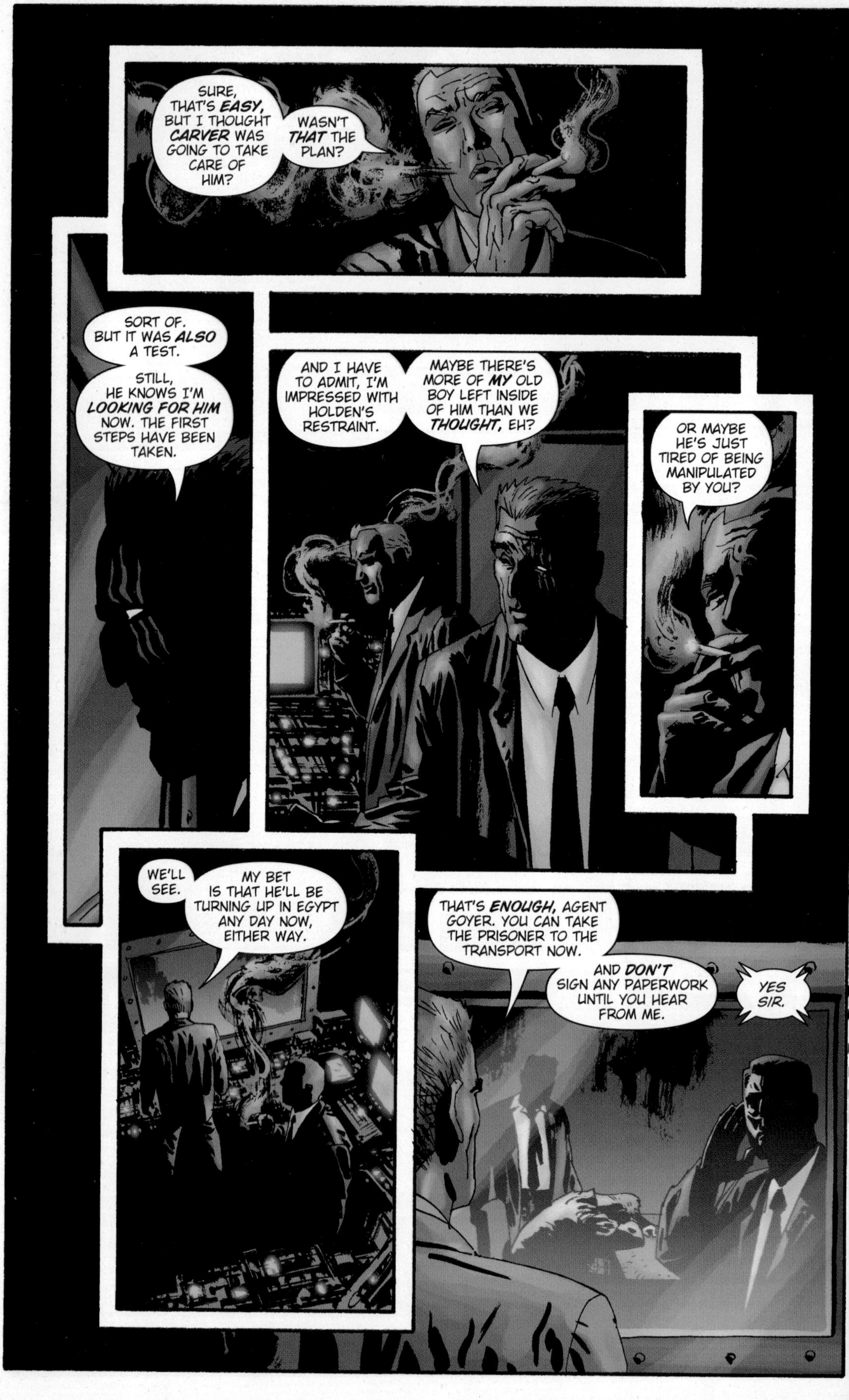
SURE, THAT'S EASY, BUT I THOUGHT CARVER WAS GOING TO TAKE CARE OF HIM?
WASN'T THAT THE PLAN?
SORT OF. BUT IT WAS ALSO A TEST.
STILL, HE KNOWS I'M LOOKING FOR HIM NOW. THE FIRST STEPS HAVE BEEN TAKEN.
AND I HAVE TO ADMIT, I'M IMPRESSED WITH HOLDEN'S RESTRAINT.
MAYBE THERE'S MORE OF MY OLD BOY LEFT INSIDE OF HIM THAN WE THOUGHT, EH?
OR MAYBE HE'S JUST TIRED OF BEING MANIPULATED BY YOU?
WE'LL SEE.
MY BET IS THAT HE'LL BE TURNING UP IN EGYPT ANY DAY NOW, EITHER WAY.
THAT'S ENOUGH, AGENT GOYER. YOU CAN TAKE THE PRISONER TO THE TRANSPORT NOW.
AND DON'T SIGN ANY PAPERWORK UNTIL YOU HEAR FROM ME.
YES SIR.

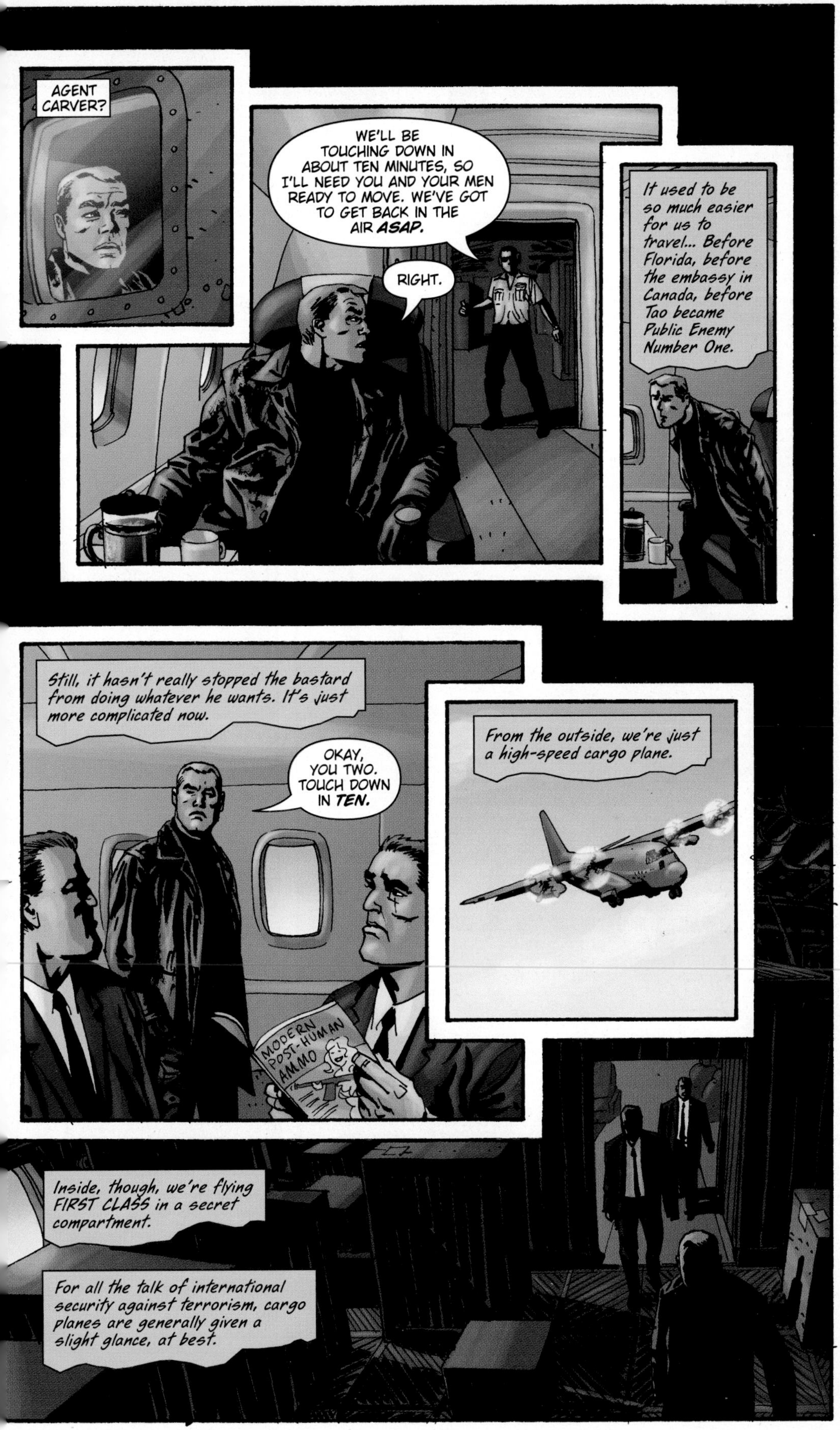

AGENT CARVER?
WE'LL BE TOUCHING DOWN IN ABOUT TEN MINUTES, SO I'LL NEED YOU AND YOUR MEN READY TO MOVE. WE'VE GOT TO GET BACK IN THE AIR *ASAP.*
RIGHT.
It used to be so much easier for us to travel... Before Florida, before the embassy in Canada, before Tao became Public Enemy Number One.
Still, it hasn't really stopped the bastard from doing whatever he wants. It's just more complicated now.
OKAY, YOU TWO. TOUCH DOWN IN *TEN.*
MODERN POST-HUMAN AMMO
From the outside, we're just a high-speed cargo plane.
Inside, though, we're flying FIRST CLASS in a secret compartment.
For all the talk of international security against terrorism, cargo planes are generally given a slight glance, at best.

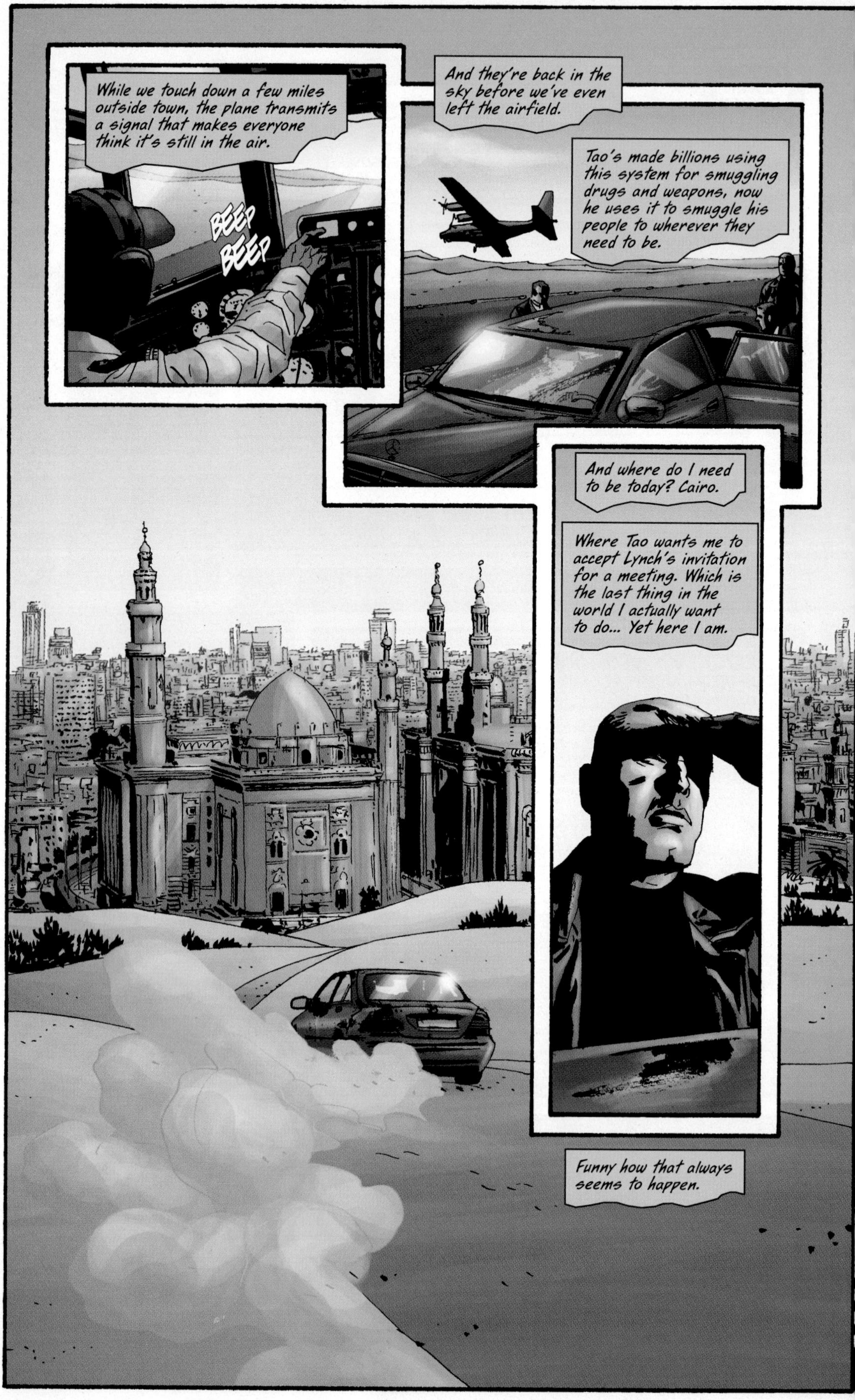

While we touch down a few miles outside town, the plane transmits a signal that makes everyone think it's still in the air.
BEEP BEEP
And they're back in the sky before we've even left the airfield.
Tao's made billions using this system for smuggling drugs and weapons, now he uses it to smuggle his people to wherever they need to be.
And where do I need to be today? Cairo.
Where Tao wants me to accept Lynch's invitation for a meeting. Which is the last thing in the world I actually want to do... Yet here I am.
Funny how that always seems to happen.

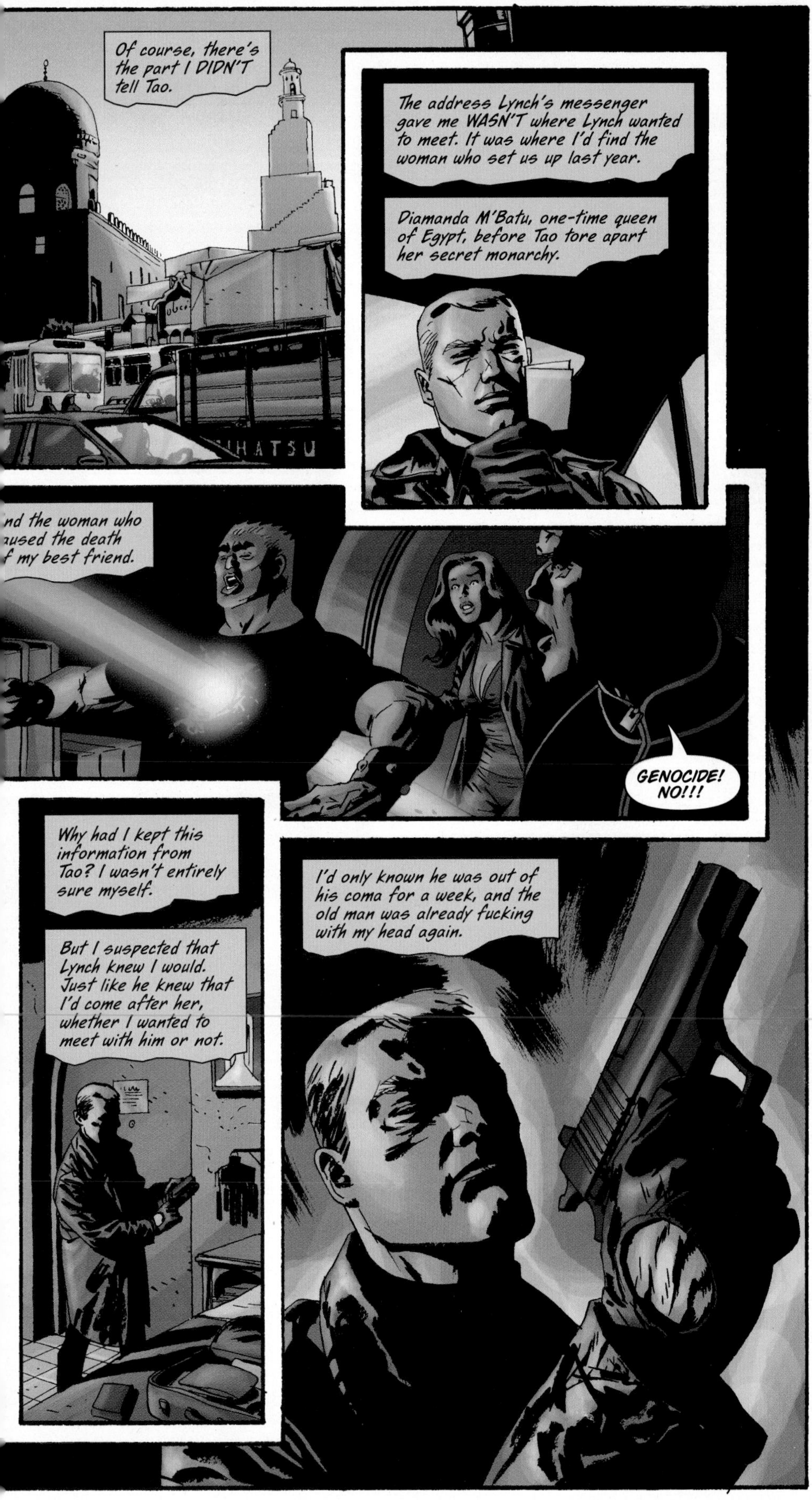

Of course, there's the part I DIDN'T tell Tao.
The address Lynch's messenger gave me WASN'T where Lynch wanted to meet. It was where I'd find the woman who set us up last year.
Diamanda M'Batu, one-time queen of Egypt, before Tao tore apart her secret monarchy.
nd the woman who aused the death f my best friend.
GENOCIDE! NO!!!
Why had I kept this information from Tao? I wasn't entirely sure myself.
But I suspected that Lynch knew I would. Just like he knew that I'd come after her, whether I wanted to meet with him or not.
I'd only known he was out of his coma for a week, and the old man was already fucking with my head again.

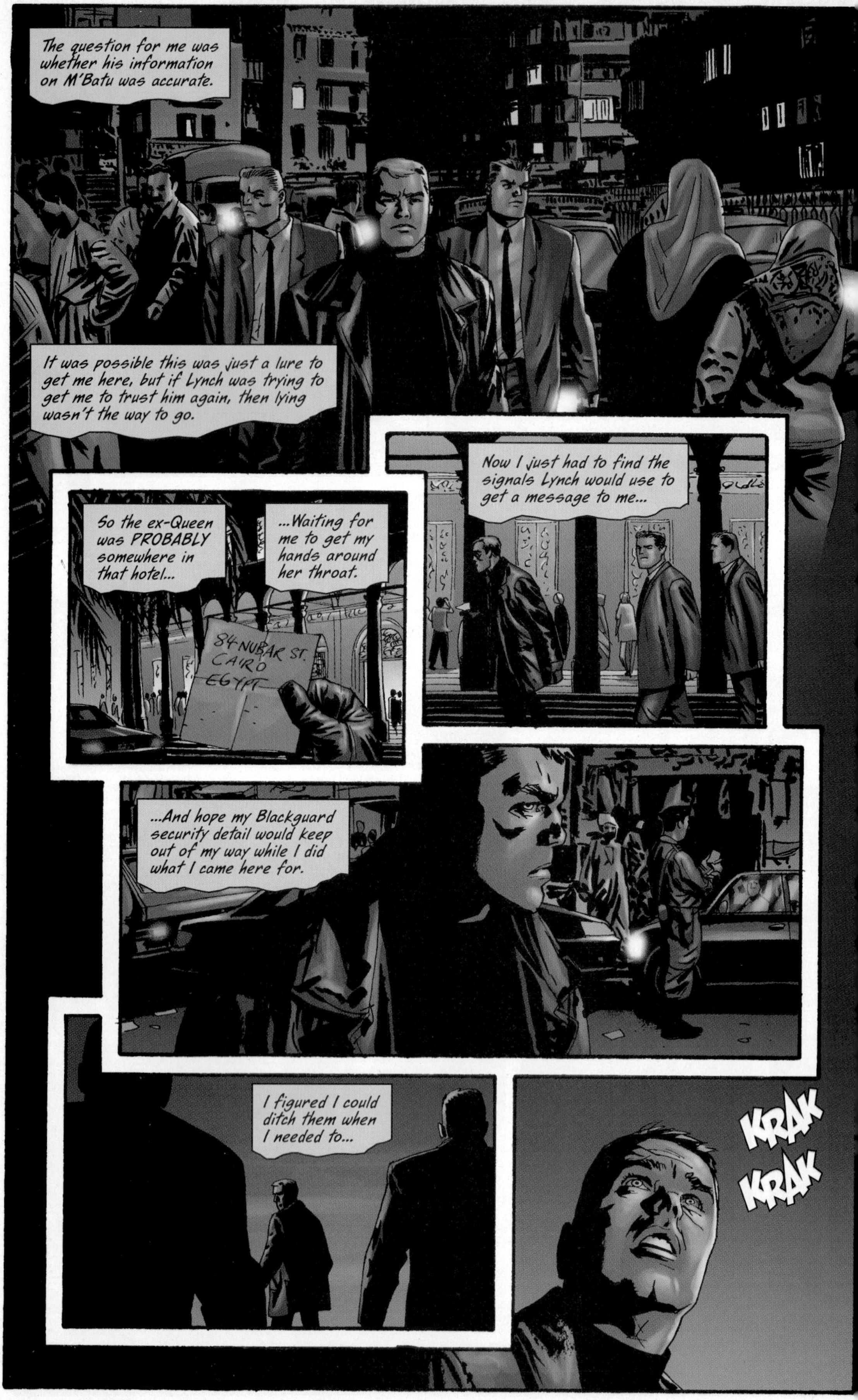
The question for me was whether his information on M'Batu was accurate.
It was possible this was just a lure to get me here, but if Lynch was trying to get me to trust him again, then lying wasn't the way to go.
So the ex-Queen was PROBABLY somewhere in that hotel...
...Waiting for me to get my hands around her throat.
84 NUBAR ST. CAIRO EGYPT
Now I just had to find the signals Lynch would use to get a message to me...
...And hope my Blackguard security detail would keep out of my way while I did what I came here for.
I figured I could ditch them when I needed to...
KRAK
KRAK

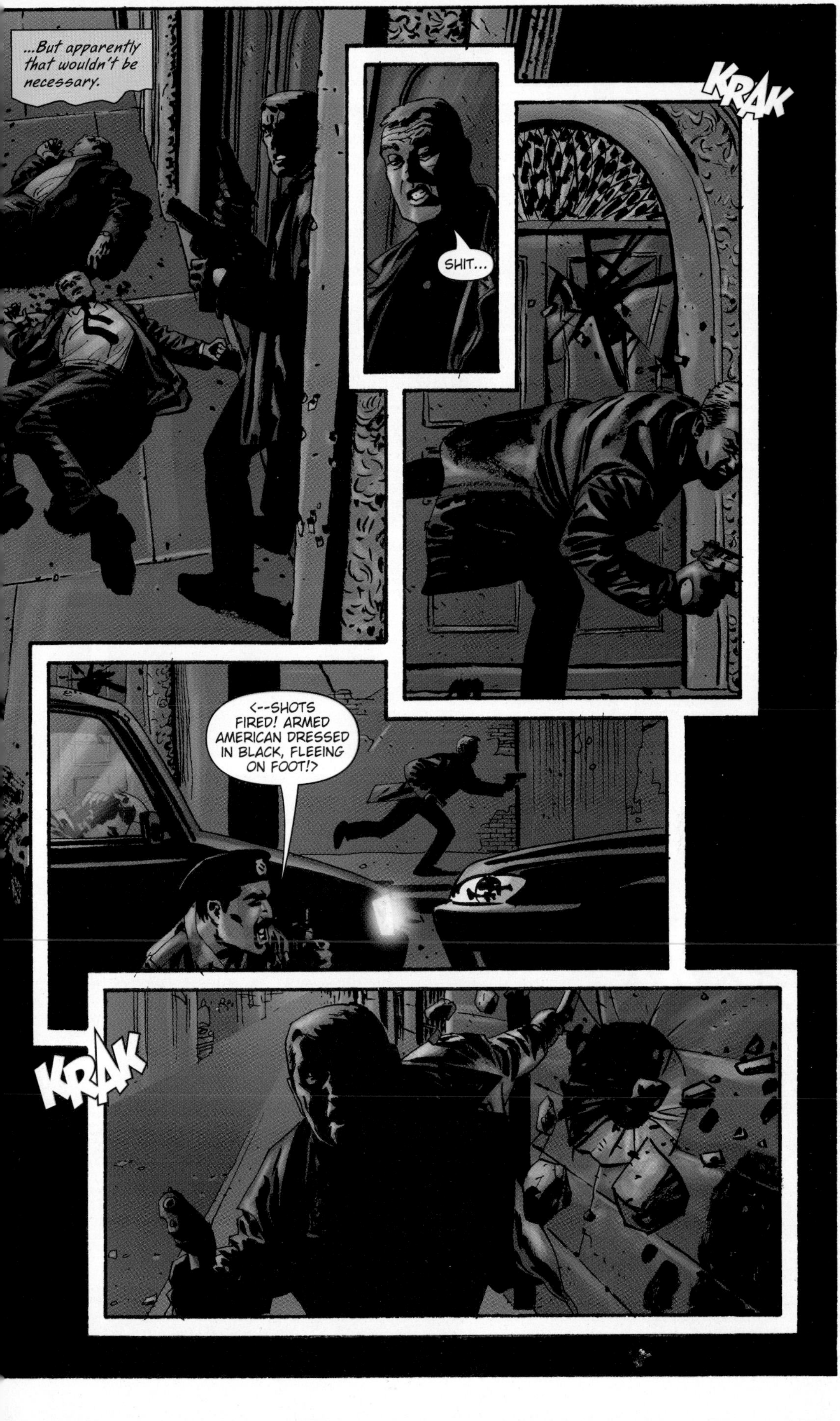
...But apparently that wouldn't be necessary.
SHIT...
KRAK
<--SHOTS FIRED! ARMED AMERICAN DRESSED IN BLACK, FLEEING ON FOOT!>
KRAK

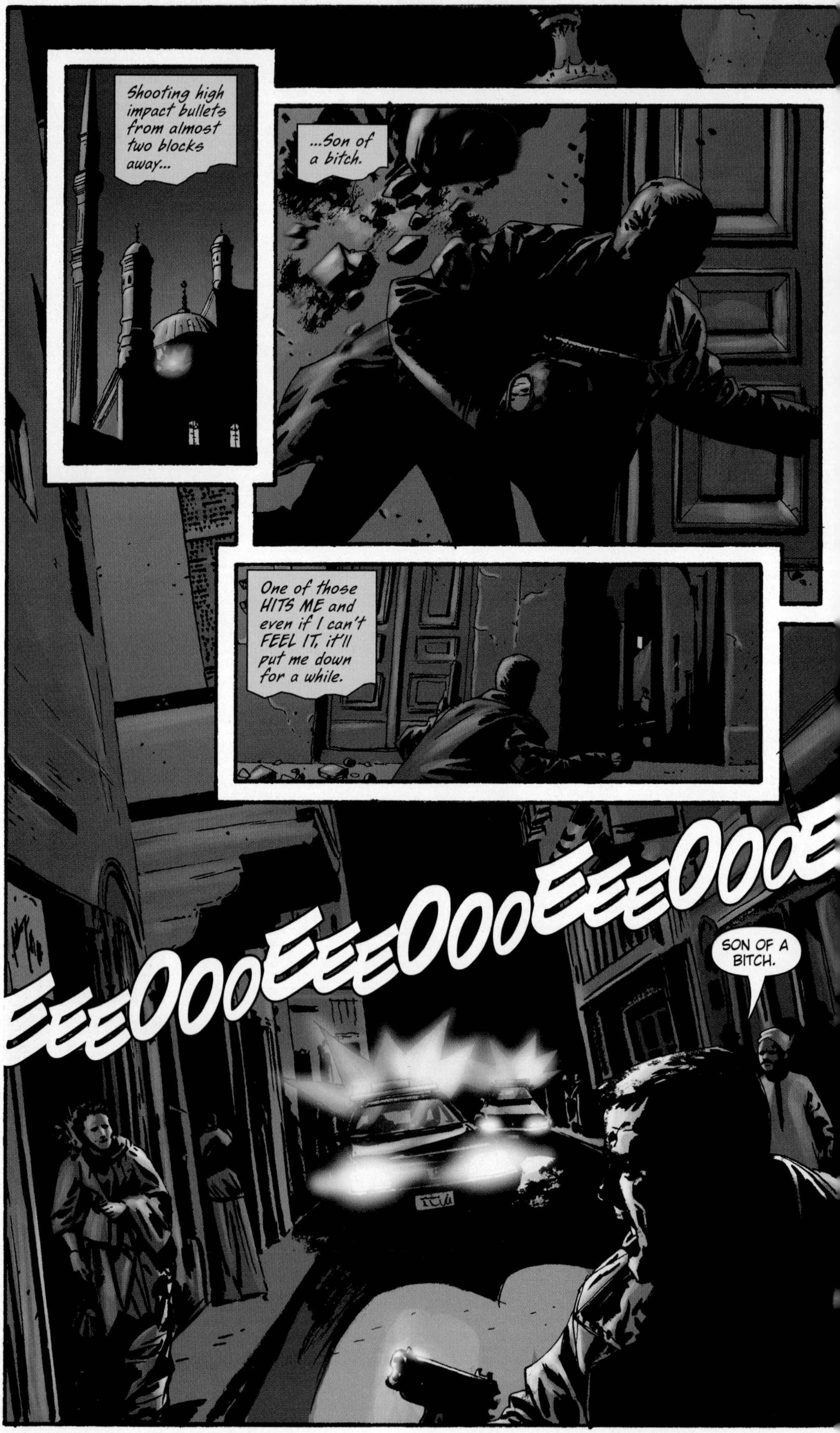
Shooting high impact bullets from almost two blocks away...
...Son of a bitch.
One of those HITS ME and even if I can't FEEL IT, it'll put me down for a while.
EEEOOOEEEOOOEEEOOOE
SON OF A BITCH.

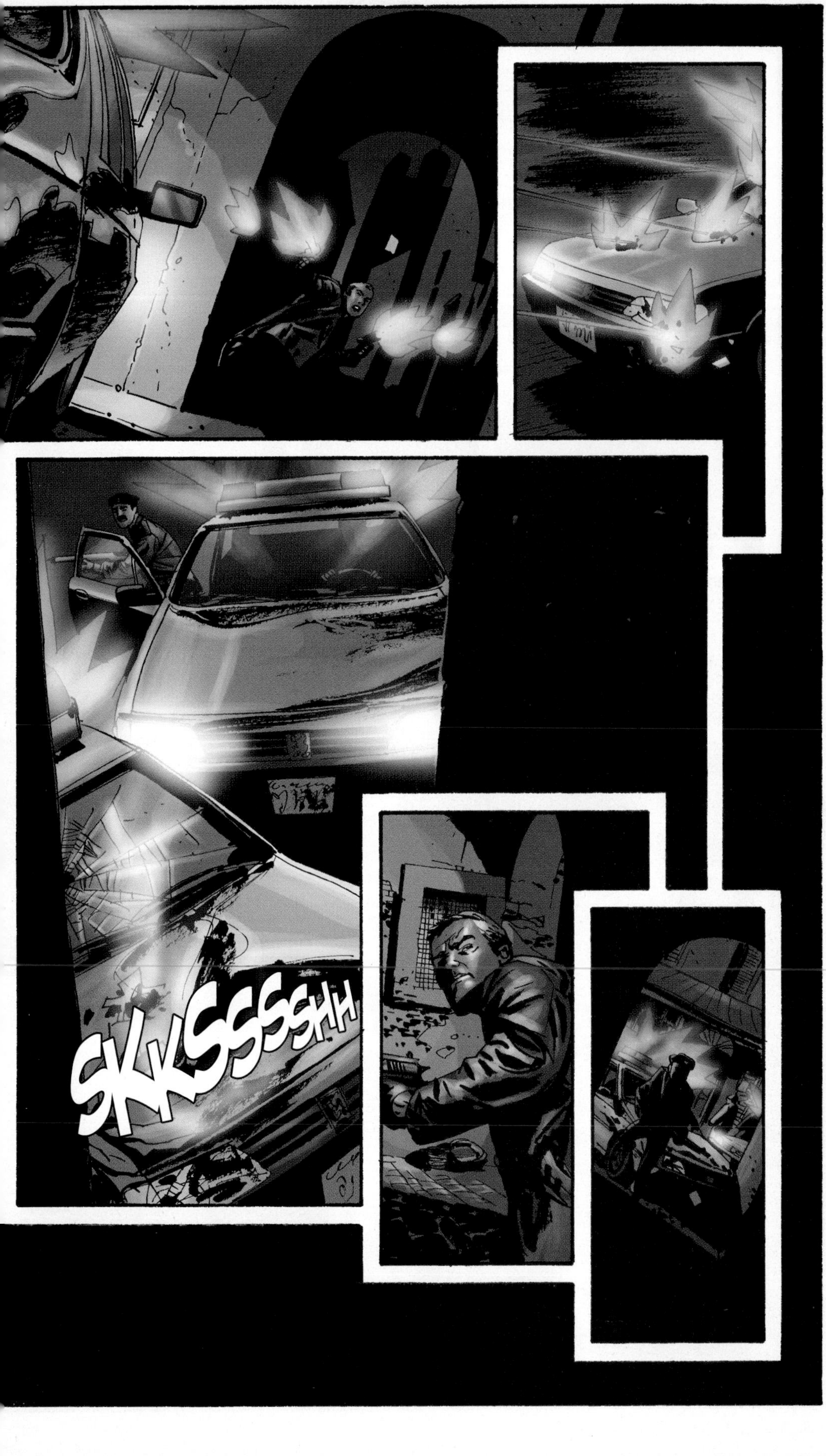
SKKSSSSHH

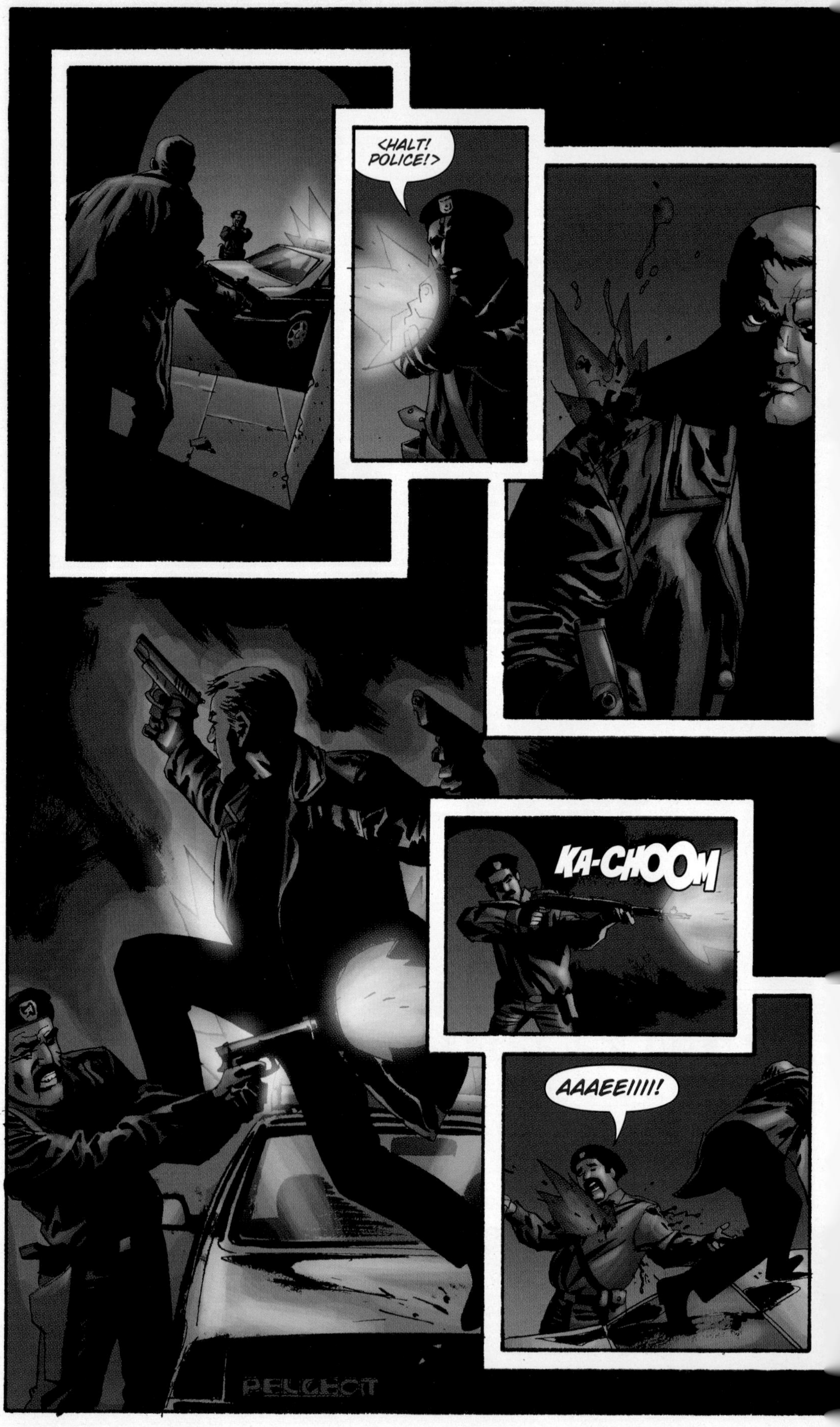
<HALT! POLICE!>
KA-CHOOM
AAAEE!!!!!
PEUGEOT

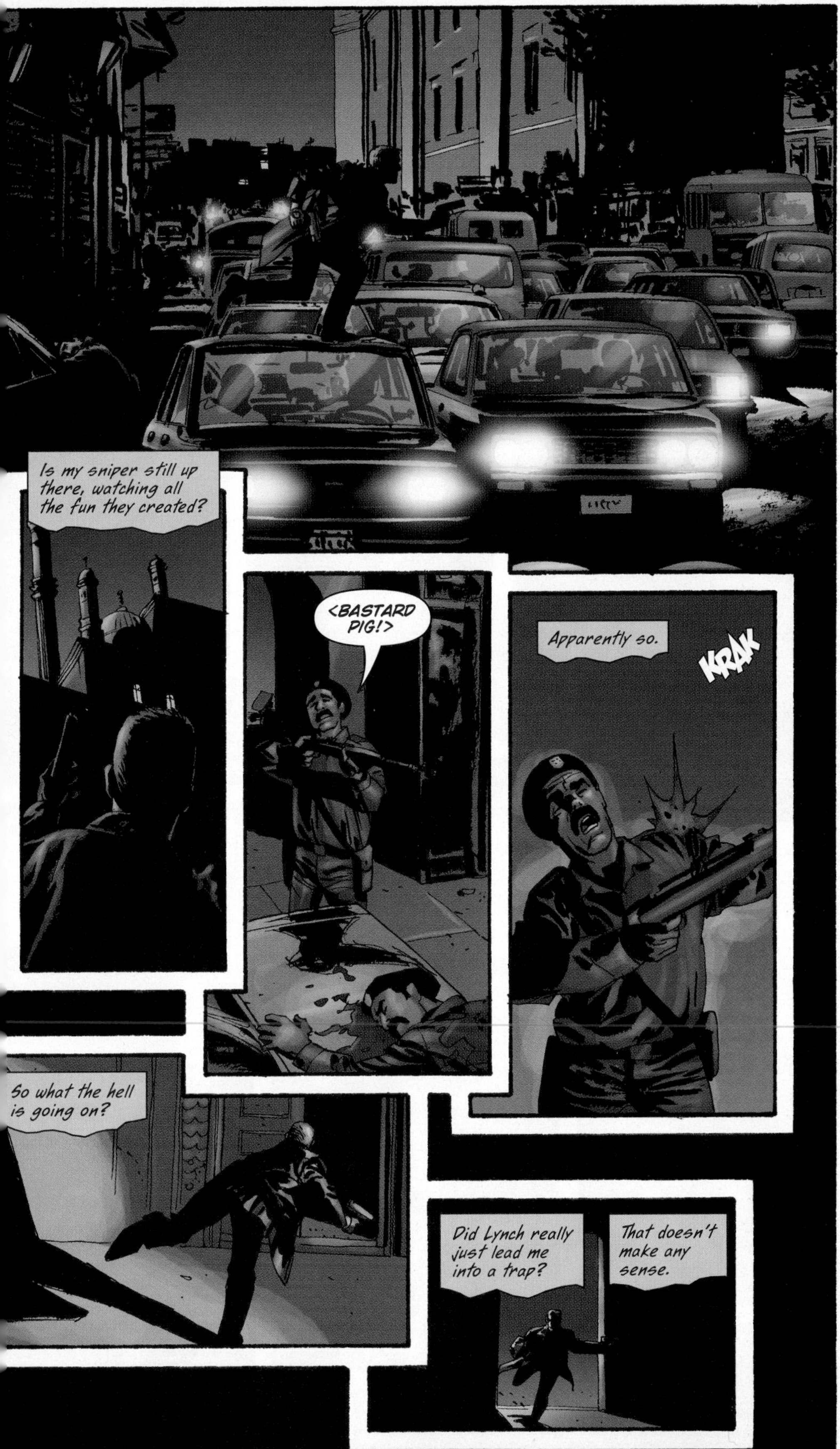
Is my sniper still up there, watching all the fun they created?
<BASTARD PIG!>
Apparently so.
KRAK
So what the hell is going on?
Did Lynch really just lead me into a trap?
That doesn't make any sense.

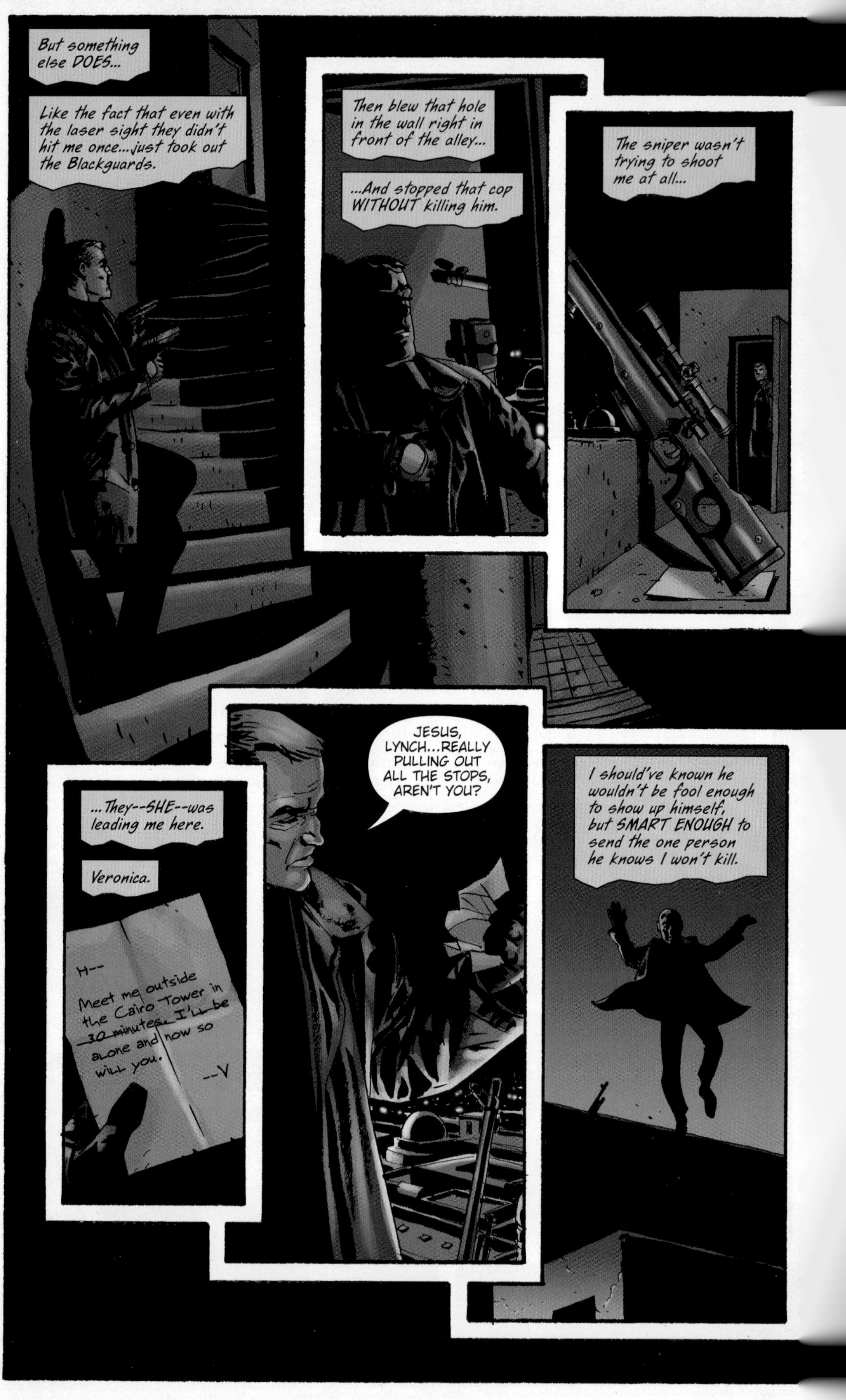
But something else DOES...
Like the fact that even with the laser sight they didn't hit me once...just took out the Blackguards.
Then blew that hole in the wall right in front of the alley...
...And stopped that cop WITHOUT killing him.
The sniper wasn't trying to shoot me at all...
...They--SHE--was leading me here.
Veronica.
H--
Meet me outside the Cairo Tower in 30 minutes. I'll be alone and now so will you.
--V
JESUS, LYNCH...REALLY PULLING OUT ALL THE STOPS, AREN'T YOU?
I should've known he wouldn't be fool enough to show up himself, but SMART ENOUGH to send the one person he knows I won't kill.

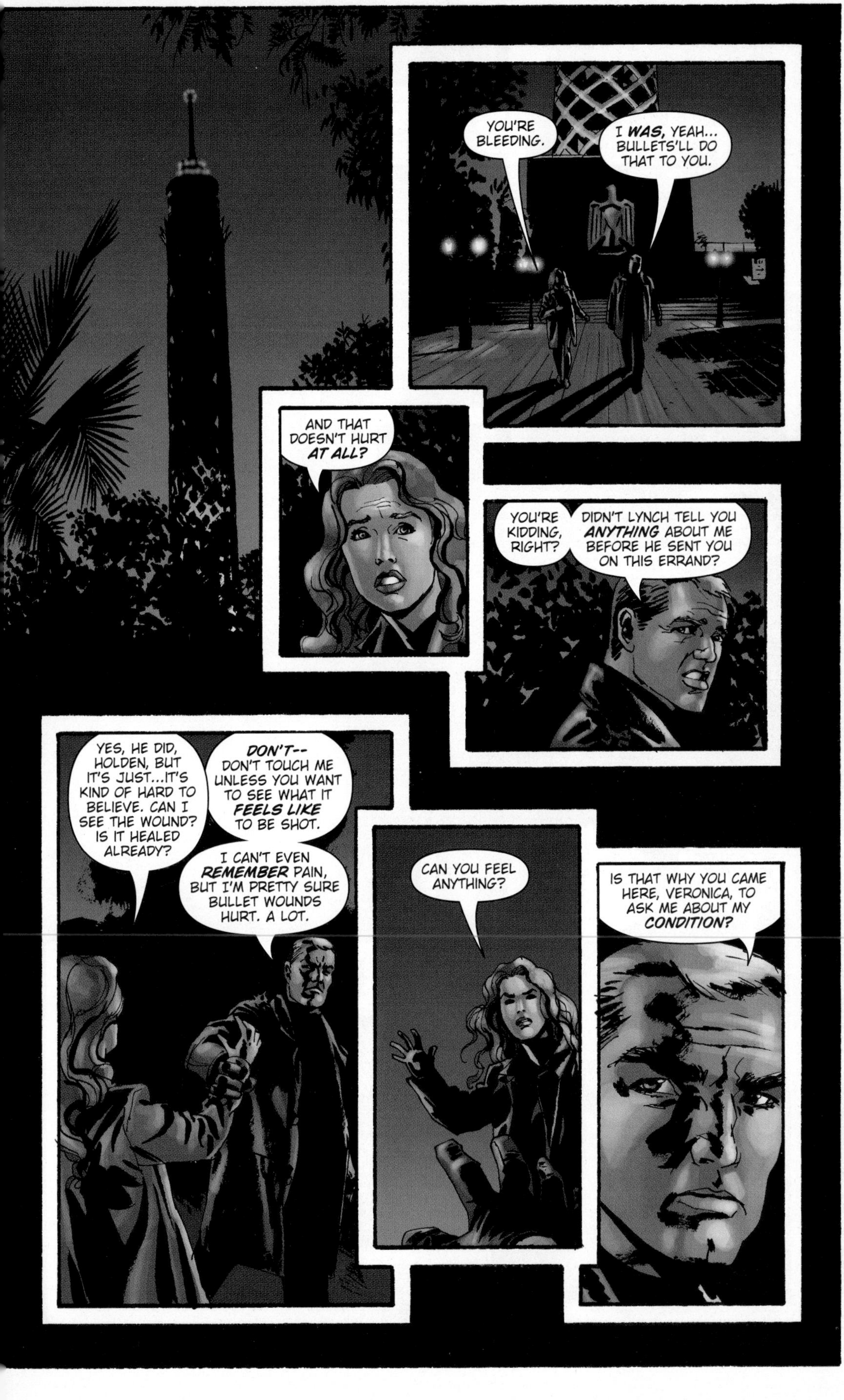
YOU'RE BLEEDING.
I WAS, YEAH... BULLETS'LL DO THAT TO YOU.
AND THAT DOESN'T HURT AT ALL?
YOU'RE KIDDING, RIGHT?
DIDN'T LYNCH TELL YOU ANYTHING ABOUT ME BEFORE HE SENT YOU ON THIS ERRAND?
YES, HE DID, HOLDEN, BUT IT'S JUST...IT'S KIND OF HARD TO BELIEVE. CAN I SEE THE WOUND? IS IT HEALED ALREADY?
DON'T-- DON'T TOUCH ME UNLESS YOU WANT TO SEE WHAT IT FEELS LIKE TO BE SHOT.
I CAN'T EVEN REMEMBER PAIN, BUT I'M PRETTY SURE BULLET WOUNDS HURT. A LOT.
CAN YOU FEEL ANYTHING?
IS THAT WHY YOU CAME HERE, VERONICA, TO ASK ME ABOUT MY CONDITION?

NO, I CAME TO TALK.

WHY?

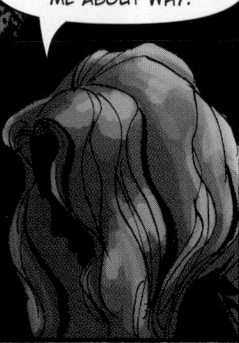

BECAUSE YOU LEFT ME, AND EVERYONE *LIED* TO ME ABOUT WHY.

AND IT *RUINED* MY LIFE...I WAS ON THE TASK-FORCE TRYING TO *CATCH YOU,* FOR GOD'S SAKE...

AND YOU WERE WORKING FOR *LYNCH* ALL ALONG.

I *HATED* YOU, YOU KNOW? OR I THOUGHT I DID.

NOT AT FIRST. AT FIRST I WAS IN DENIAL, COULDN'T BELIEVE THE MAN I WAS GOING TO *MARRY* COULD TURN TRAITOR.

BUT YOU DID BELIEVE IT, EVENTUALLY.

YES...ALL THE *EVIDENCE* THEY HAD AGAINST YOU, AND...AND I DON'T KNOW...

WHAT?

SOMEWHERE INSIDE, IT MADE *SENSE.* I'D SEE YOU WHEN YOU GOT HOME FROM LYNCH'S MISSIONS.

YOU NEVER TALKED ABOUT THEM, BUT...I KNEW WHAT YOU WERE. I KNEW WHAT *BLACK OPS* MEANT.

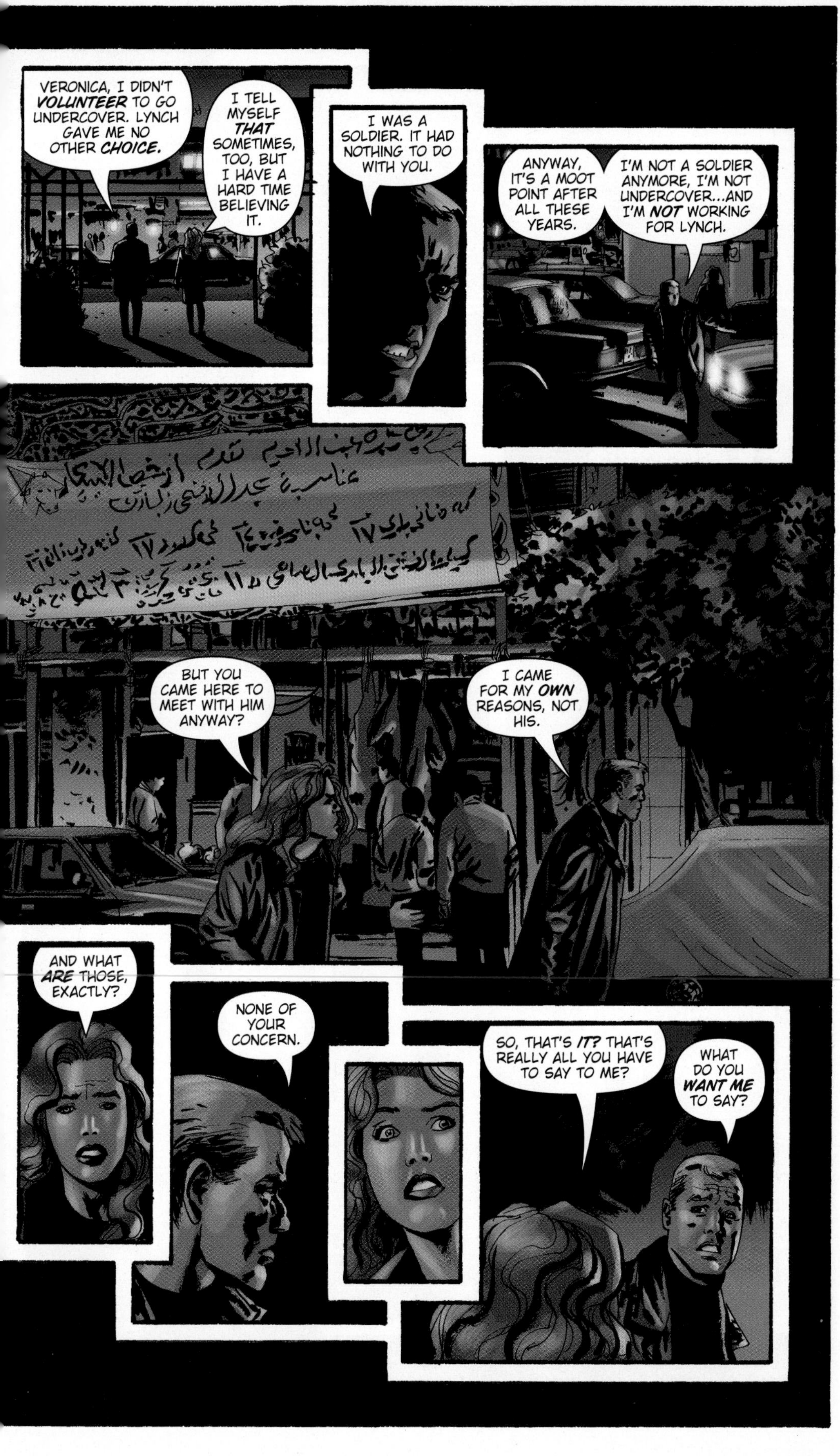
VERONICA, I DIDN'T VOLUNTEER TO GO UNDERCOVER. LYNCH GAVE ME NO OTHER CHOICE.
I TELL MYSELF THAT SOMETIMES, TOO, BUT I HAVE A HARD TIME BELIEVING IT.
I WAS A SOLDIER. IT HAD NOTHING TO DO WITH YOU.
ANYWAY, IT'S A MOOT POINT AFTER ALL THESE YEARS.
I'M NOT A SOLDIER ANYMORE, I'M NOT UNDERCOVER...AND I'M NOT WORKING FOR LYNCH.
BUT YOU CAME HERE TO MEET WITH HIM ANYWAY?
I CAME FOR MY OWN REASONS, NOT HIS.
AND WHAT ARE THOSE, EXACTLY?
NONE OF YOUR CONCERN.
SO, THAT'S IT? THAT'S REALLY ALL YOU HAVE TO SAY TO ME?
WHAT DO YOU WANT ME TO SAY?

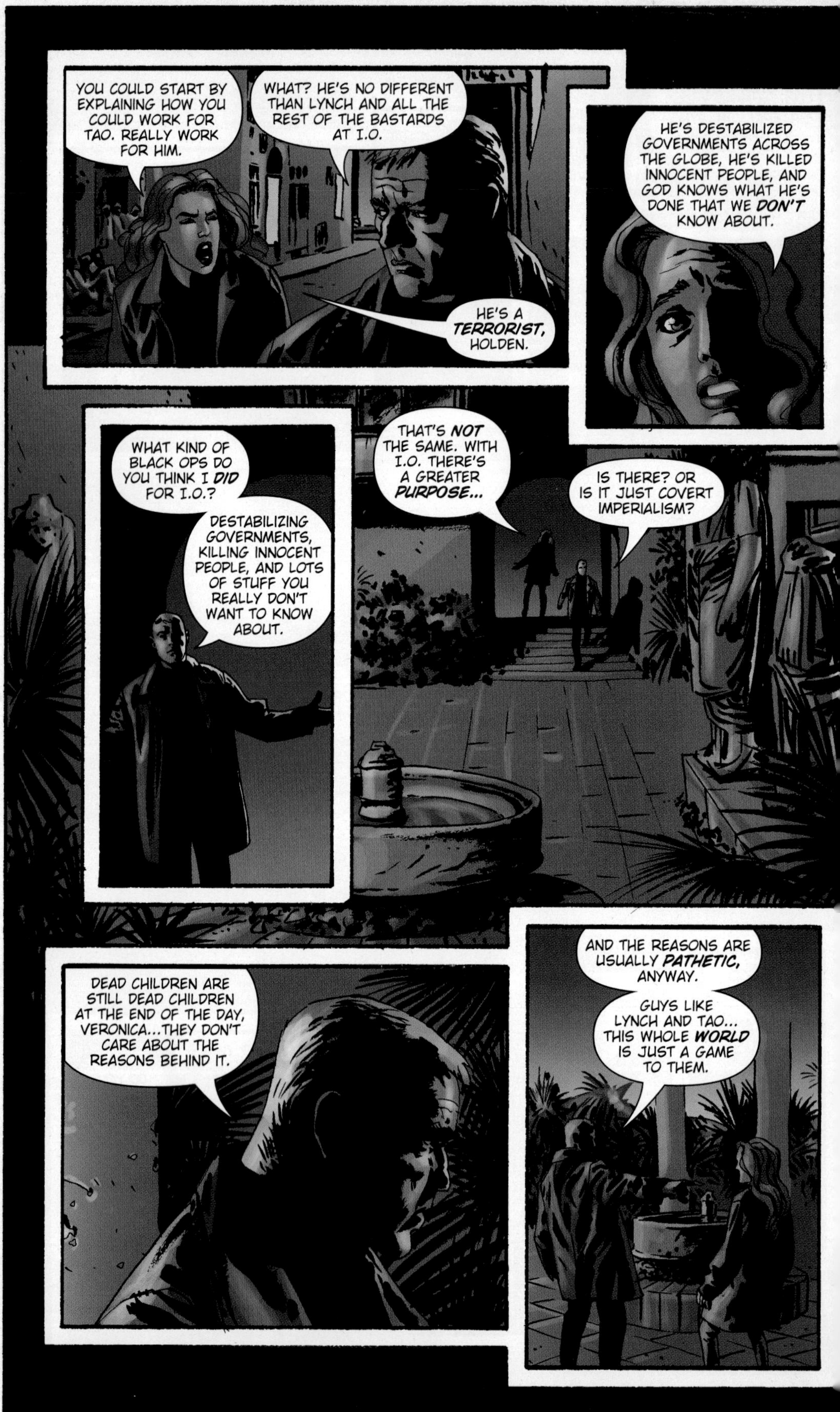
YOU COULD START BY EXPLAINING HOW YOU COULD WORK FOR TAO. REALLY WORK FOR HIM.
WHAT? HE'S NO DIFFERENT THAN LYNCH AND ALL THE REST OF THE BASTARDS AT I.O.
HE'S A *TERRORIST,* HOLDEN.
HE'S DESTABILIZED GOVERNMENTS ACROSS THE GLOBE, HE'S KILLED INNOCENT PEOPLE, AND GOD KNOWS WHAT HE'S DONE THAT WE *DON'T* KNOW ABOUT.
WHAT KIND OF BLACK OPS DO YOU THINK I *DID* FOR I.O.?
DESTABILIZING GOVERNMENTS, KILLING INNOCENT PEOPLE, AND LOTS OF STUFF YOU REALLY DON'T WANT TO KNOW ABOUT.
THAT'S *NOT* THE SAME. WITH I.O. THERE'S A GREATER *PURPOSE...*
IS THERE? OR IS IT JUST COVERT IMPERIALISM?
DEAD CHILDREN ARE STILL DEAD CHILDREN AT THE END OF THE DAY, VERONICA...THEY DON'T CARE ABOUT THE REASONS BEHIND IT.
AND THE REASONS ARE USUALLY *PATHETIC,* ANYWAY.
GUYS LIKE LYNCH AND TAO... THIS WHOLE *WORLD* IS JUST A GAME TO THEM.

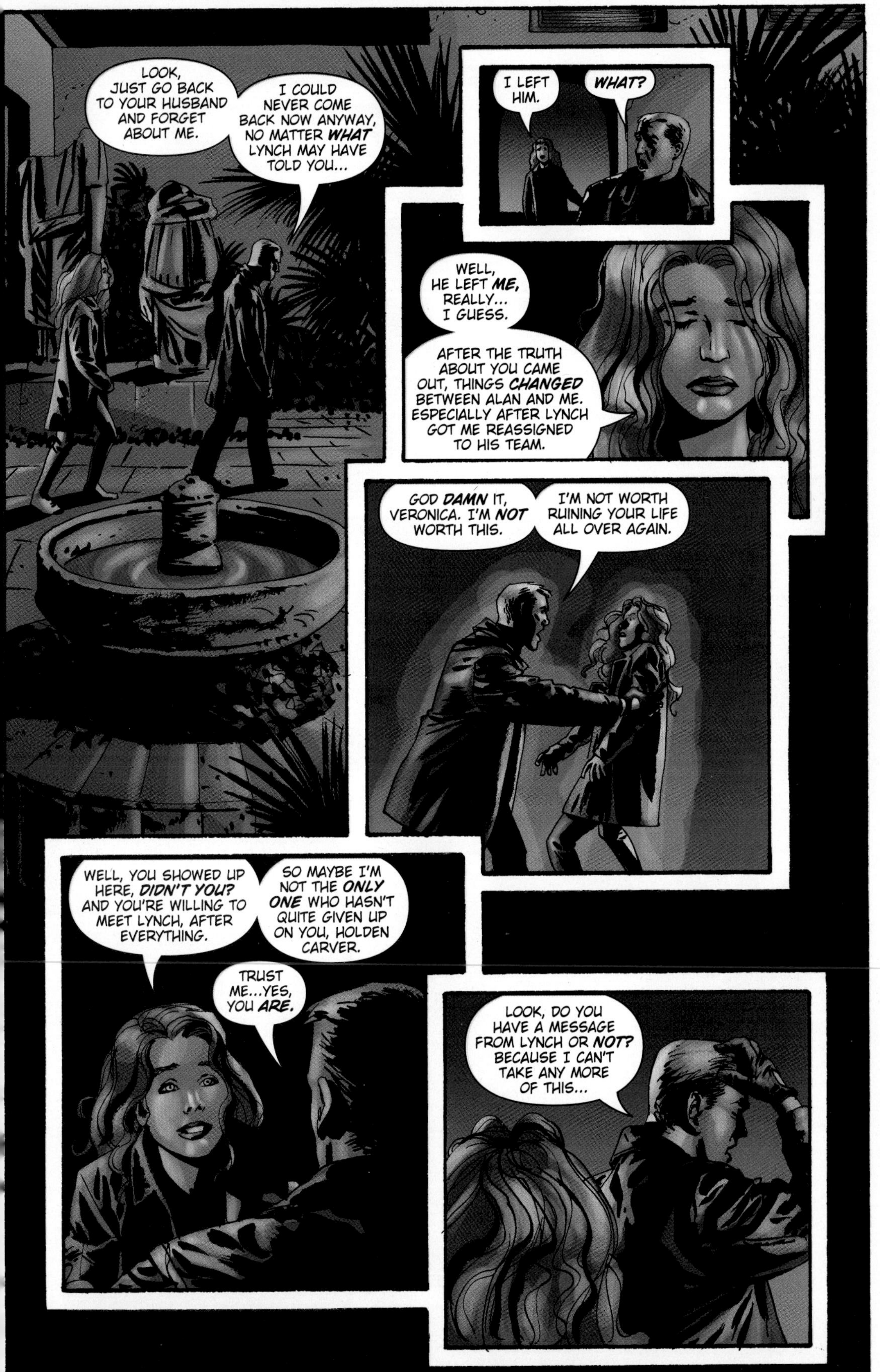
LOOK, JUST GO BACK TO YOUR HUSBAND AND FORGET ABOUT ME.
I COULD NEVER COME BACK NOW ANYWAY, NO MATTER WHAT LYNCH MAY HAVE TOLD YOU...
I LEFT HIM.
WHAT?
WELL, HE LEFT ME, REALLY... I GUESS.
AFTER THE TRUTH ABOUT YOU CAME OUT, THINGS CHANGED BETWEEN ALAN AND ME. ESPECIALLY AFTER LYNCH GOT ME REASSIGNED TO HIS TEAM.
GOD DAMN IT, VERONICA. I'M NOT WORTH THIS.
I'M NOT WORTH RUINING YOUR LIFE ALL OVER AGAIN.
WELL, YOU SHOWED UP HERE, DIDN'T YOU? AND YOU'RE WILLING TO MEET LYNCH, AFTER EVERYTHING.
SO MAYBE I'M NOT THE ONLY ONE WHO HASN'T QUITE GIVEN UP ON YOU, HOLDEN CARVER.
TRUST ME...YES, YOU ARE.
LOOK, DO YOU HAVE A MESSAGE FROM LYNCH OR NOT? BECAUSE I CAN'T TAKE ANY MORE OF THIS...

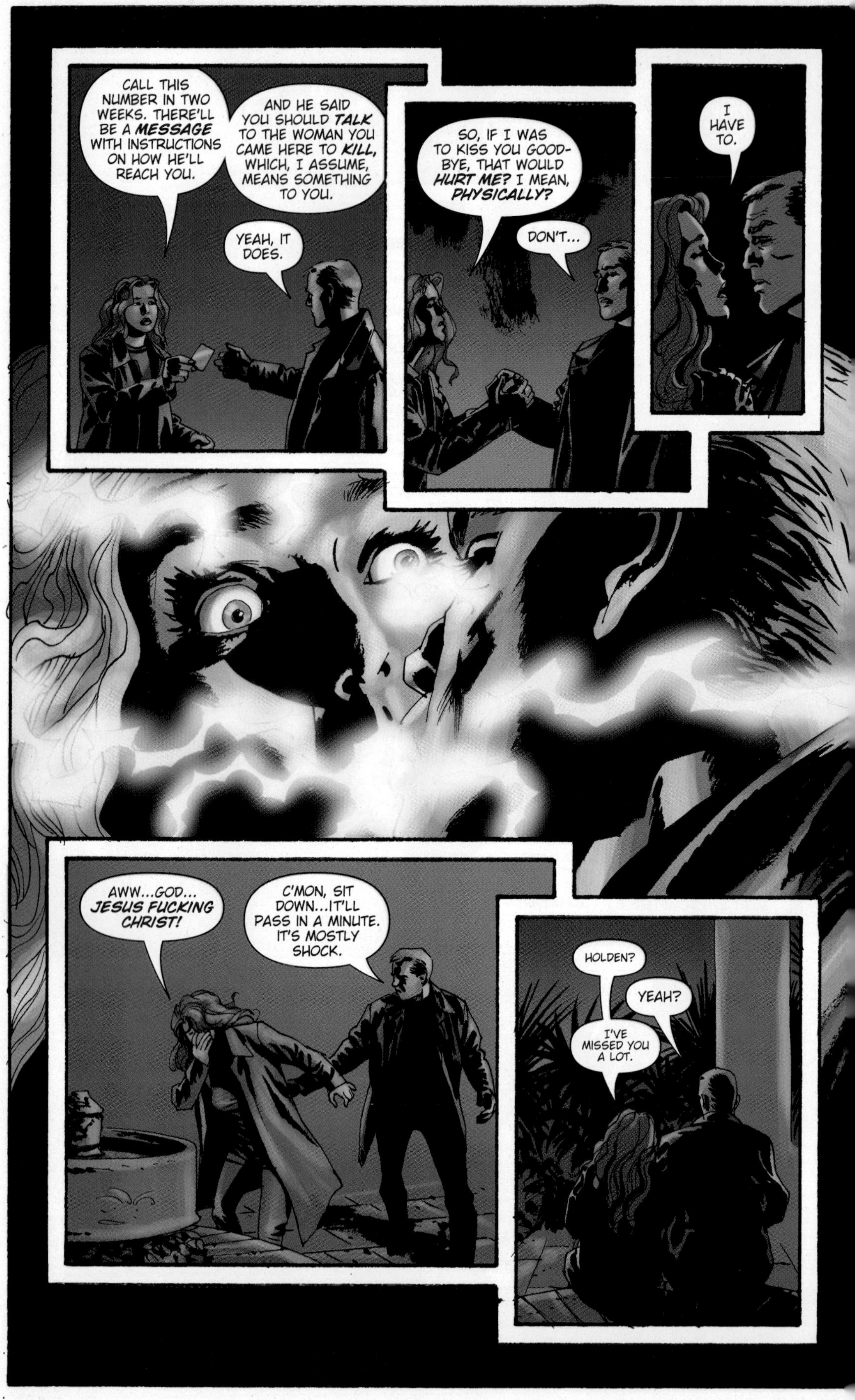
CALL THIS NUMBER IN TWO WEEKS. THERE'LL BE A MESSAGE WITH INSTRUCTIONS ON HOW HE'LL REACH YOU.
AND HE SAID YOU SHOULD TALK TO THE WOMAN YOU CAME HERE TO KILL, WHICH, I ASSUME, MEANS SOMETHING TO YOU.
YEAH, IT DOES.
SO, IF I WAS TO KISS YOU GOOD-BYE, THAT WOULD HURT ME? I MEAN, PHYSICALLY?
DON'T...
I HAVE TO.
AWW...GOD... JESUS FUCKING CHRIST!
C'MON, SIT DOWN...IT'LL PASS IN A MINUTE. IT'S MOSTLY SHOCK.
HOLDEN?
YEAH?
I'VE MISSED YOU A LOT.

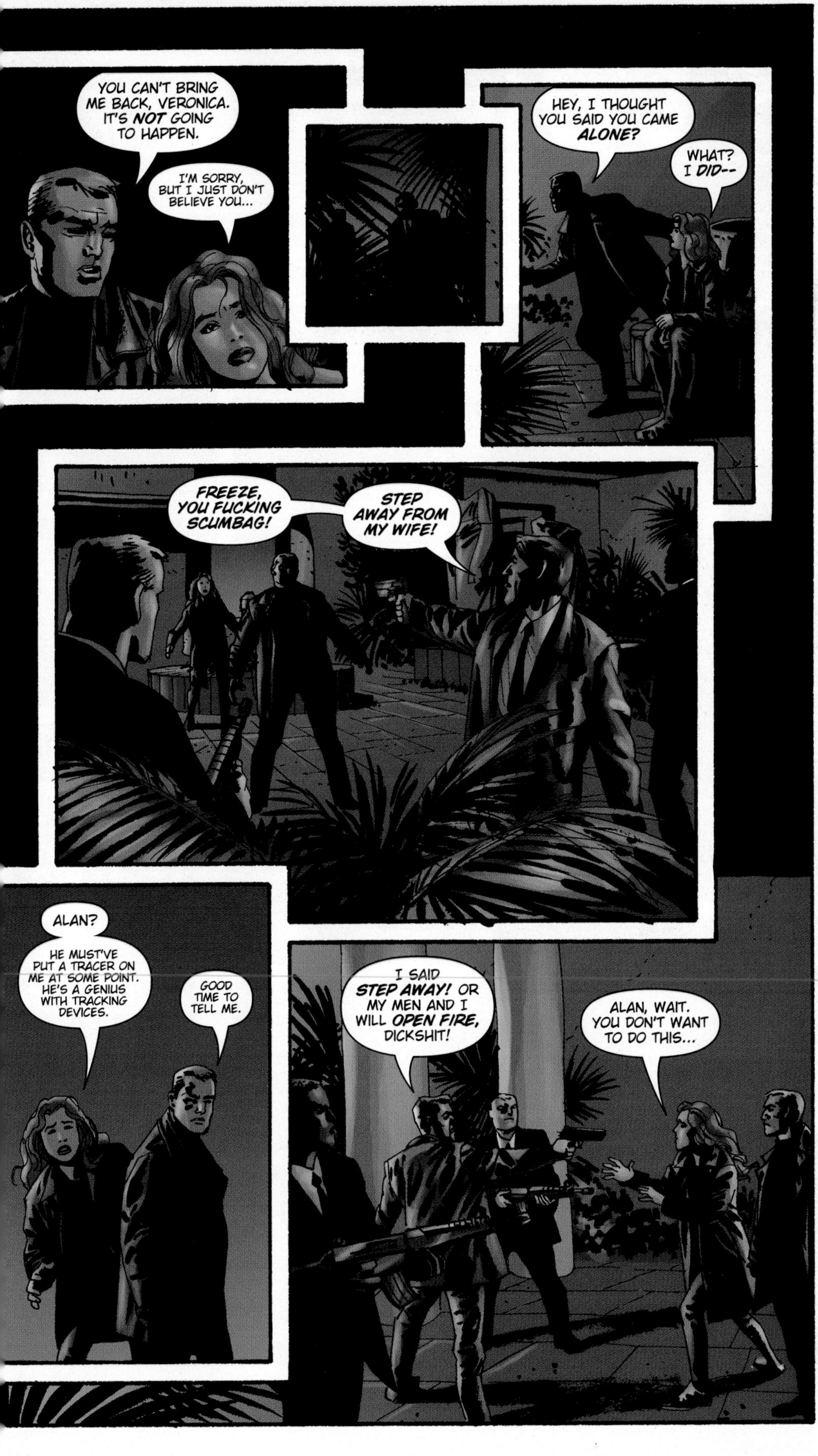
YOU CAN'T BRING ME BACK, VERONICA. IT'S **NOT** GOING TO HAPPEN.
I'M SORRY, BUT I JUST DON'T BELIEVE YOU...
HEY, I THOUGHT YOU SAID YOU CAME **ALONE?**
WHAT? I **DID--**
FREEZE, YOU FUCKING SCUMBAG!
STEP AWAY FROM MY WIFE!
ALAN?
HE MUST'VE PUT A TRACER ON ME AT SOME POINT. HE'S A GENIUS WITH TRACKING DEVICES.
GOOD TIME TO TELL ME.
I SAID **STEP AWAY!** OR MY MEN AND I WILL **OPEN FIRE,** DICKSHIT!
ALAN, WAIT. YOU DON'T WANT TO DO THIS...

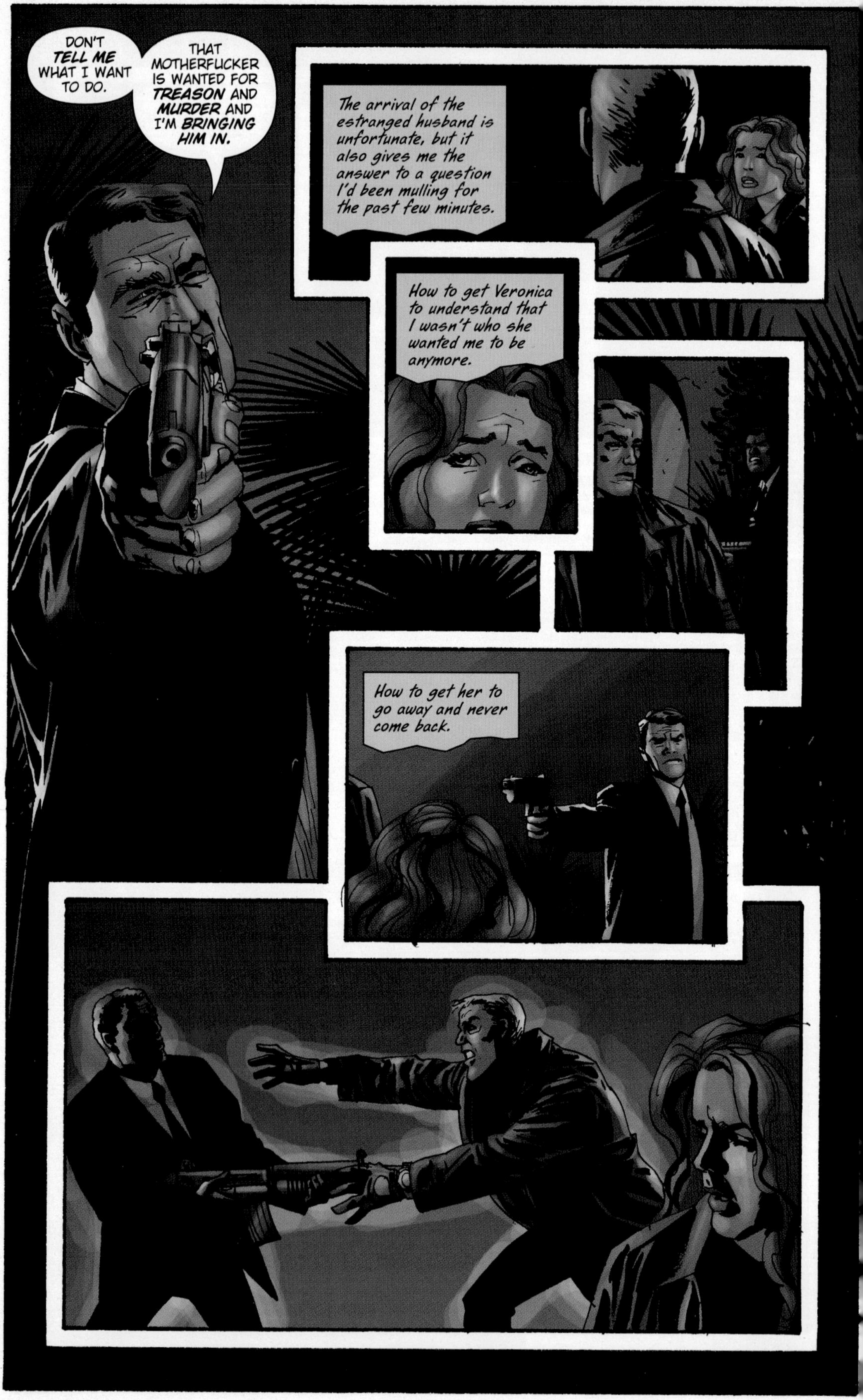
DON'T TELL ME WHAT I WANT TO DO.
THAT MOTHERFUCKER IS WANTED FOR TREASON AND MURDER AND I'M BRINGING HIM IN.
The arrival of the estranged husband is unfortunate, but it also gives me the answer to a question I'd been mulling for the past few minutes.
How to get Veronica to understand that I wasn't who she wanted me to be anymore.
How to get her to go away and never come back.

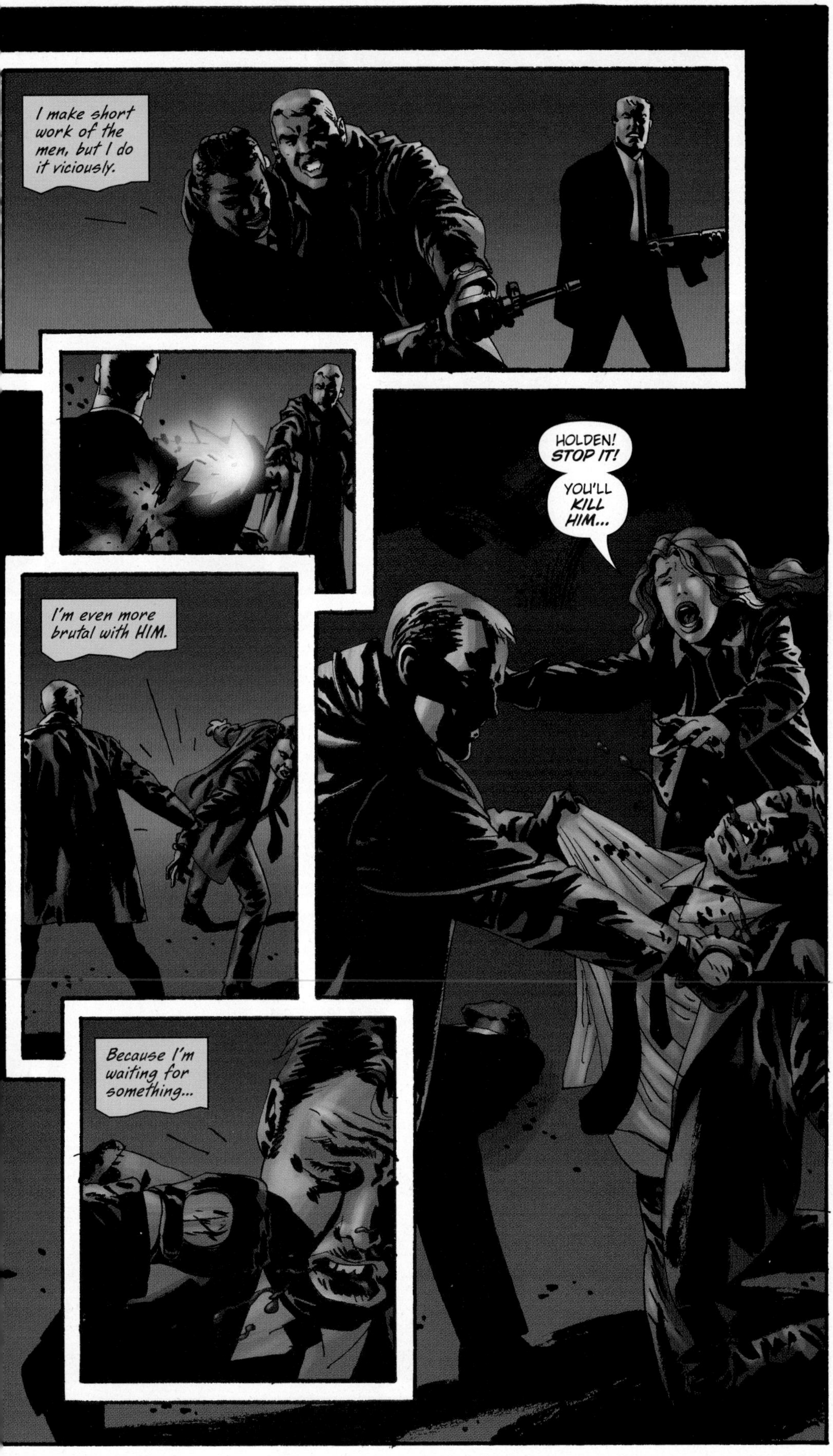
I make short work of the men, but I do it viciously.
HOLDEN! STOP IT!
YOU'LL KILL HIM...
I'm even more brutal with HIM.
Because I'm waiting for something...

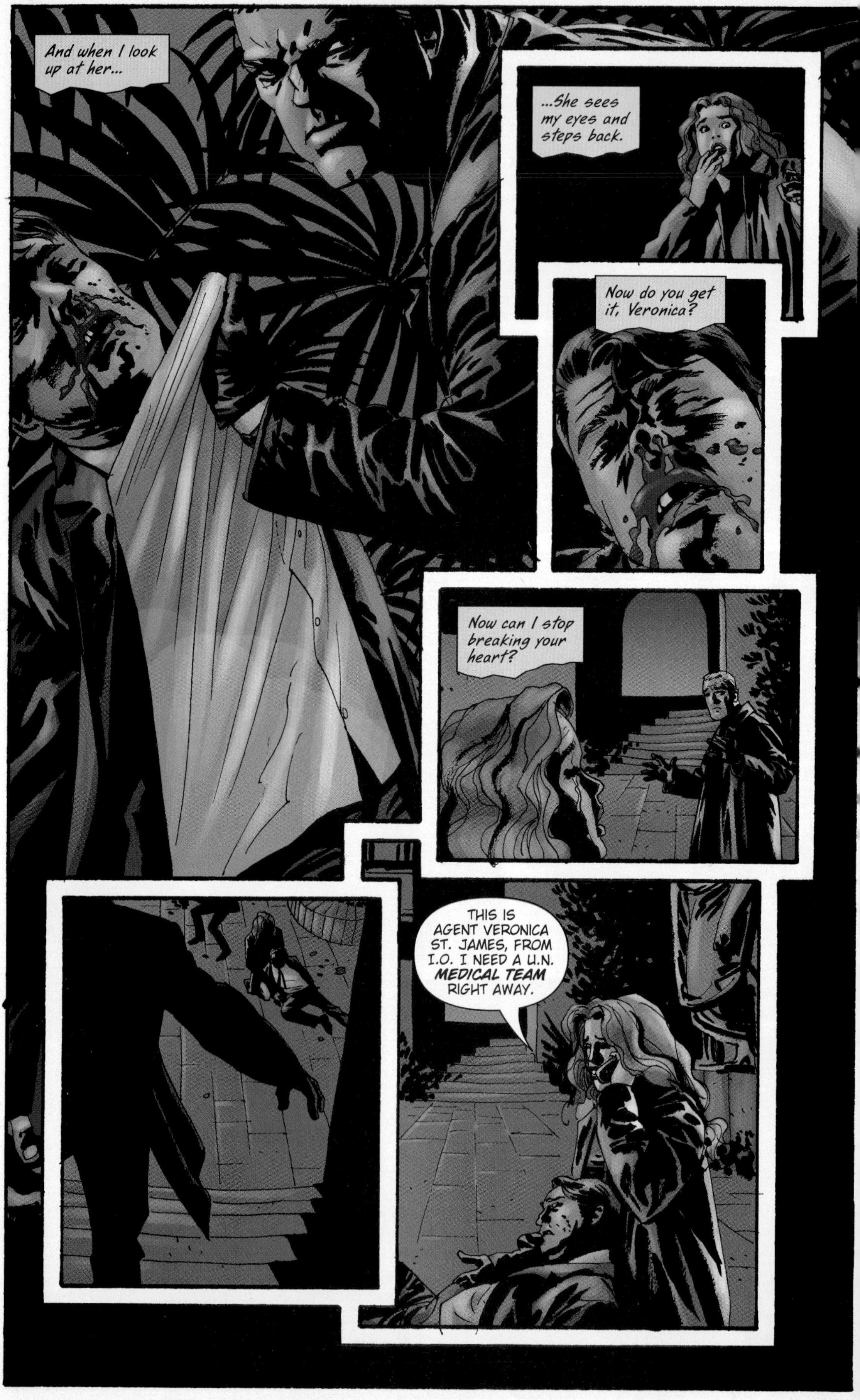

And when I look up at her...
...She sees my eyes and steps back.
Now do you get it, Veronica?
Now can I stop breaking your heart?
THIS IS AGENT VERONICA ST. JAMES, FROM I.O. I NEED A U.N. MEDICAL TEAM RIGHT AWAY.

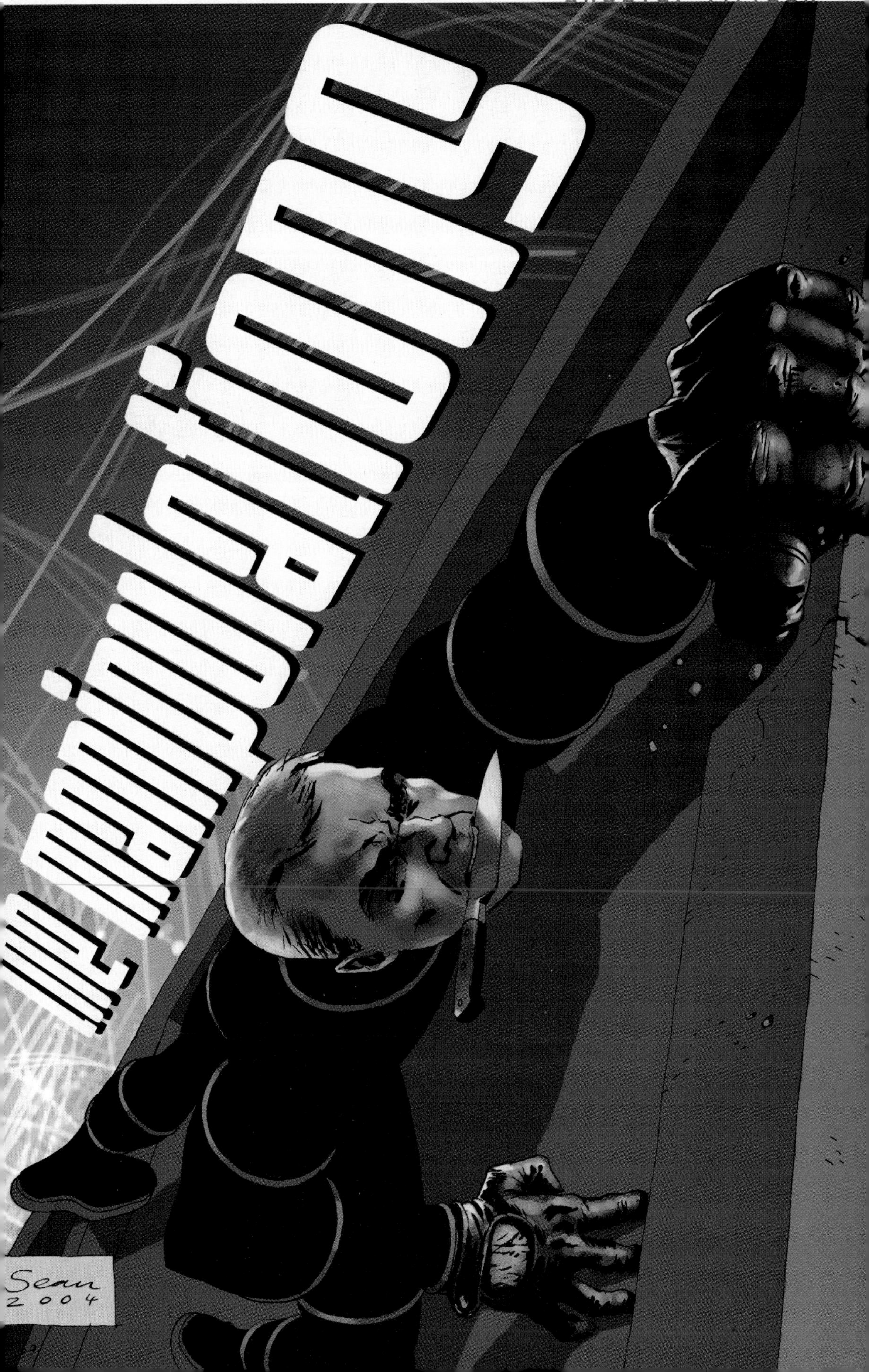
the manipulations
Sean 2004

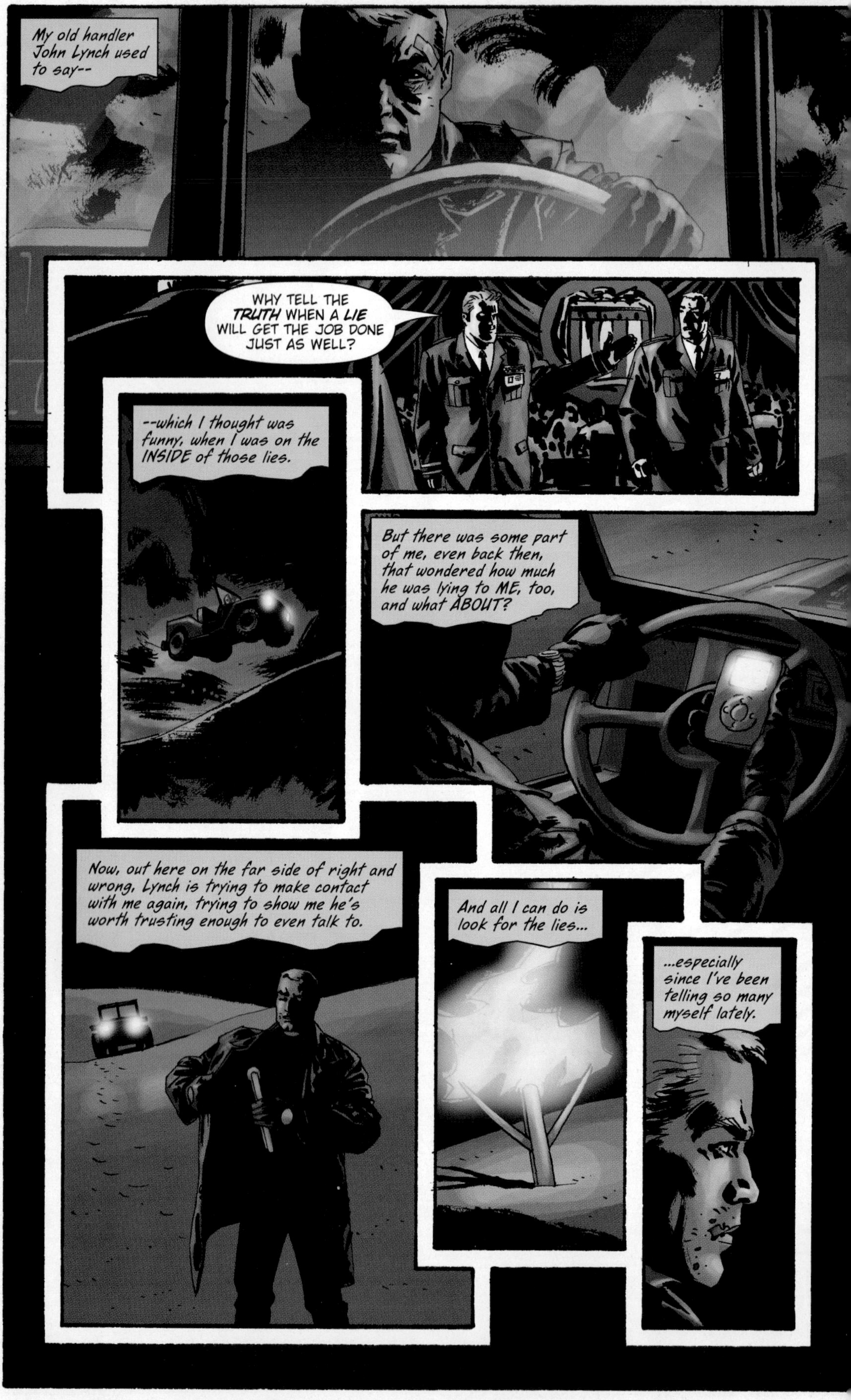
My old handler John Lynch used to say--
WHY TELL THE TRUTH WHEN A LIE WILL GET THE JOB DONE JUST AS WELL?
--which I thought was funny, when I was on the INSIDE of those lies.
But there was some part of me, even back then, that wondered how much he was lying to ME, too, and what ABOUT?
Now, out here on the far side of right and wrong, Lynch is trying to make contact with me again, trying to show me he's worth trusting enough to even talk to.
And all I can do is look for the lies...
...especially since I've been telling so many myself lately.

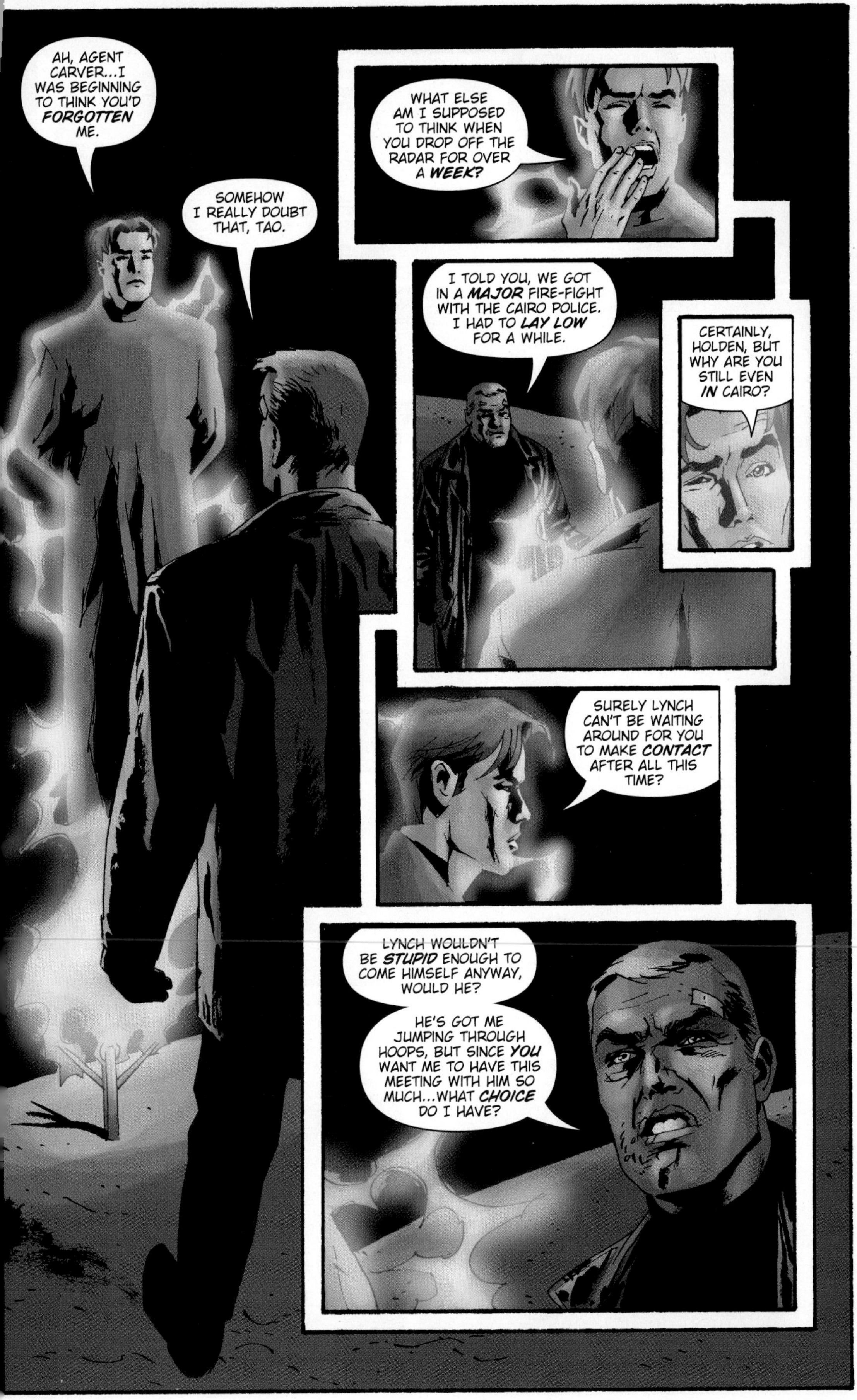
AH, AGENT CARVER...I WAS BEGINNING TO THINK YOU'D FORGOTTEN ME.
SOMEHOW I REALLY DOUBT THAT, TAO.
WHAT ELSE AM I SUPPOSED TO THINK WHEN YOU DROP OFF THE RADAR FOR OVER A WEEK?
I TOLD YOU, WE GOT IN A MAJOR FIRE-FIGHT WITH THE CAIRO POLICE. I HAD TO LAY LOW FOR A WHILE.
CERTAINLY, HOLDEN, BUT WHY ARE YOU STILL EVEN IN CAIRO?
SURELY LYNCH CAN'T BE WAITING AROUND FOR YOU TO MAKE CONTACT AFTER ALL THIS TIME?
LYNCH WOULDN'T BE STUPID ENOUGH TO COME HIMSELF ANYWAY, WOULD HE?
HE'S GOT ME JUMPING THROUGH HOOPS, BUT SINCE YOU WANT ME TO HAVE THIS MEETING WITH HIM SO MUCH...WHAT CHOICE DO I HAVE?

WHAT **HOOPS**, EXACTLY?

WELL, THAT FIRE-FIGHT WITH THE POLICE, FOR ONE.

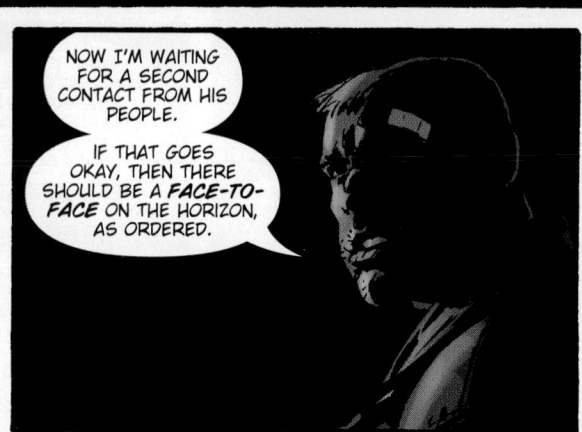

NOW I'M WAITING FOR A SECOND CONTACT FROM HIS PEOPLE.

IF THAT GOES OKAY, THEN THERE SHOULD BE A **FACE-TO-FACE** ON THE HORIZON, AS ORDERED.

OH, COME **ON**, HOLDEN. YOU HAVE TO AT LEAST BE CURIOUS TO SEE WHAT THE OLD BASTARD HAS TO SAY FOR HIMSELF.

NOT REALLY. I'M MORE INTERESTED IN WHY LYNCH MEANS MORE TO YOU THAN ANY **OTHER** GOVERNMENT SPOOK.

WHATEVER GAVE YOU **THAT** IDEA?

I'M **HERE**, AREN'T I? MUST MEAN **SOMETHING** TO YOU.

CLEVER BOY... LISTEN, JUST FINISH UP AND GET BACK TO HOME BASE. MISS MISERY'S BEEN GETTING **RESTLESS** WITHOUT YOU AROUND.

SHE'S MAIMED SOME VALUABLE PEOPLE.

I'LL BET SHE HAS.

OH, AND HOLDEN...IF YOU'RE KEEPING A **LOW PROFILE**, HOW DID YOU MANAGE TO GET BEATEN EARLIER TONIGHT? JUDGING BY YOUR **FACE**.

OH, **THIS**? LET'S JUST SAY, IT WAS A PRETTY **DIVEY** BAR AND MY ARABIC IS REAL **RUSTY**...

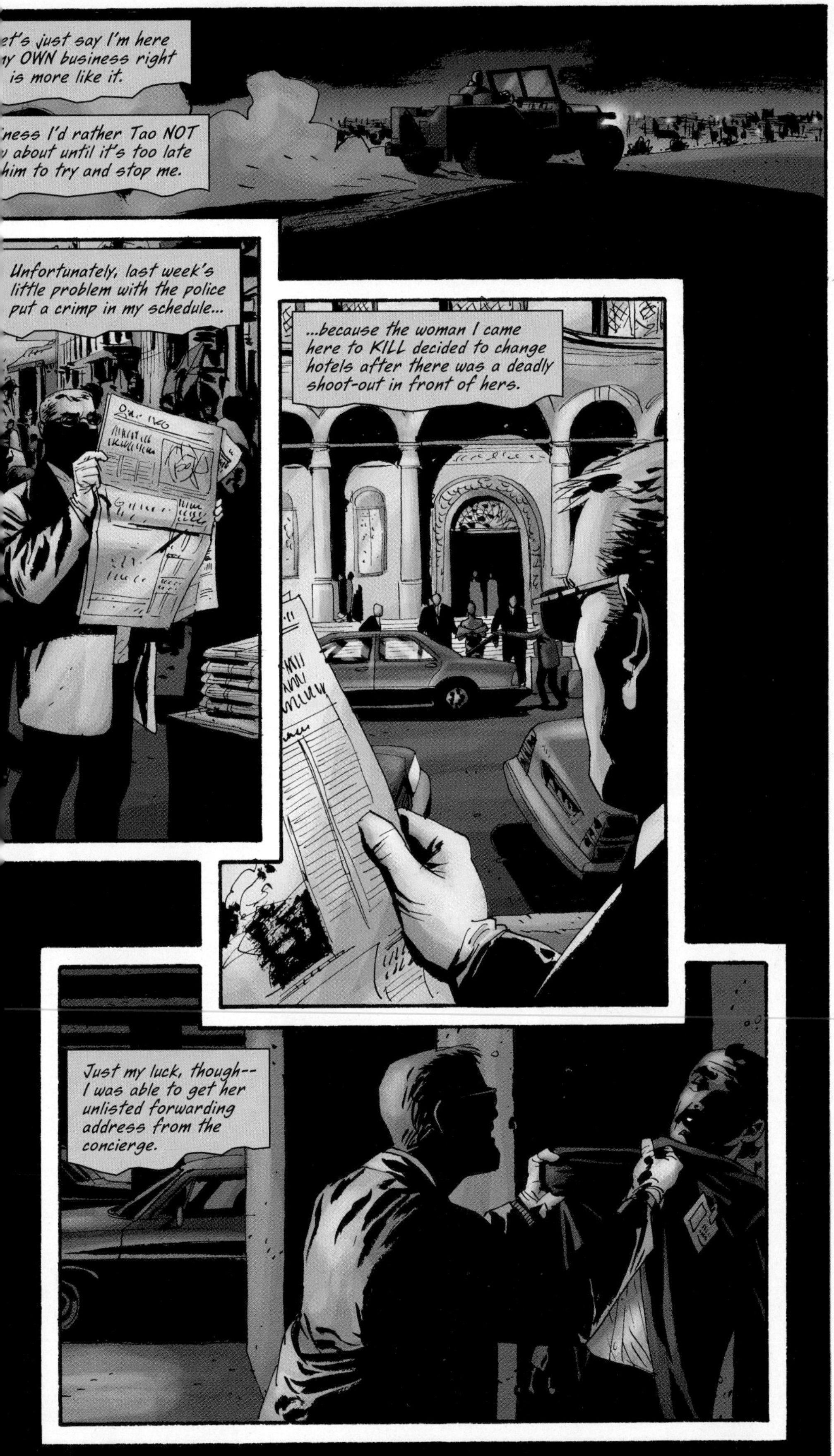
et's just say I'm here
ny OWN business right
is more like it.
iness I'd rather Tao NOT
about until it's too late
him to try and stop me.
Unfortunately, last week's little problem with the police put a crimp in my schedule...
...because the woman I came here to KILL decided to change hotels after there was a deadly shoot-out in front of hers.
Just my luck, though-- I was able to get her unlisted forwarding address from the concierge.

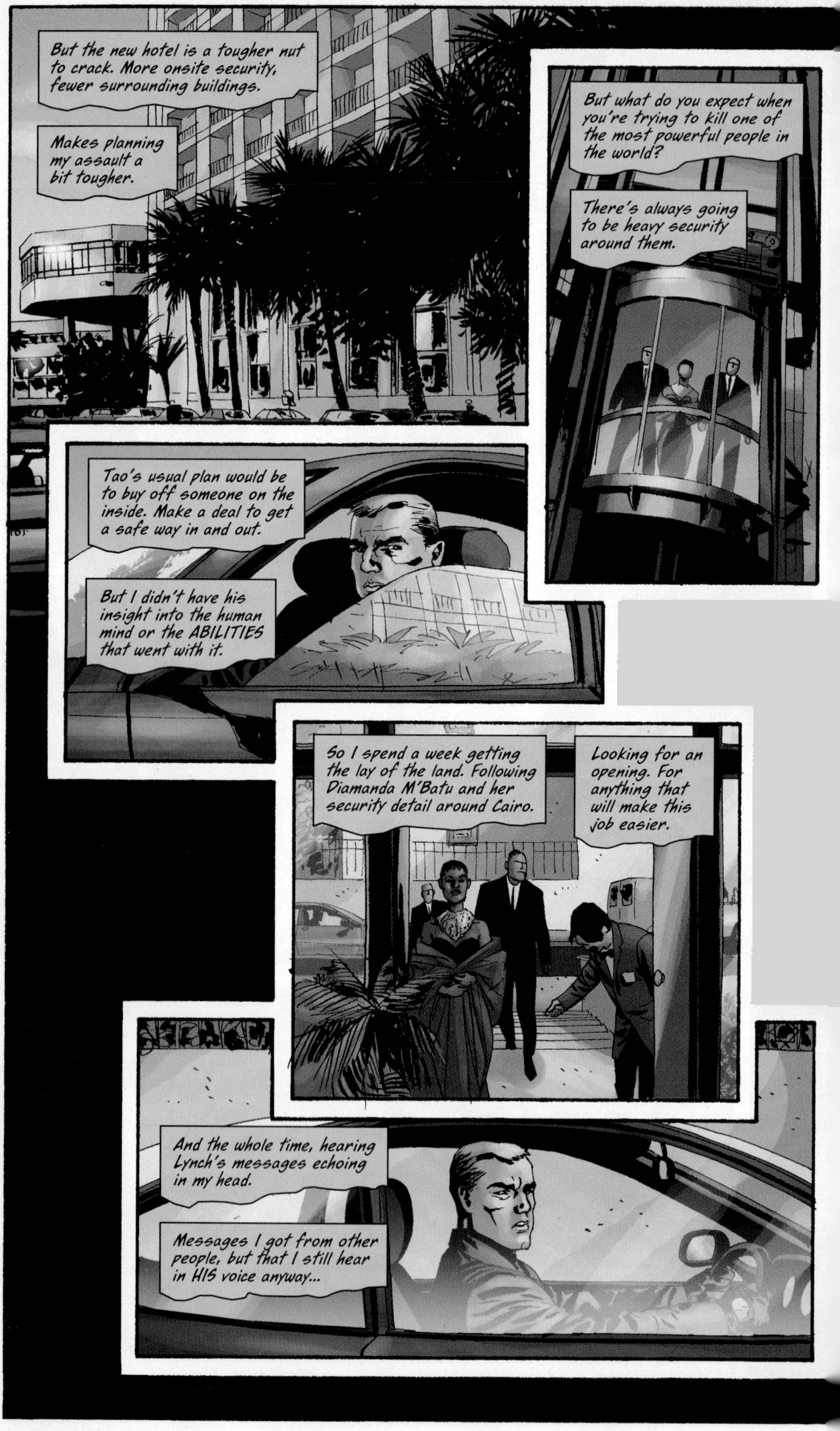
But the new hotel is a tougher nut to crack. More onsite security, fewer surrounding buildings.
Makes planning my assault a bit tougher.
But what do you expect when you're trying to kill one of the most powerful people in the world?
There's always going to be heavy security around them.
Tao's usual plan would be to buy off someone on the inside. Make a deal to get a safe way in and out.
But I didn't have his insight into the human mind or the ABILITIES that went with it.
So I spend a week getting the lay of the land. Following Diamanda M'Batu and her security detail around Cairo.
Looking for an opening. For anything that will make this job easier.
And the whole time, hearing Lynch's messages echoing in my head.
Messages I got from other people, but that I still hear in HIS voice anyway...

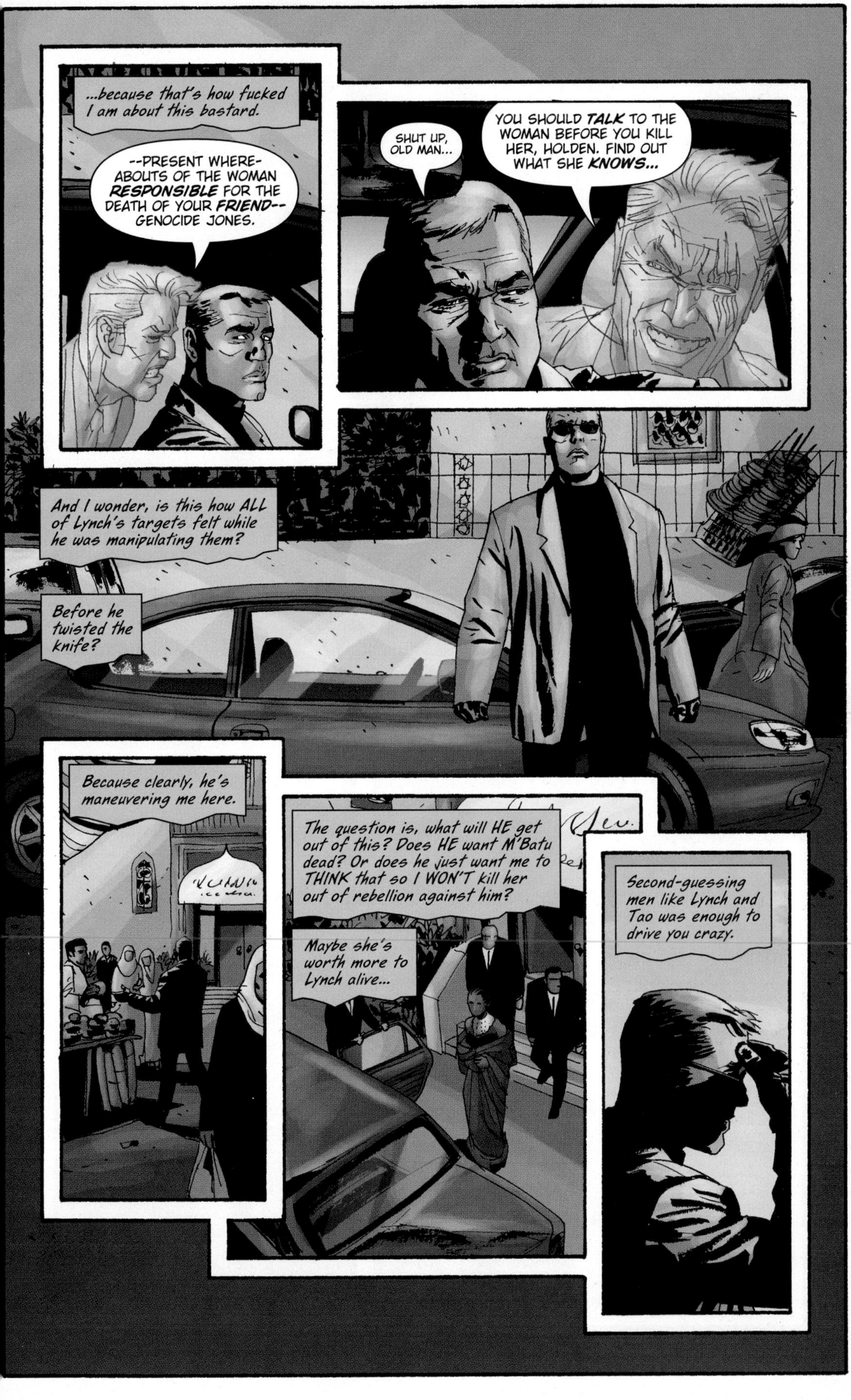
...because that's how fucked I am about this bastard.
--PRESENT WHERE-ABOUTS OF THE WOMAN RESPONSIBLE FOR THE DEATH OF YOUR FRIEND--GENOCIDE JONES.
SHUT UP, OLD MAN...
YOU SHOULD TALK TO THE WOMAN BEFORE YOU KILL HER, HOLDEN. FIND OUT WHAT SHE KNOWS...
And I wonder, is this how ALL of Lynch's targets felt while he was manipulating them?
Before he twisted the knife?
Because clearly, he's maneuvering me here.
The question is, what will HE get out of this? Does HE want M'Batu dead? Or does he just want me to THINK that so I WON'T kill her out of rebellion against him?
Maybe she's worth more to Lynch alive...
Second-guessing men like Lynch and Tao was enough to drive you crazy.

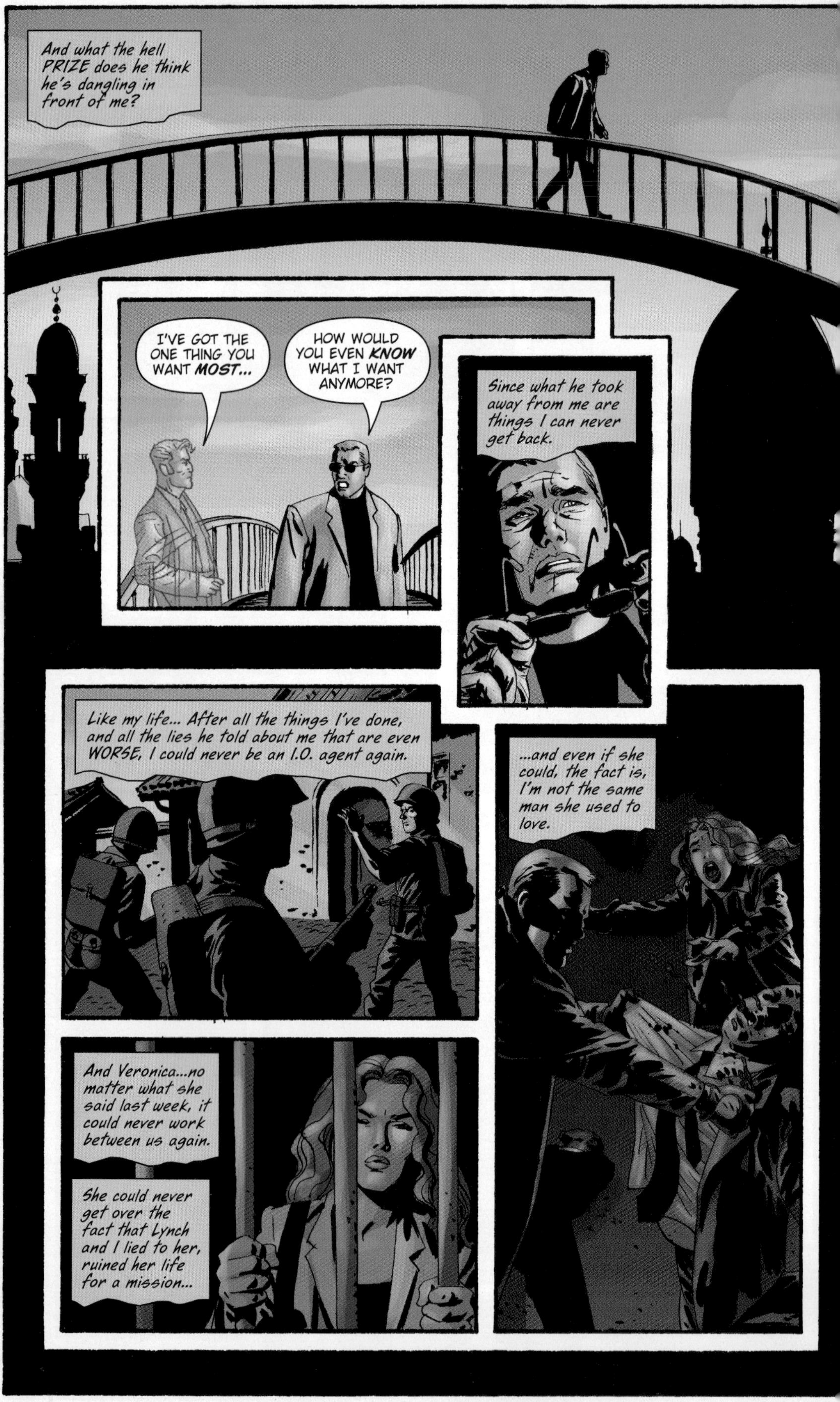
And what the hell PRIZE does he think he's dangling in front of me?
I'VE GOT THE ONE THING YOU WANT MOST...
HOW WOULD YOU EVEN KNOW WHAT I WANT ANYMORE?
Since what he took away from me are things I can never get back.
Like my life... After all the things I've done, and all the lies he told about me that are even WORSE, I could never be an I.O. agent again.
And Veronica...no matter what she said last week, it could never work between us again.
She could never get over the fact that Lynch and I lied to her, ruined her life for a mission...
...and even if she could, the fact is, I'm not the same man she used to love.

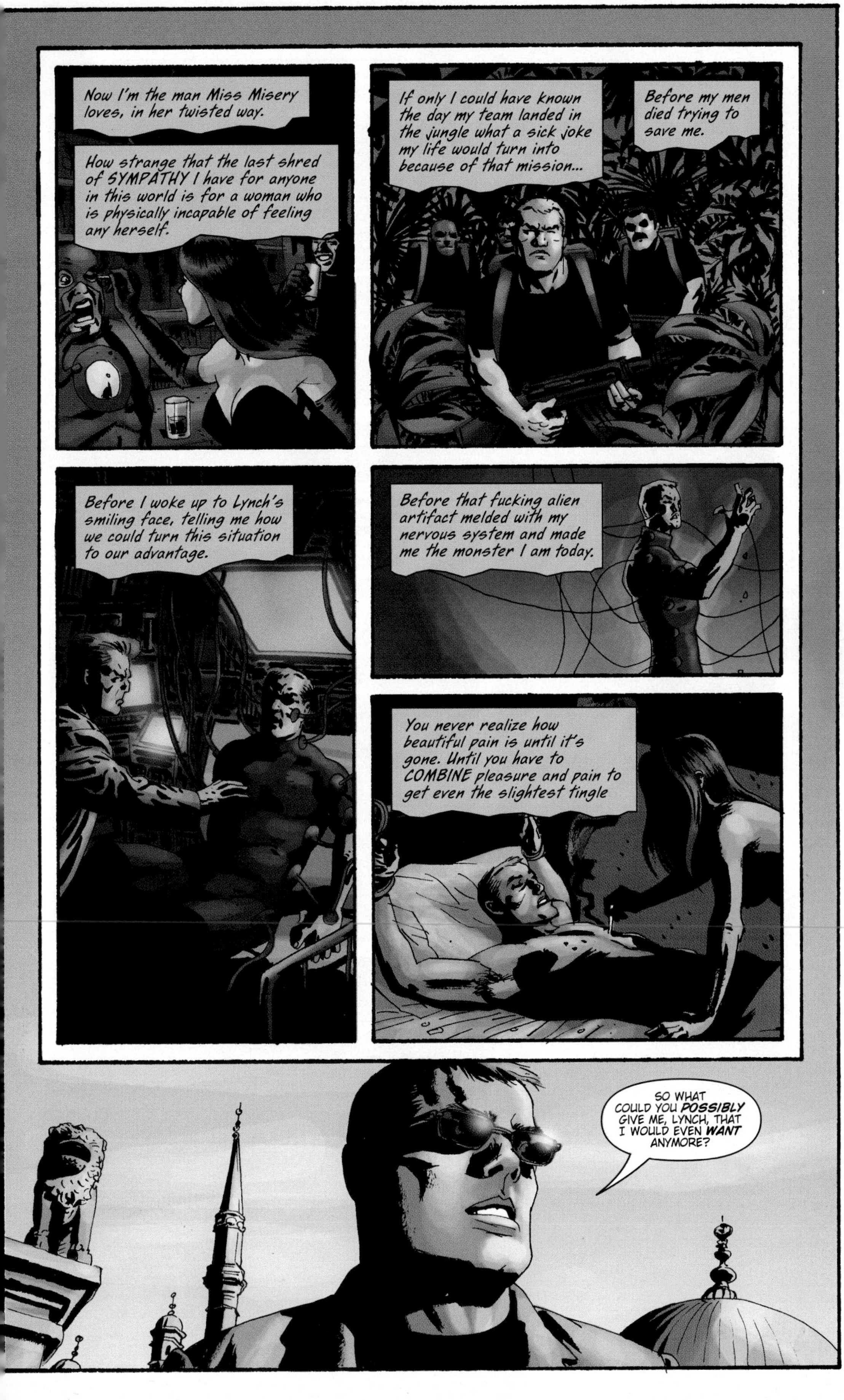

Now I'm the man Miss Misery loves, in her twisted way.
How strange that the last shred of SYMPATHY I have for anyone in this world is for a woman who is physically incapable of feeling any herself.
If only I could have known the day my team landed in the jungle what a sick joke my life would turn into because of that mission...
Before my men died trying to save me.
Before I woke up to Lynch's smiling face, telling me how we could turn this situation to our advantage.
Before that fucking alien artifact melded with my nervous system and made me the monster I am today.
You never realize how beautiful pain is until it's gone. Until you have to COMBINE pleasure and pain to get even the slightest tingle
SO WHAT COULD YOU POSSIBLY GIVE ME, LYNCH, THAT I WOULD EVEN WANT ANYMORE?

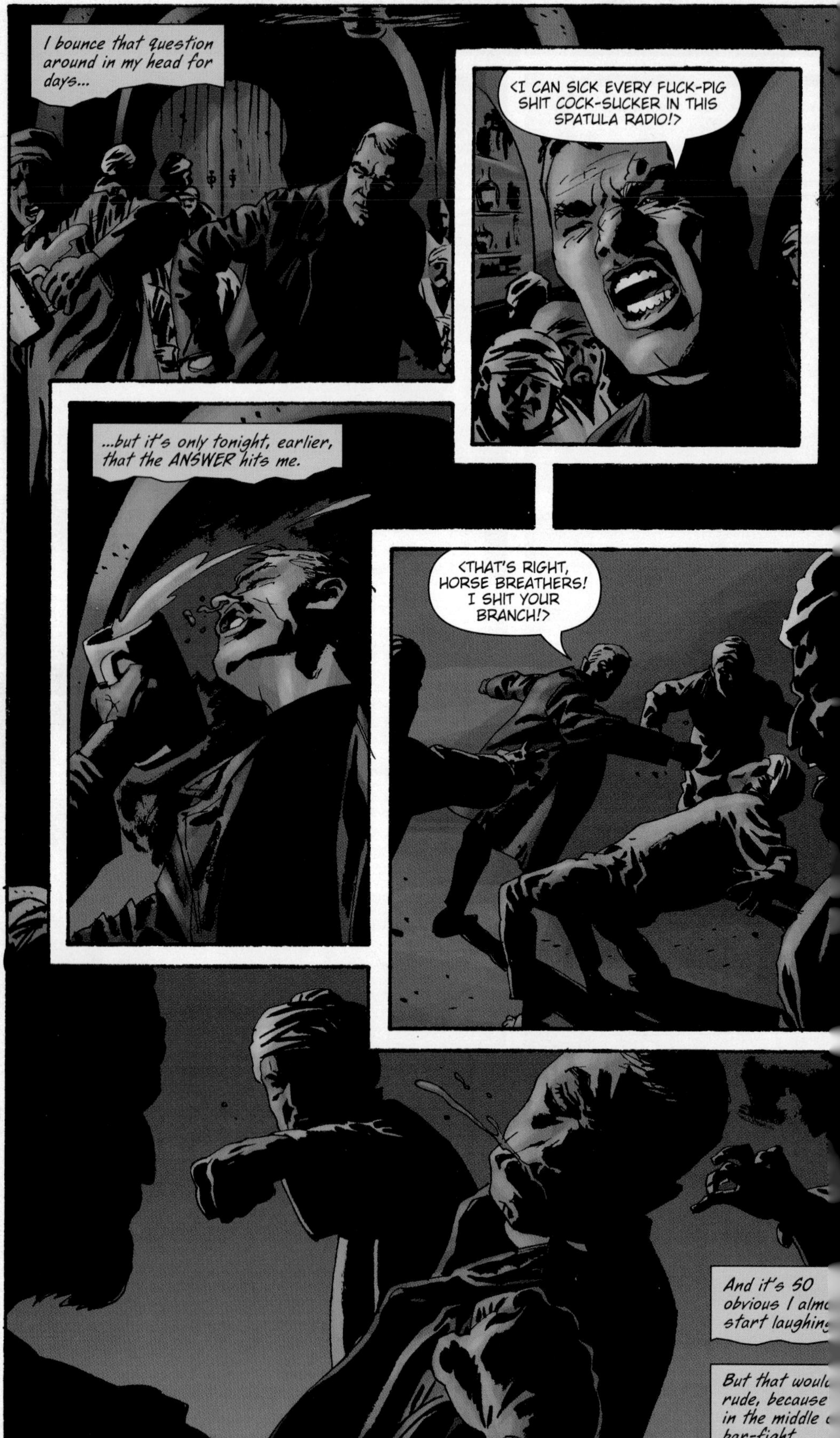
I bounce that question around in my head for days...
<I CAN SICK EVERY FUCK-PIG SHIT COCK-SUCKER IN THIS SPATULA RADIO!>
...but it's only tonight, earlier, that the ANSWER hits me.
<THAT'S RIGHT, HORSE BREATHERS! I SHIT YOUR BRANCH!>
And it's SO obvious I alm start laughin
But that woul rude, because in the middle bar-fight.

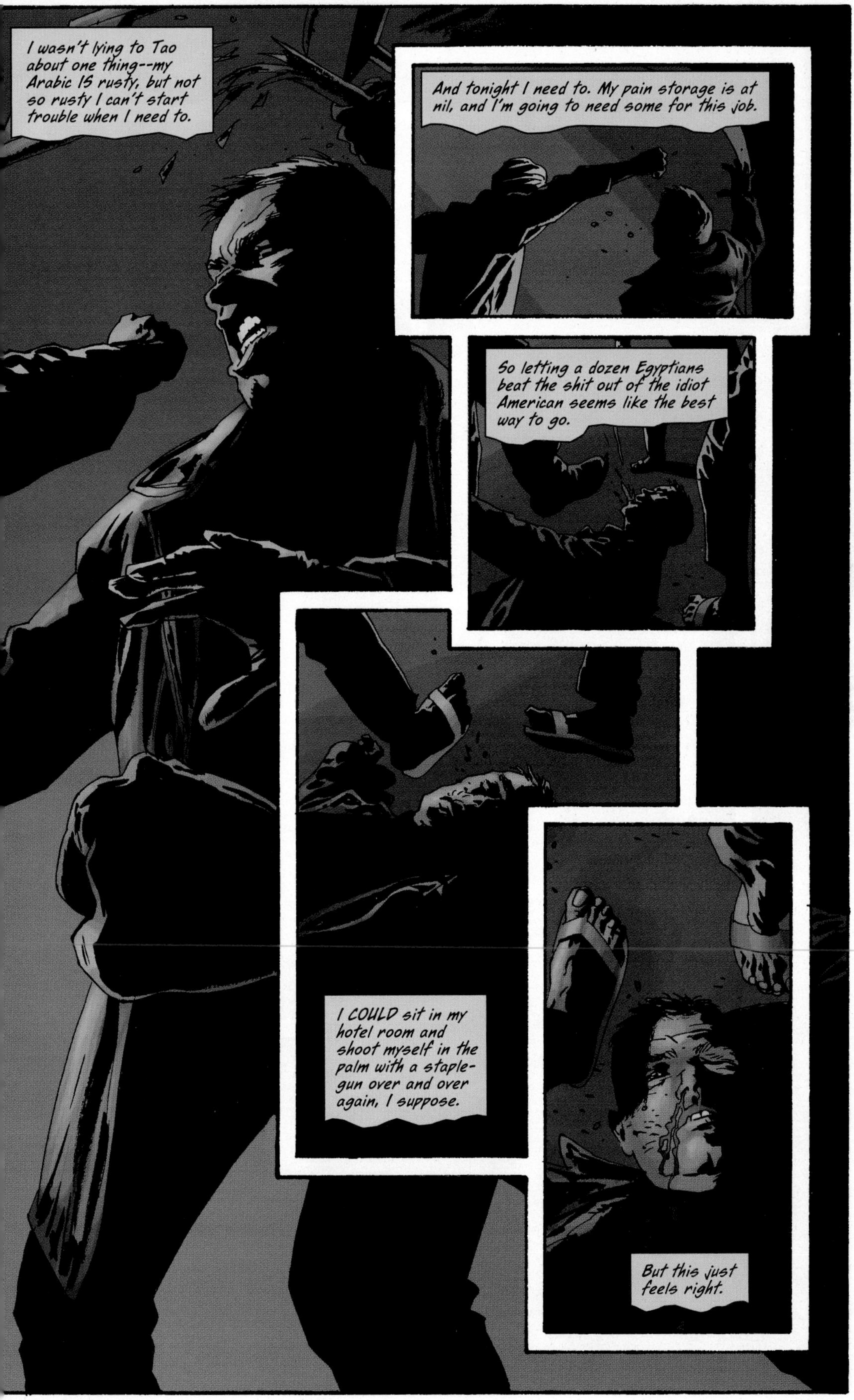
I wasn't lying to Tao about one thing--my Arabic IS rusty, but not so rusty I can't start trouble when I need to.
And tonight I need to. My pain storage is at nil, and I'm going to need some for this job.
So letting a dozen Egyptians beat the shit out of the idiot American seems like the best way to go.
I COULD sit in my hotel room and shoot myself in the palm with a staple-gun over and over again, I suppose.
But this just feels right.

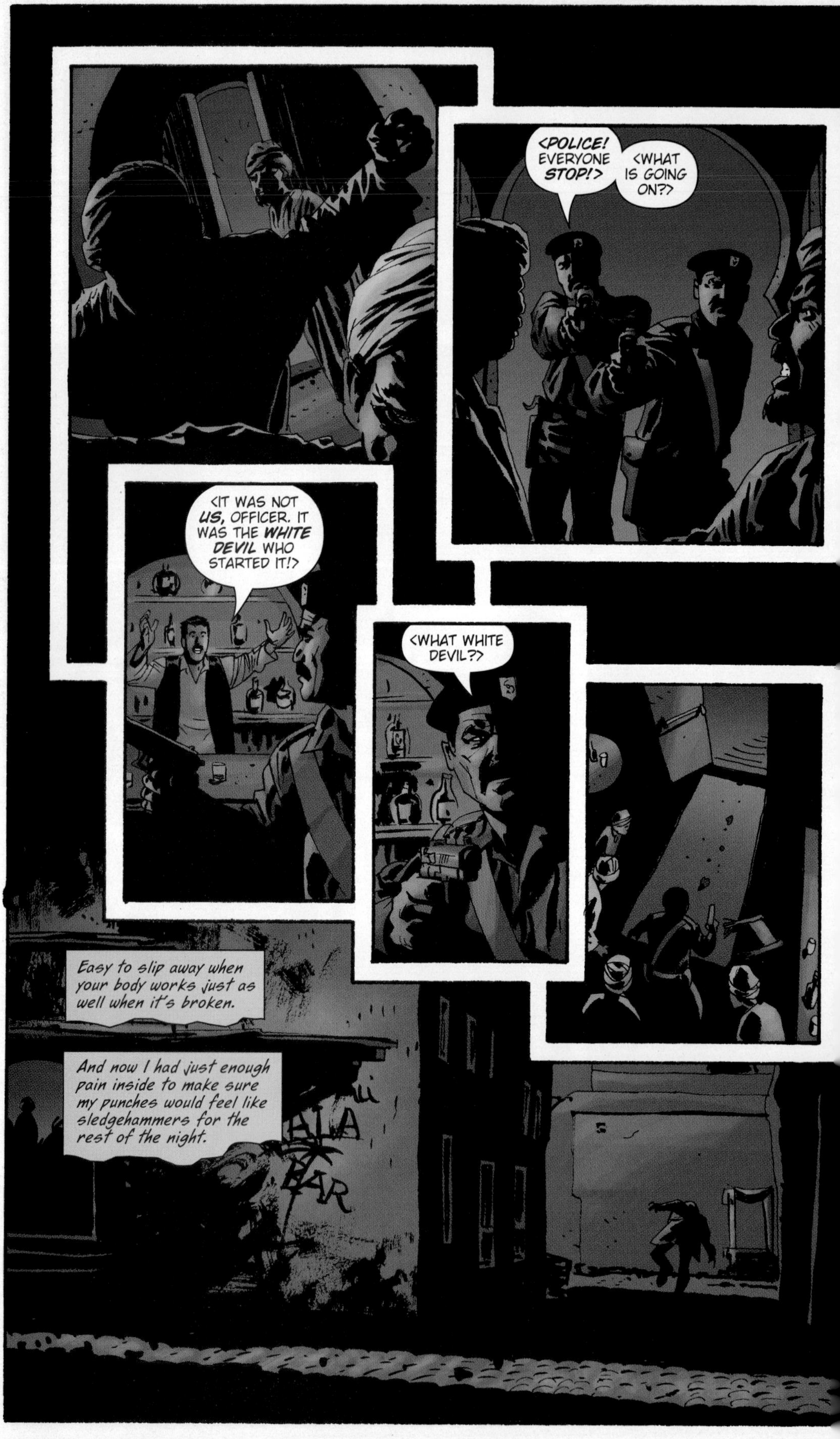
<POLICE! EVERYONE STOP!>
<WHAT IS GOING ON?>
<IT WAS NOT US, OFFICER. IT WAS THE WHITE DEVIL WHO STARTED IT!>
<WHAT WHITE DEVIL?>
Easy to slip away when your body works just as well when it's broken.
And now I had just enough pain inside to make sure my punches would feel like sledgehammers for the rest of the night.
ALA BAR

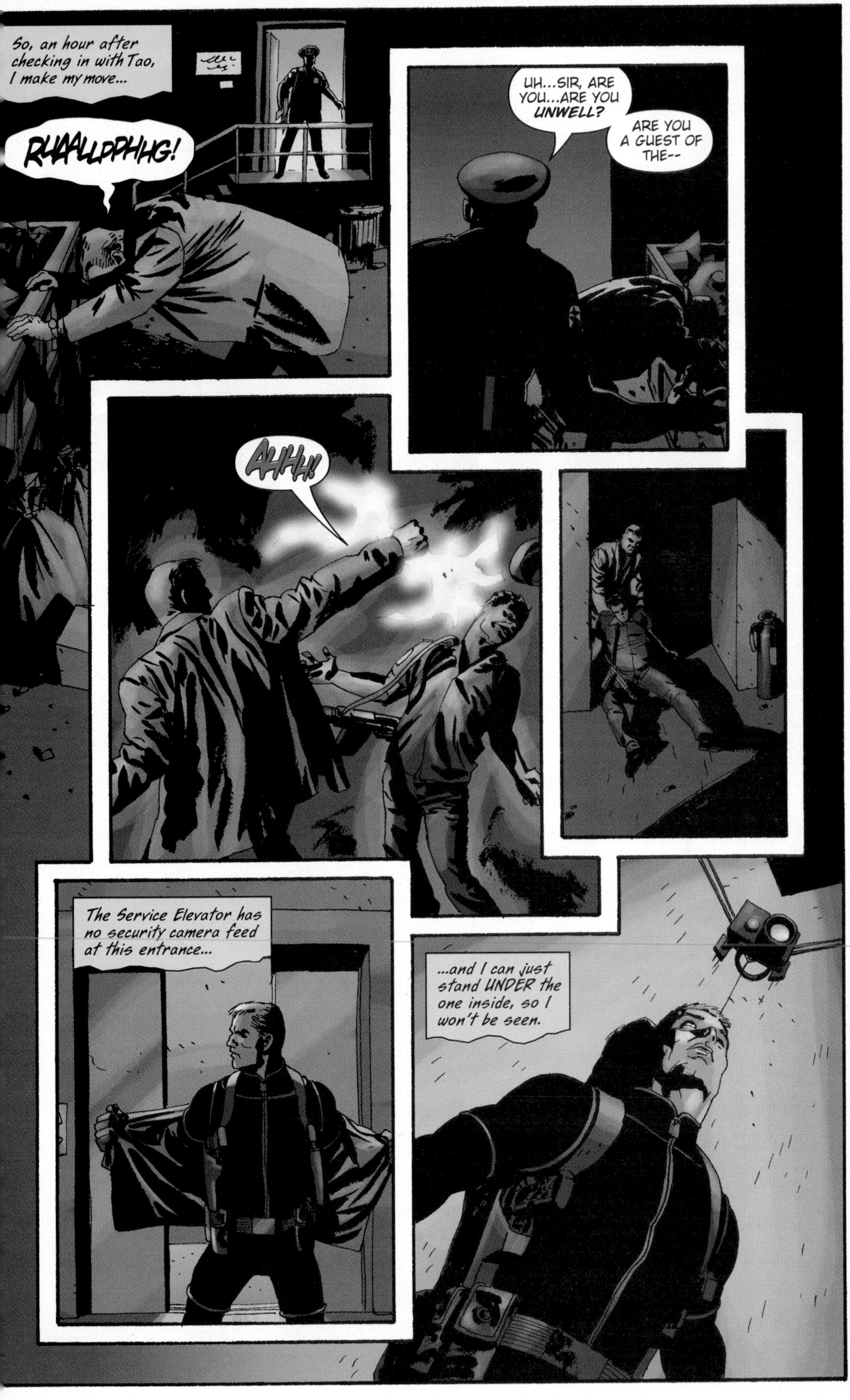
So, an hour after checking in with Tao, I make my move...
RHAALLPPHHG!
UH...SIR, ARE YOU...ARE YOU UNWELL?
ARE YOU A GUEST OF THE--
AHHH!
The Service Elevator has no security camera feed at this entrance...
...and I can just stand UNDER the one inside, so I won't be seen.

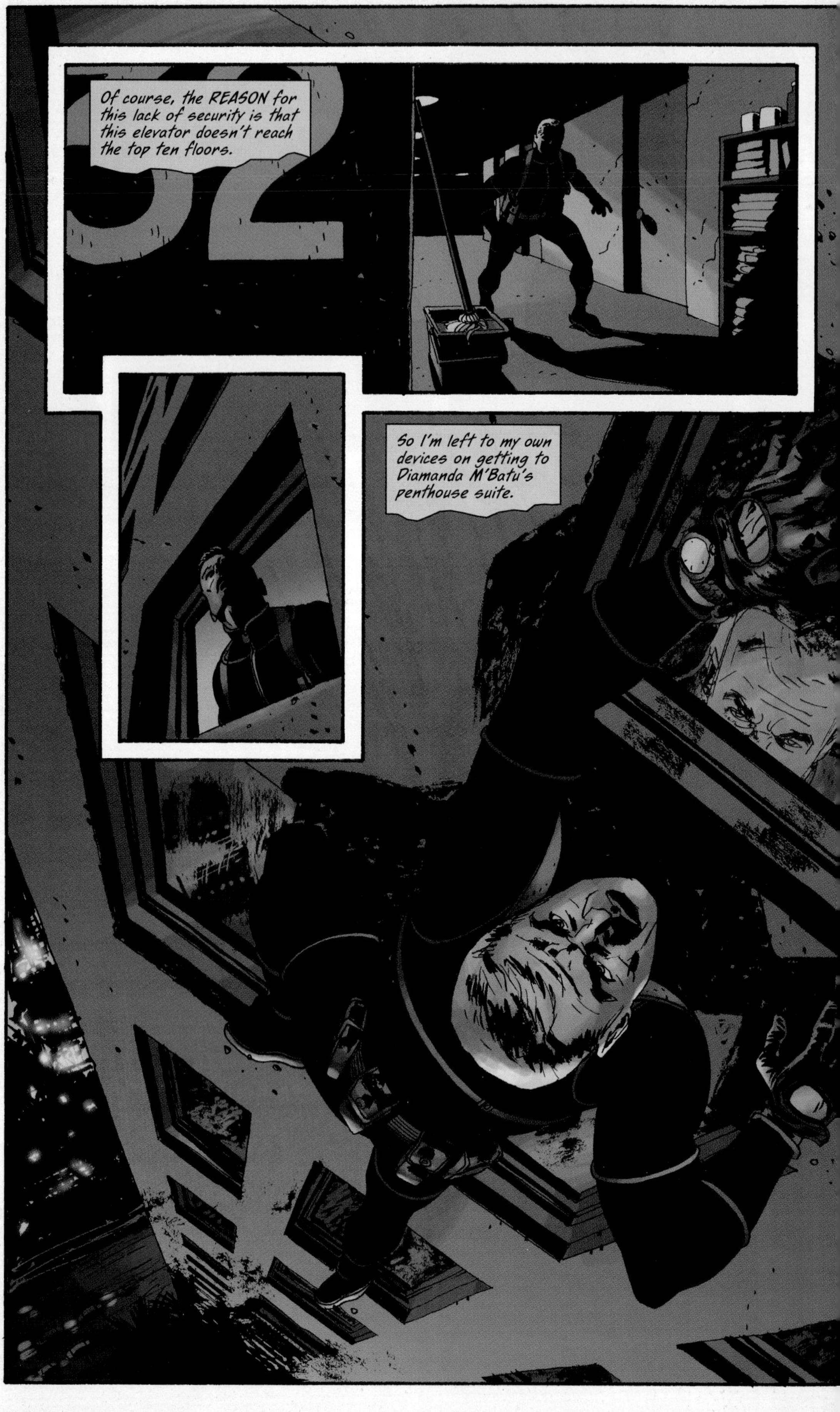
Of course, the REASON for this lack of security is that this elevator doesn't reach the top ten floors.
So I'm left to my own devices on getting to Diamanda M'Batu's penthouse suite.

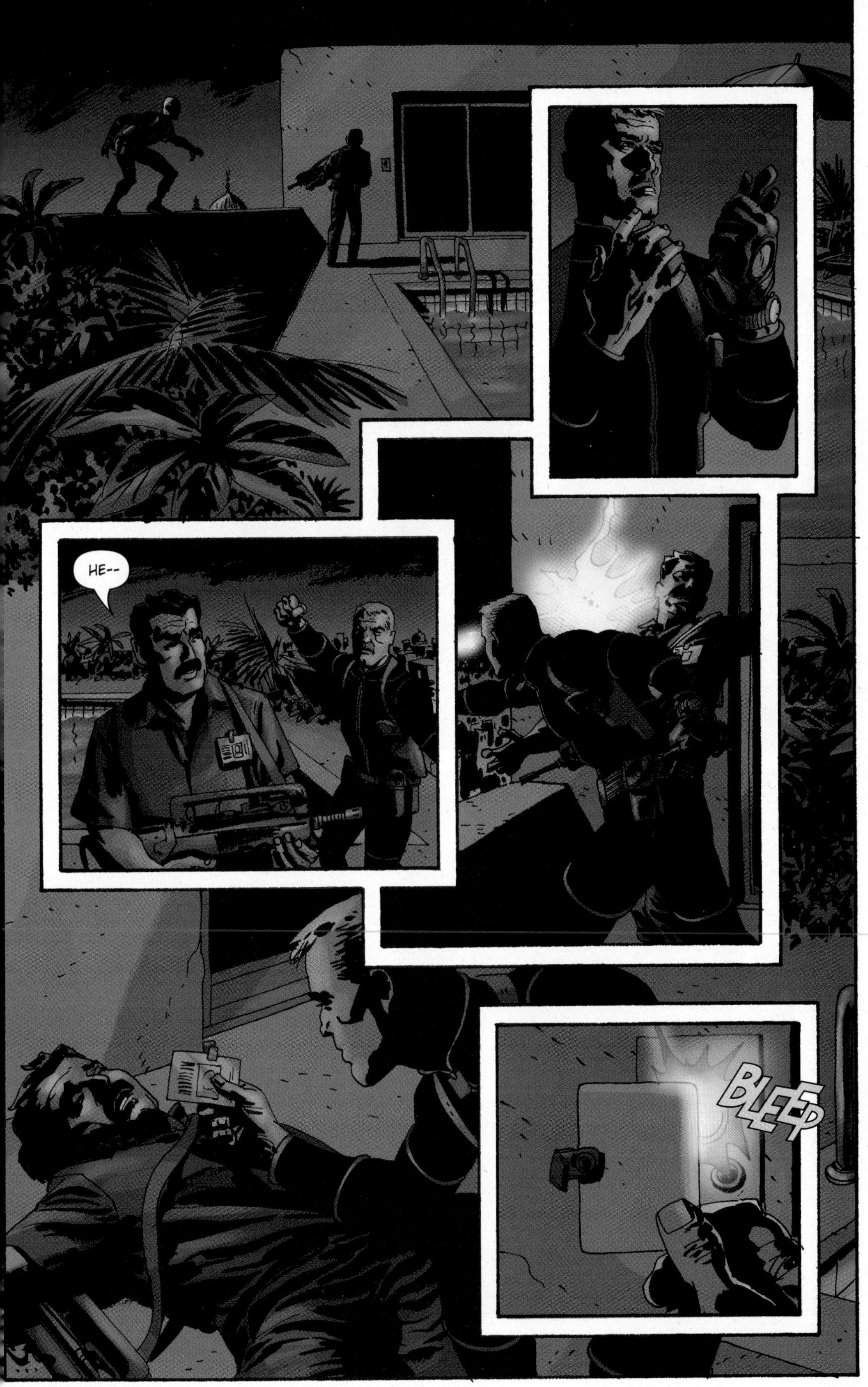
HE--
BLEEP

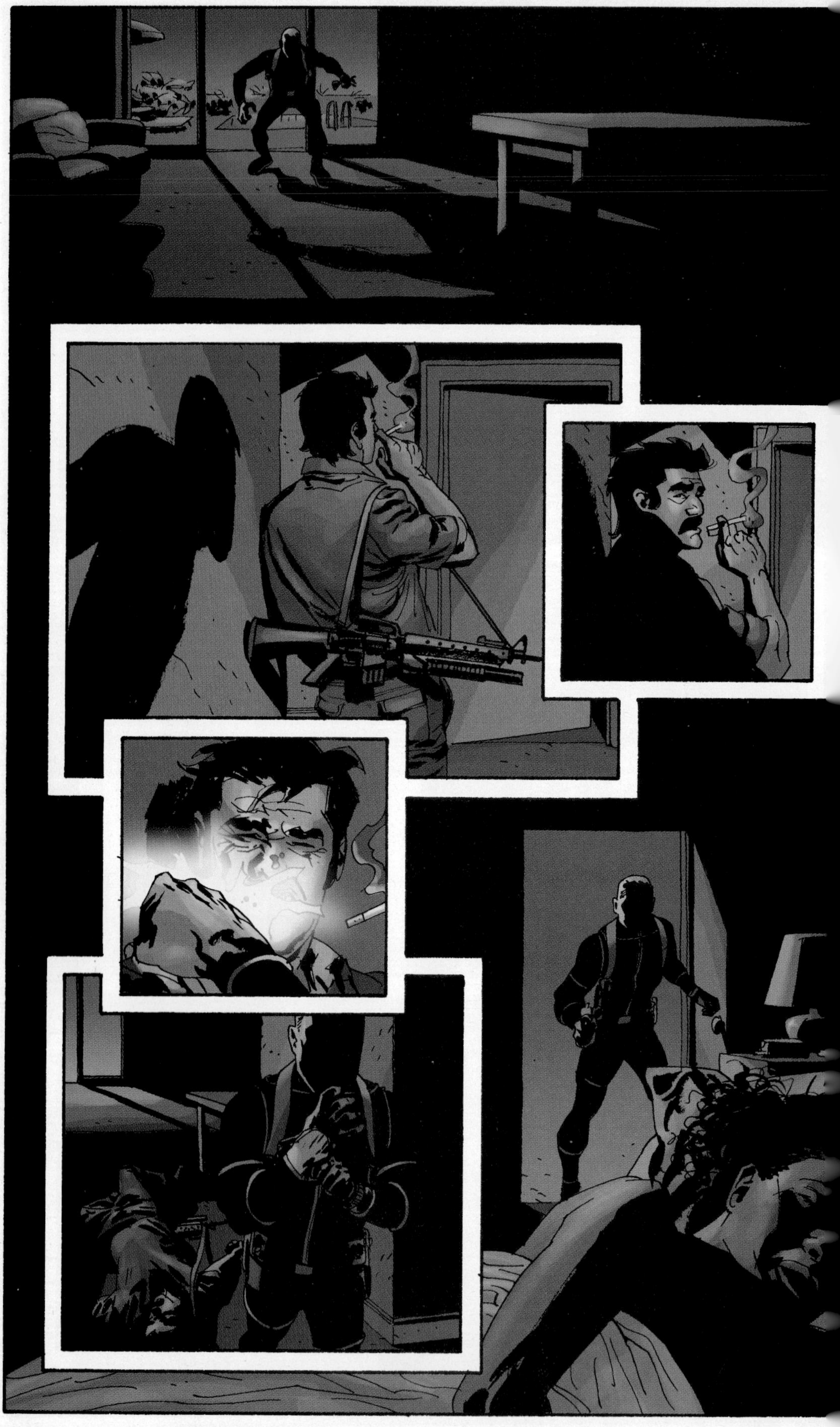

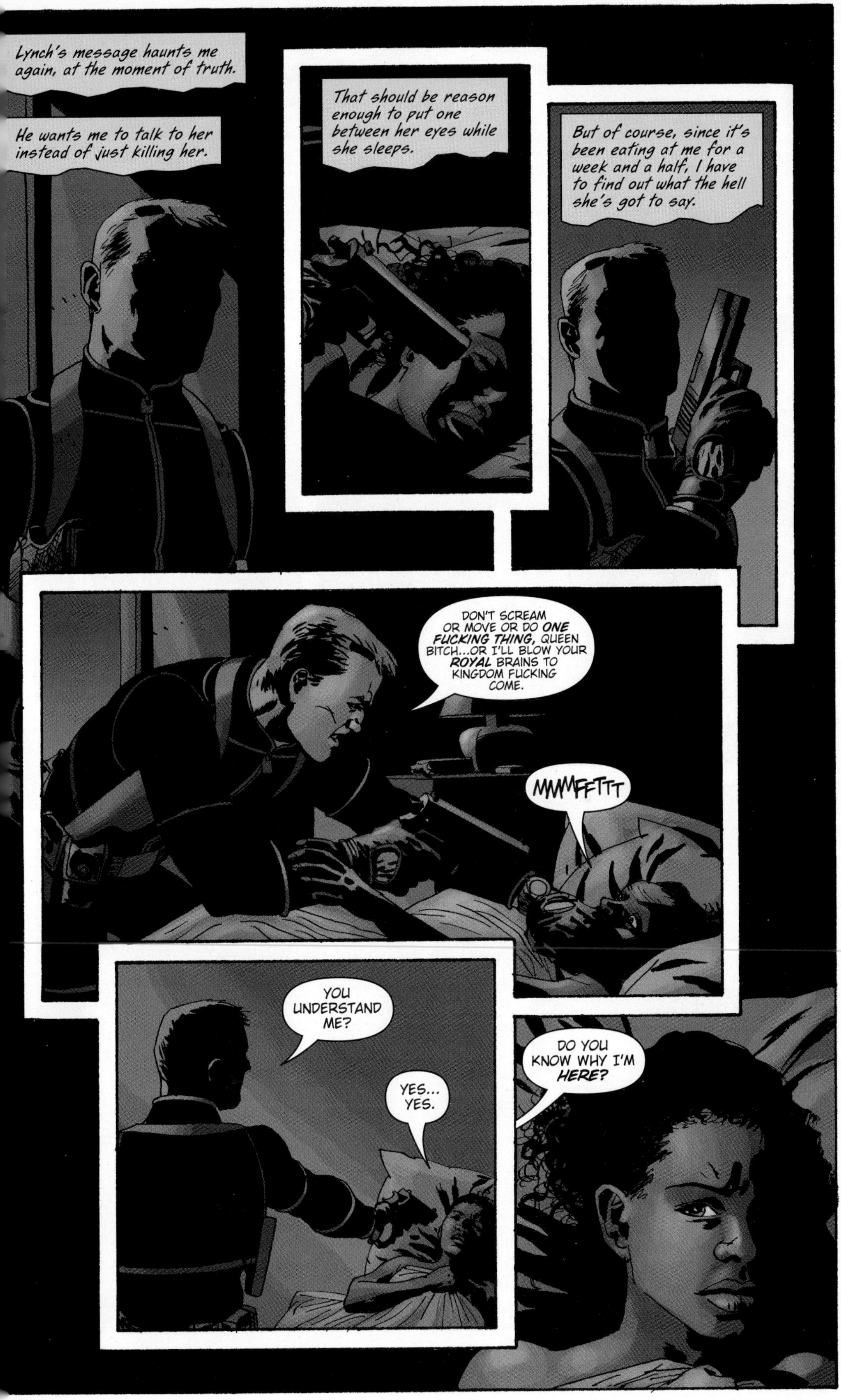
Lynch's message haunts me again, at the moment of truth.
He wants me to talk to her instead of just killing her.
That should be reason enough to put one between her eyes while she sleeps.
But of course, since it's been eating at me for a week and a half, I have to find out what the hell she's got to say.
DON'T SCREAM OR MOVE OR DO ONE FUCKING THING, QUEEN BITCH...OR I'LL BLOW YOUR ROYAL BRAINS TO KINGDOM FUCKING COME.
MMMFFTTT
YOU UNDERSTAND ME?
YES... YES.
DO YOU KNOW WHY I'M HERE?

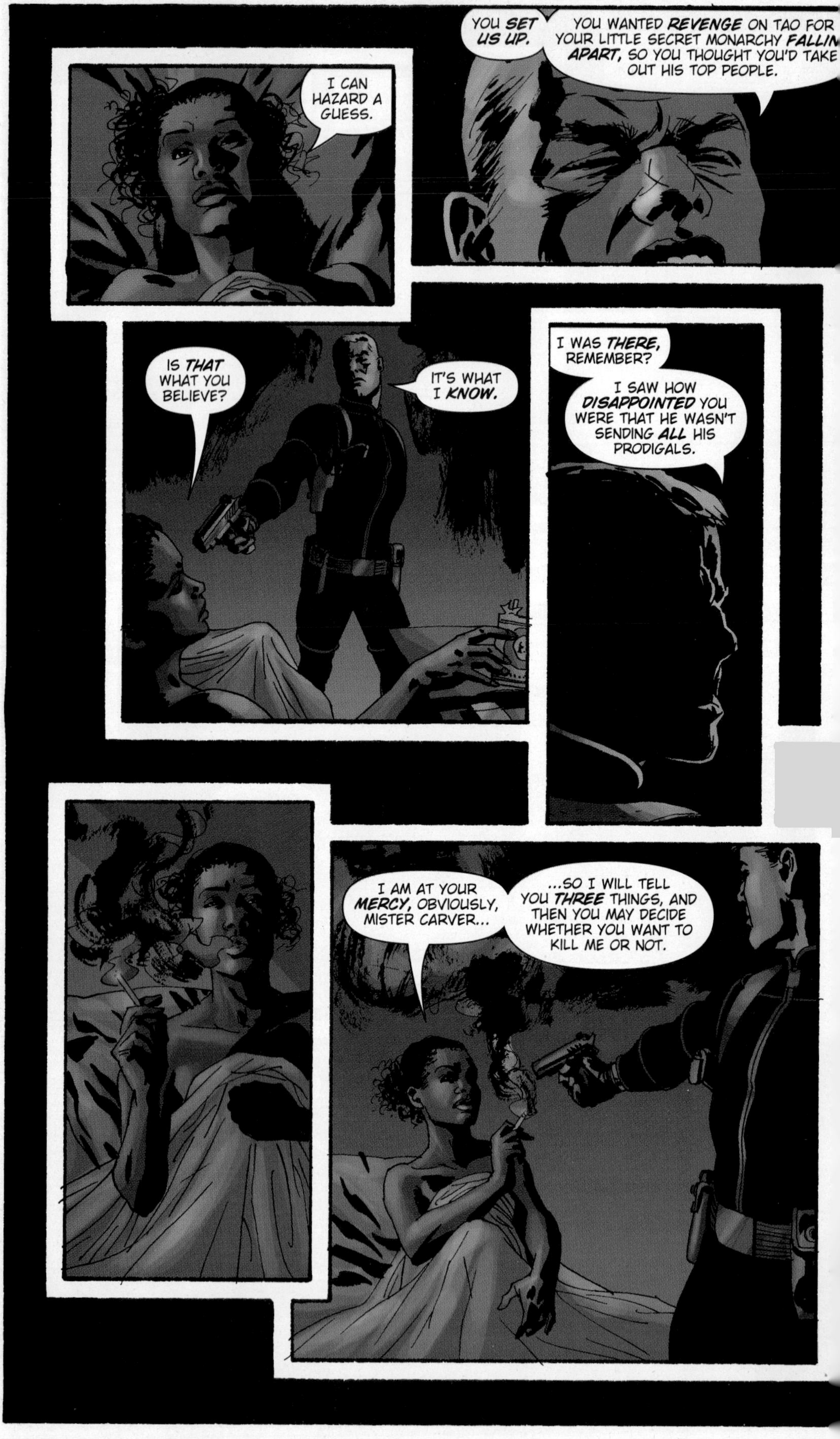

I CAN HAZARD A GUESS.
YOU SET US UP.
YOU WANTED REVENGE ON TAO FOR YOUR LITTLE SECRET MONARCHY FALLIN APART, SO YOU THOUGHT YOU'D TAKE OUT HIS TOP PEOPLE.
IS THAT WHAT YOU BELIEVE?
IT'S WHAT I KNOW.
I WAS THERE, REMEMBER?
I SAW HOW DISAPPOINTED YOU WERE THAT HE WASN'T SENDING ALL HIS PRODIGALS.
I AM AT YOUR MERCY, OBVIOUSLY, MISTER CARVER...
...SO I WILL TELL YOU THREE THINGS, AND THEN YOU MAY DECIDE WHETHER YOU WANT TO KILL ME OR NOT.

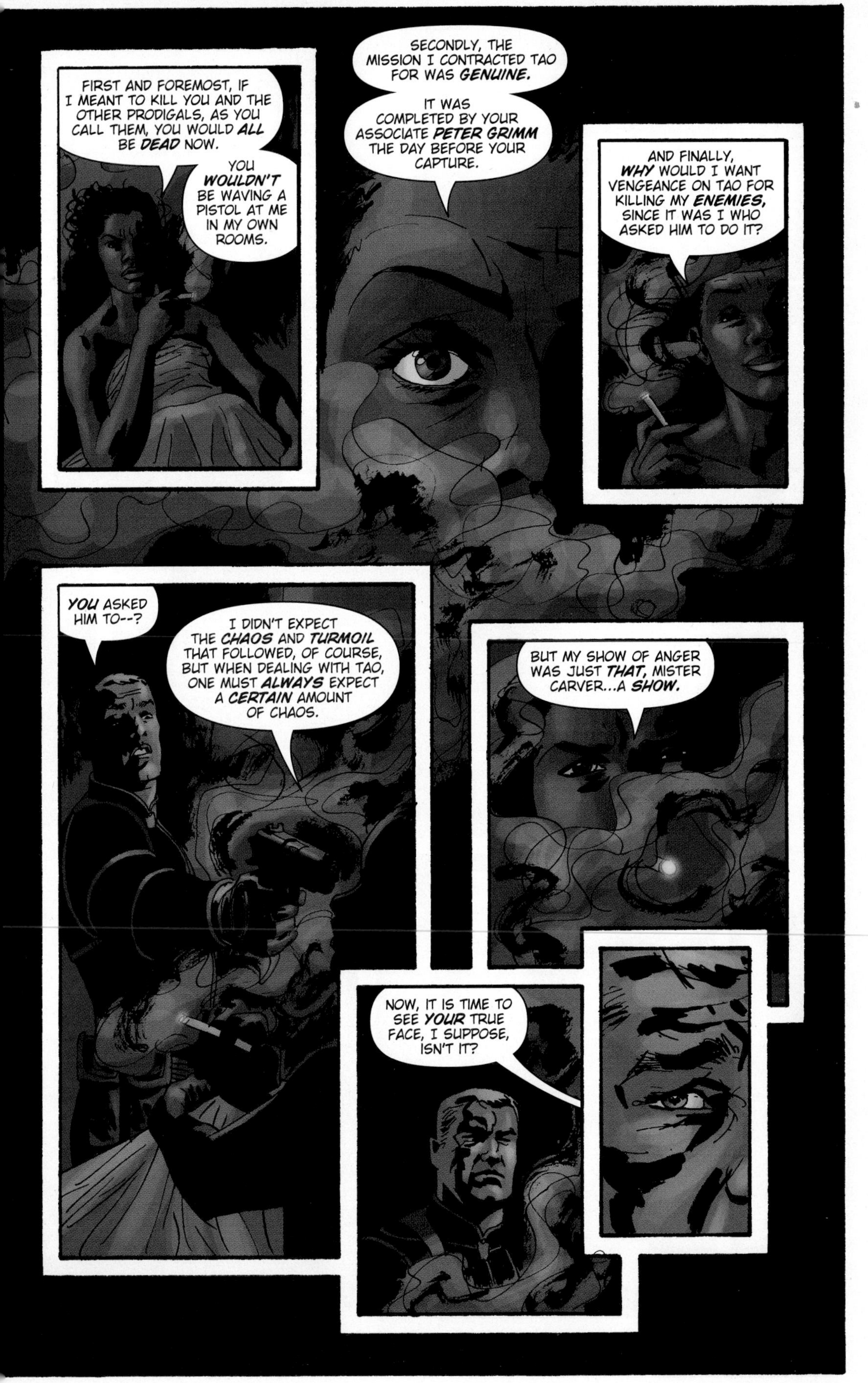
FIRST AND FOREMOST, IF I MEANT TO KILL YOU AND THE OTHER PRODIGALS, AS YOU CALL THEM, YOU WOULD ALL BE DEAD NOW.
YOU WOULDN'T BE WAVING A PISTOL AT ME IN MY OWN ROOMS.
SECONDLY, THE MISSION I CONTRACTED TAO FOR WAS GENUINE.
IT WAS COMPLETED BY YOUR ASSOCIATE PETER GRIMM THE DAY BEFORE YOUR CAPTURE.
AND FINALLY, WHY WOULD I WANT VENGEANCE ON TAO FOR KILLING MY ENEMIES, SINCE IT WAS I WHO ASKED HIM TO DO IT?
YOU ASKED HIM TO--?
I DIDN'T EXPECT THE CHAOS AND TURMOIL THAT FOLLOWED, OF COURSE, BUT WHEN DEALING WITH TAO, ONE MUST ALWAYS EXPECT A CERTAIN AMOUNT OF CHAOS.
BUT MY SHOW OF ANGER WAS JUST THAT, MISTER CARVER...A SHOW.
NOW, IT IS TIME TO SEE YOUR TRUE FACE, I SUPPOSE, ISN'T IT?

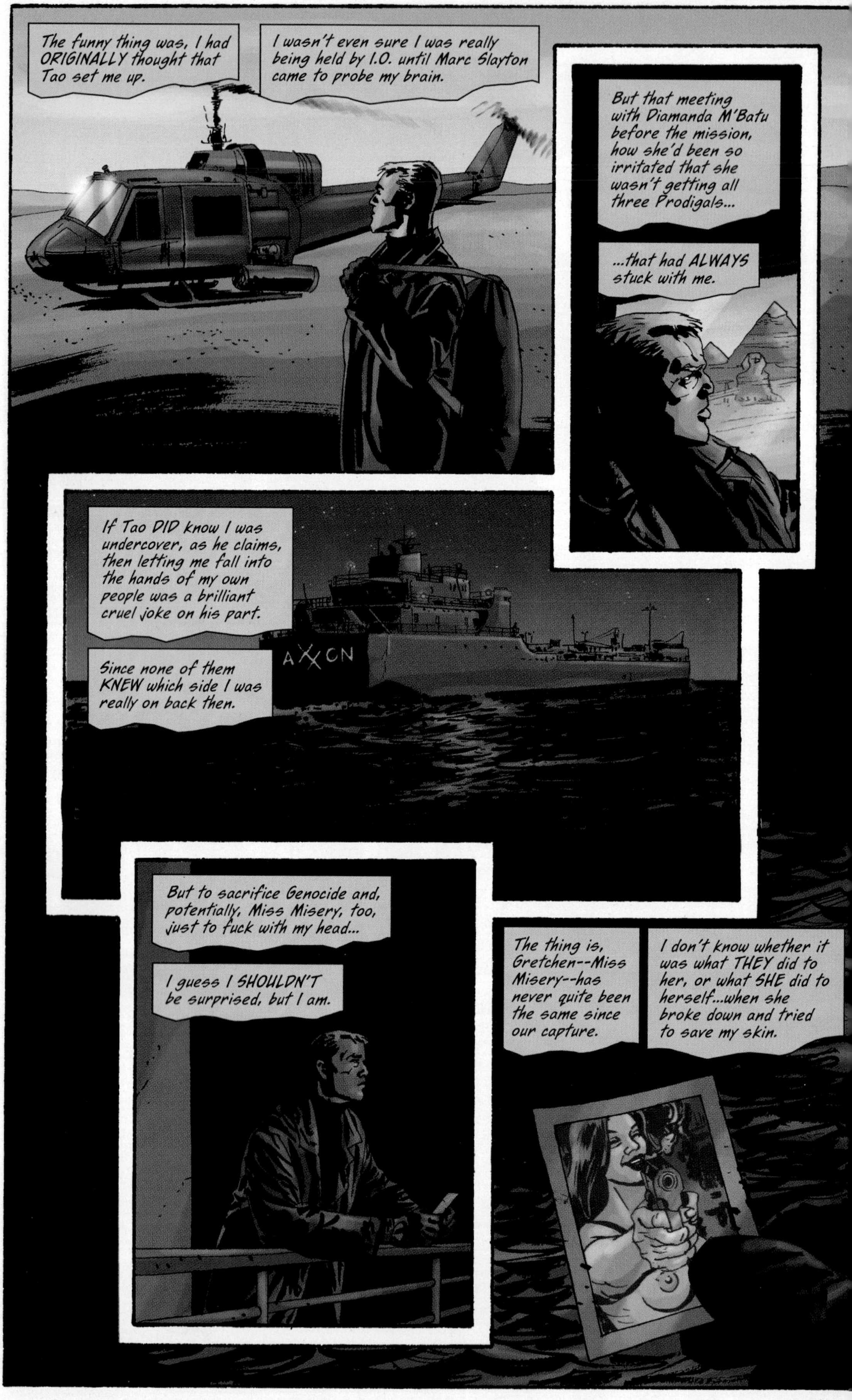
The funny thing was, I had ORIGINALLY thought that Tao set me up.
I wasn't even sure I was really being held by I.O. until Marc Slayton came to probe my brain.
But that meeting with Diamanda M'Batu before the mission, how she'd been so irritated that she wasn't getting all three Prodigals...
...that had ALWAYS stuck with me.
If Tao DID know I was undercover, as he claims, then letting me fall into the hands of my own people was a brilliant cruel joke on his part.
Since none of them KNEW which side I was really on back then.
But to sacrifice Genocide and, potentially, Miss Misery, too, just to fuck with my head...
I guess I SHOULDN'T be surprised, but I am.
The thing is, Gretchen--Miss Misery--has never quite been the same since our capture.
I don't know whether it was what THEY did to her, or what SHE did to herself...when she broke down and tried to save my skin.

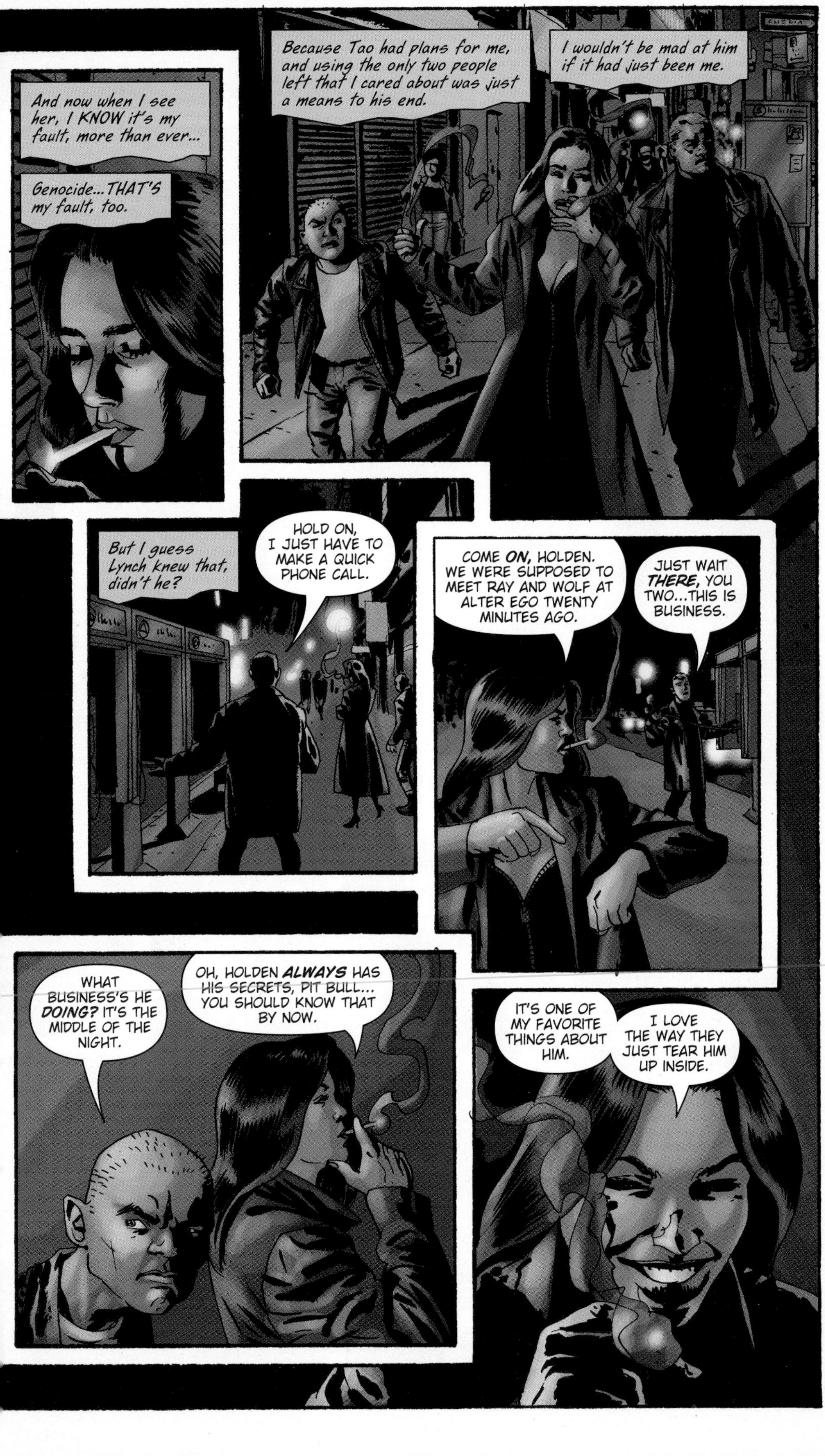
And now when I see her, I KNOW it's my fault, more than ever...
Genocide...THAT'S my fault, too.
Because Tao had plans for me, and using the only two people left that I cared about was just a means to his end.
I wouldn't be mad at him if it had just been me.
But I guess Lynch knew that, didn't he?
HOLD ON, I JUST HAVE TO MAKE A QUICK PHONE CALL.
COME ON, HOLDEN. WE WERE SUPPOSED TO MEET RAY AND WOLF AT ALTER EGO TWENTY MINUTES AGO.
JUST WAIT THERE, YOU TWO...THIS IS BUSINESS.
WHAT BUSINESS'S HE DOING? IT'S THE MIDDLE OF THE NIGHT.
OH, HOLDEN ALWAYS HAS HIS SECRETS, PIT BULL... YOU SHOULD KNOW THAT BY NOW.
IT'S ONE OF MY FAVORITE THINGS ABOUT HIM.
I LOVE THE WAY THEY JUST TEAR HIM UP INSIDE.

AT THE TONE, PLEASE STATE YOUR NAME AND CALL SIGN...
BEEP
HOLDEN CARVER, NO CALL SIGN.
VOICE ANALYSIS ACTIVATED...PLEASE WAIT...BRRRK... CLIK...BRRRK...
PLEASE HANG UP PHONE AND WAIT TEN SECONDS.
BRRRNNG
BRRRNNG
BRRRNNG
YOU THERE, OLD MAN?

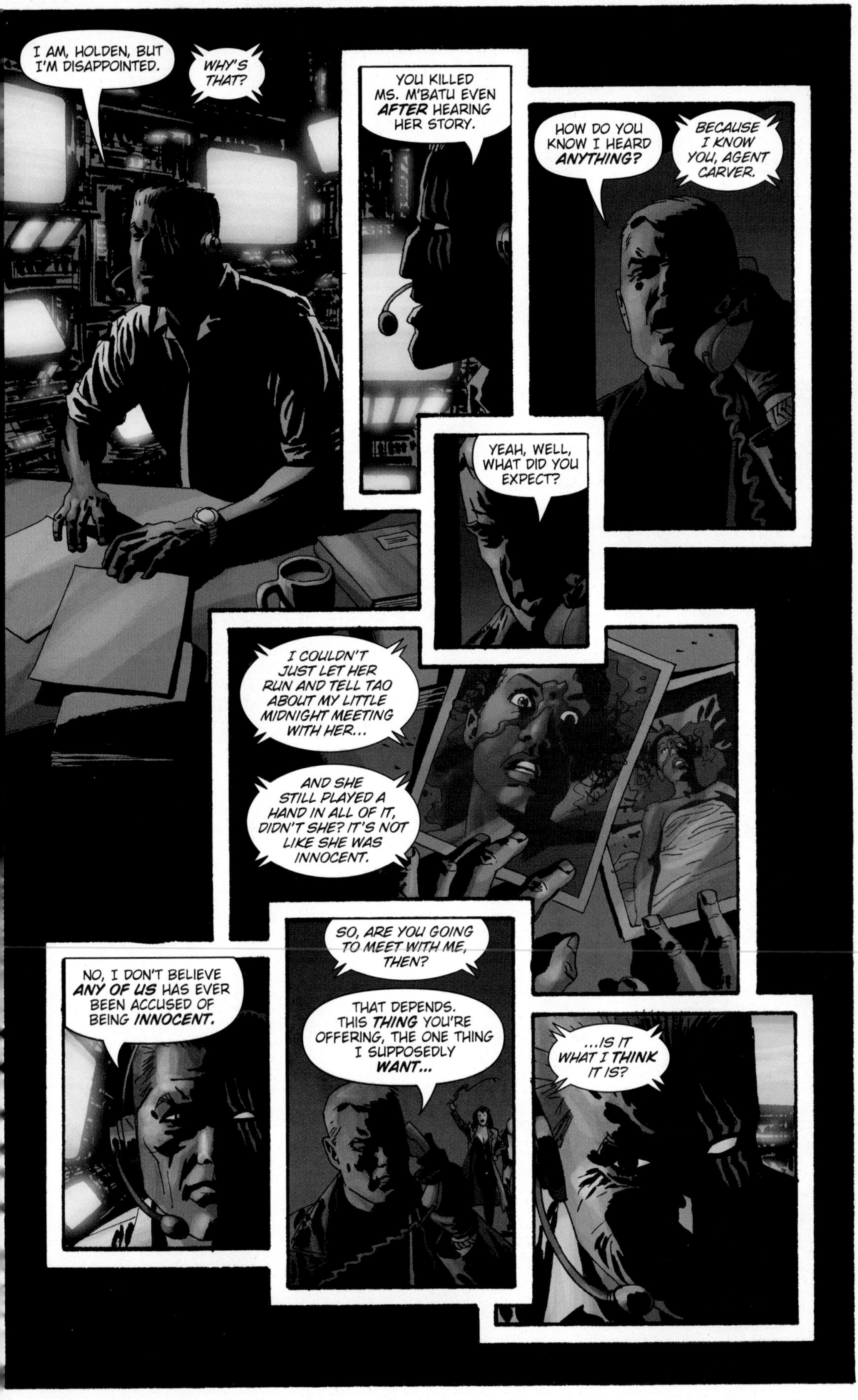
I AM, HOLDEN, BUT I'M DISAPPOINTED.
WHY'S THAT?
YOU KILLED MS. M'BATU EVEN AFTER HEARING HER STORY.
HOW DO YOU KNOW I HEARD ANYTHING?
BECAUSE I KNOW YOU, AGENT CARVER.
YEAH, WELL, WHAT DID YOU EXPECT?
I COULDN'T JUST LET HER RUN AND TELL TAO ABOUT MY LITTLE MIDNIGHT MEETING WITH HER...
AND SHE STILL PLAYED A HAND IN ALL OF IT, DIDN'T SHE? IT'S NOT LIKE SHE WAS INNOCENT.
NO, I DON'T BELIEVE ANY OF US HAS EVER BEEN ACCUSED OF BEING INNOCENT.
SO, ARE YOU GOING TO MEET WITH ME, THEN?
THAT DEPENDS. THIS THING YOU'RE OFFERING, THE ONE THING I SUPPOSEDLY WANT...
...IS IT WHAT I THINK IT IS?

chapter sixteen

face / two face

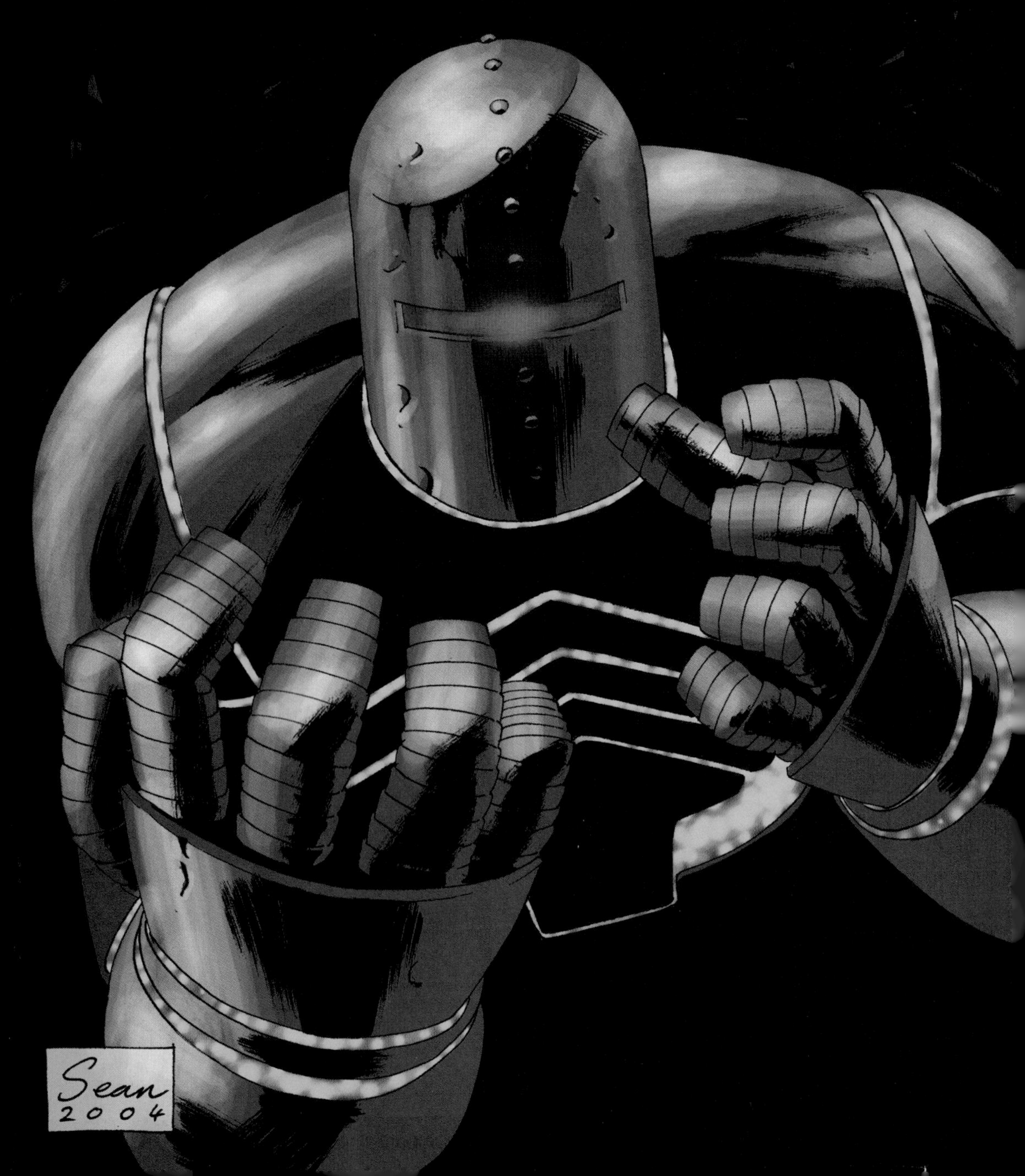
Sean
2004

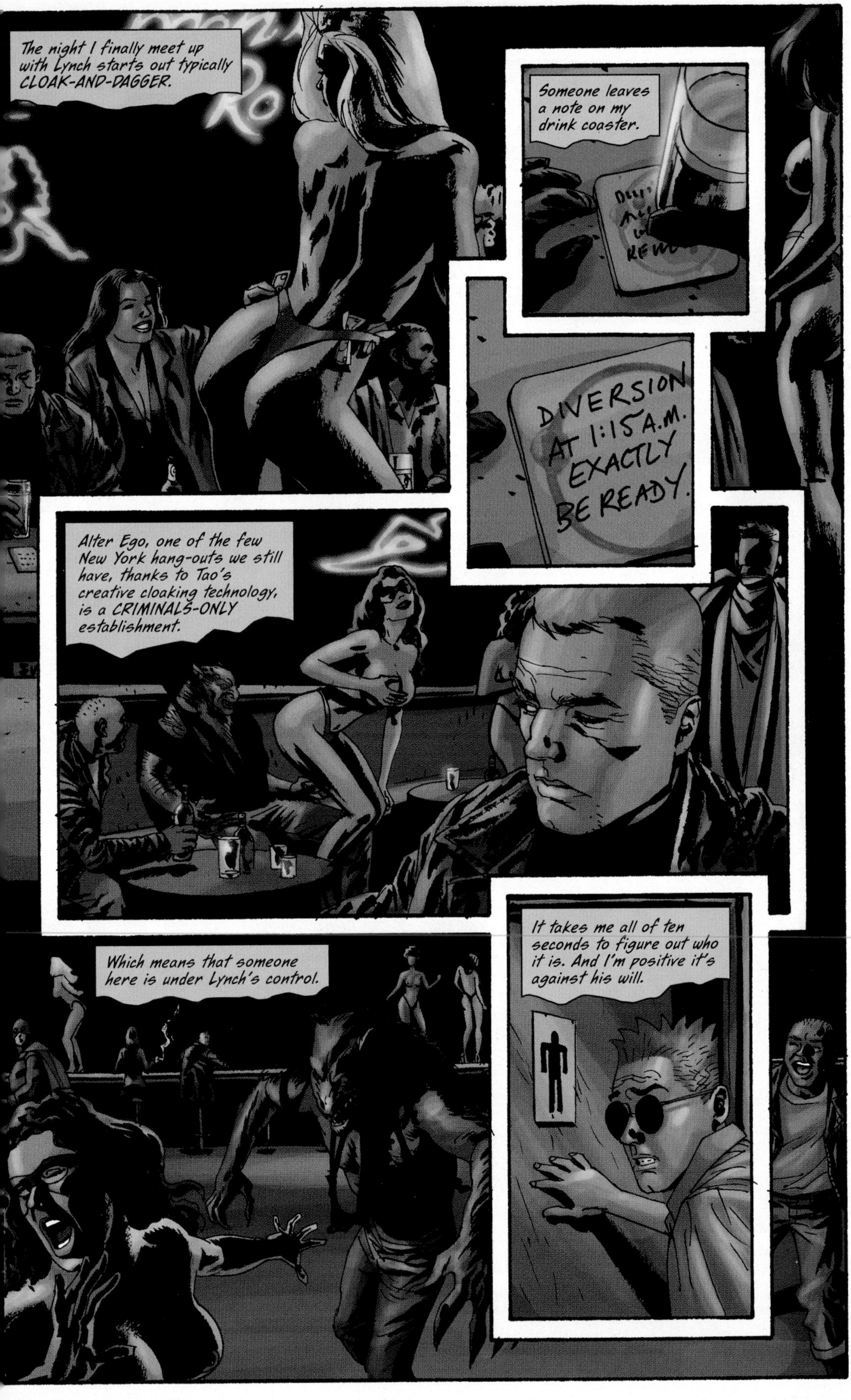
The night I finally meet up with Lynch starts out typically CLOAK-AND-DAGGER.
Someone leaves a note on my drink coaster.
DIVERSION AT 1:15 A.M. EXACTLY BE READY.
Alter Ego, one of the few New York hang-outs we still have, thanks to Tao's creative cloaking technology, is a CRIMINALS-ONLY establishment.
Which means that someone here is under Lynch's control.
It takes me all of ten seconds to figure out who it is. And I'm positive it's against his will.

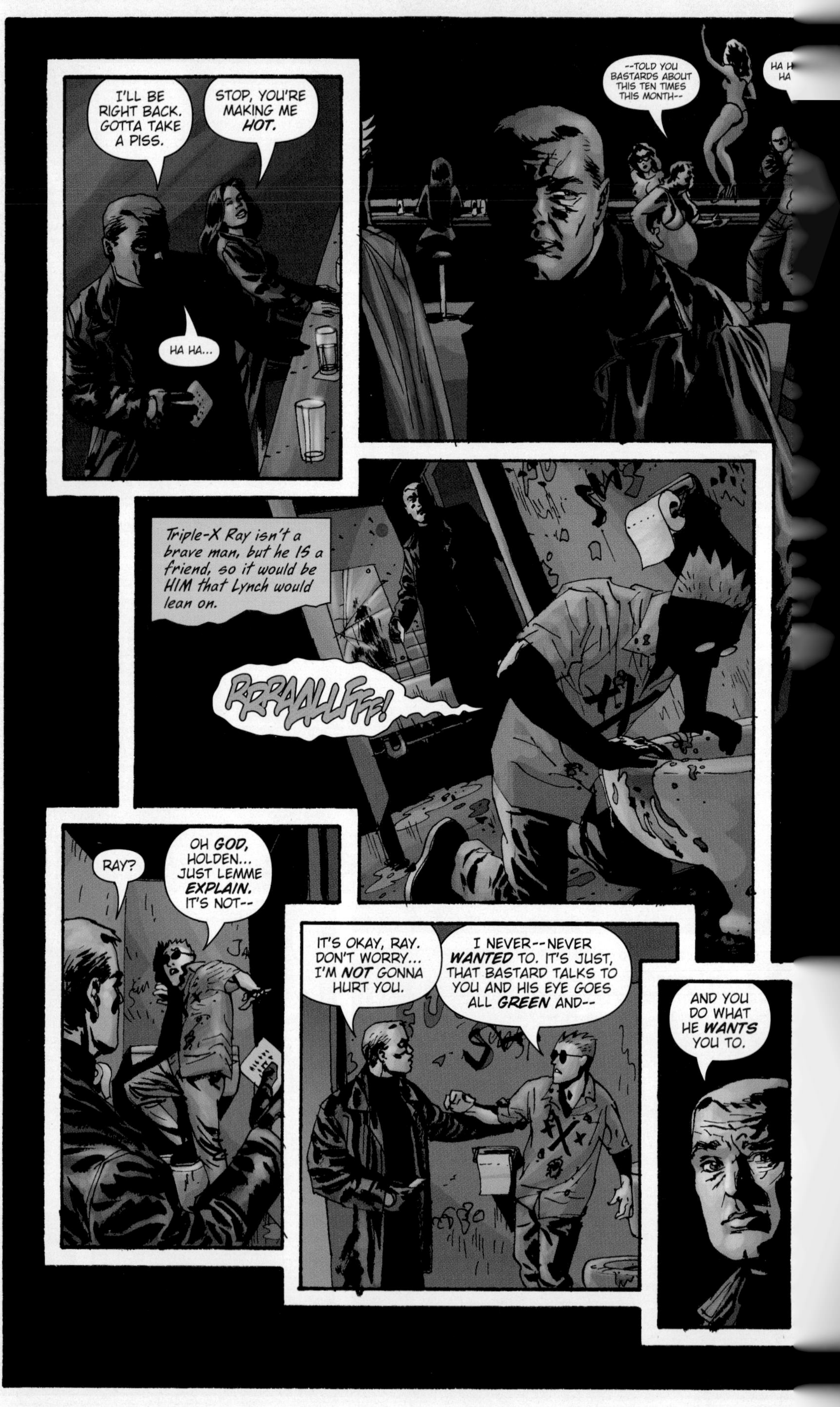

I'LL BE RIGHT BACK. GOTTA TAKE A PISS.
STOP, YOU'RE MAKING ME HOT.
HA HA...
--TOLD YOU BASTARDS ABOUT THIS TEN TIMES THIS MONTH--
Triple-X Ray isn't a brave man, but he IS a friend, so it would be HIM that Lynch would lean on.
RRRAALLFFF!
RAY?
OH GOD, HOLDEN... JUST LEMME EXPLAIN. IT'S NOT--
IT'S OKAY, RAY. DON'T WORRY... I'M NOT GONNA HURT YOU.
I NEVER--NEVER WANTED TO. IT'S JUST, THAT BASTARD TALKS TO YOU AND HIS EYE GOES ALL GREEN AND--
AND YOU DO WHAT HE WANTS YOU TO.

YEAH... I MEAN, I *TRIED*...

BUT *YEAH*.

THAT'S WHAT LYNCH *DOES*. HE GETS INSIDE AND BENDS YOU OVER.

HE'S JUST LIKE *TAO*, IN A LOT OF WAYS.

SO--SO, YOU'RE *NOT* GONNA KILL ME?

IT WAS ME THAT TOLD 'IM HOW TO GET TO YOU WITH THAT JOB LAST MONTH, THAT HIJACKING THING.

NO, RAY, I'M NOT GOING TO KILL YOU... THIS'LL JUST BE OUR LITTLE SECRET, OKAY?

YOU JUST STEER CLEAR OF HIM FROM NOW ON AND DON'T TELL *ANYONE ELSE* ABOUT THIS.

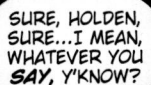

SURE, HOLDEN, SURE...I MEAN, WHATEVER YOU *SAY*, Y'KNOW?

NOW I'VE GOT ANOTHER JOB FOR YOU. SOMETHING YOU'RE CONVENIENTLY PREPPED FOR ALREADY.

WHAT?

I WANT YOU TO HELP ME GET MISS MISERY *OUT OF HERE* BEFORE THIS PLACE GOES TO HELL IN HALF AN HOUR. SO, JUST ACT LIKE YOU'RE SICK, *REALLY* SICK.

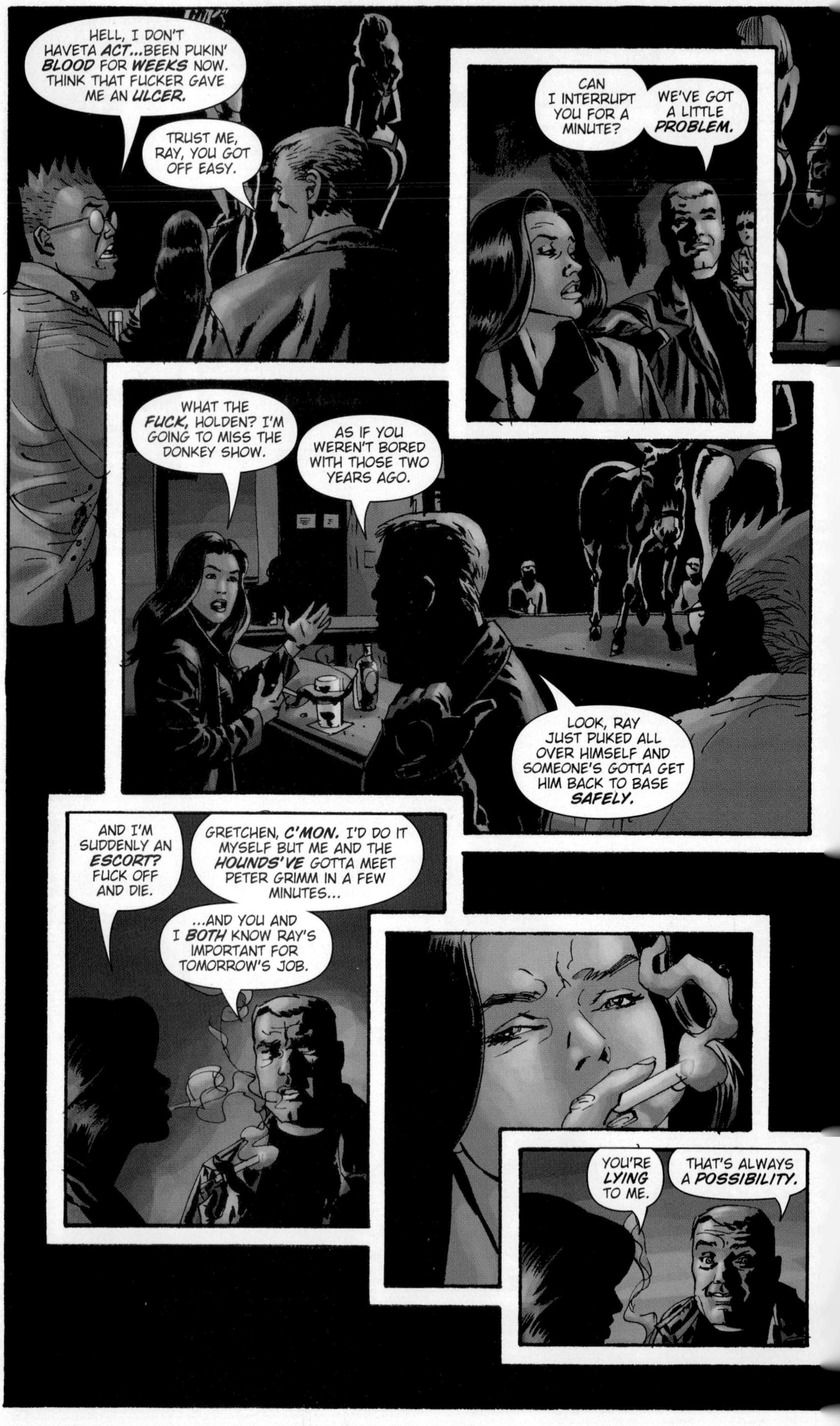
HELL, I DON'T HAVETA ACT...BEEN PUKIN' BLOOD FOR WEEKS NOW. THINK THAT FUCKER GAVE ME AN ULCER.
TRUST ME, RAY, YOU GOT OFF EASY.
CAN I INTERRUPT YOU FOR A MINUTE?
WE'VE GOT A LITTLE PROBLEM.
WHAT THE FUCK, HOLDEN? I'M GOING TO MISS THE DONKEY SHOW.
AS IF YOU WEREN'T BORED WITH THOSE TWO YEARS AGO.
LOOK, RAY JUST PUKED ALL OVER HIMSELF AND SOMEONE'S GOTTA GET HIM BACK TO BASE SAFELY.
AND I'M SUDDENLY AN ESCORT? FUCK OFF AND DIE.
GRETCHEN, C'MON. I'D DO IT MYSELF BUT ME AND THE HOUNDS'VE GOTTA MEET PETER GRIMM IN A FEW MINUTES...
...AND YOU AND I BOTH KNOW RAY'S IMPORTANT FOR TOMORROW'S JOB.
YOU'RE LYING TO ME.
THAT'S ALWAYS A POSSIBILITY.

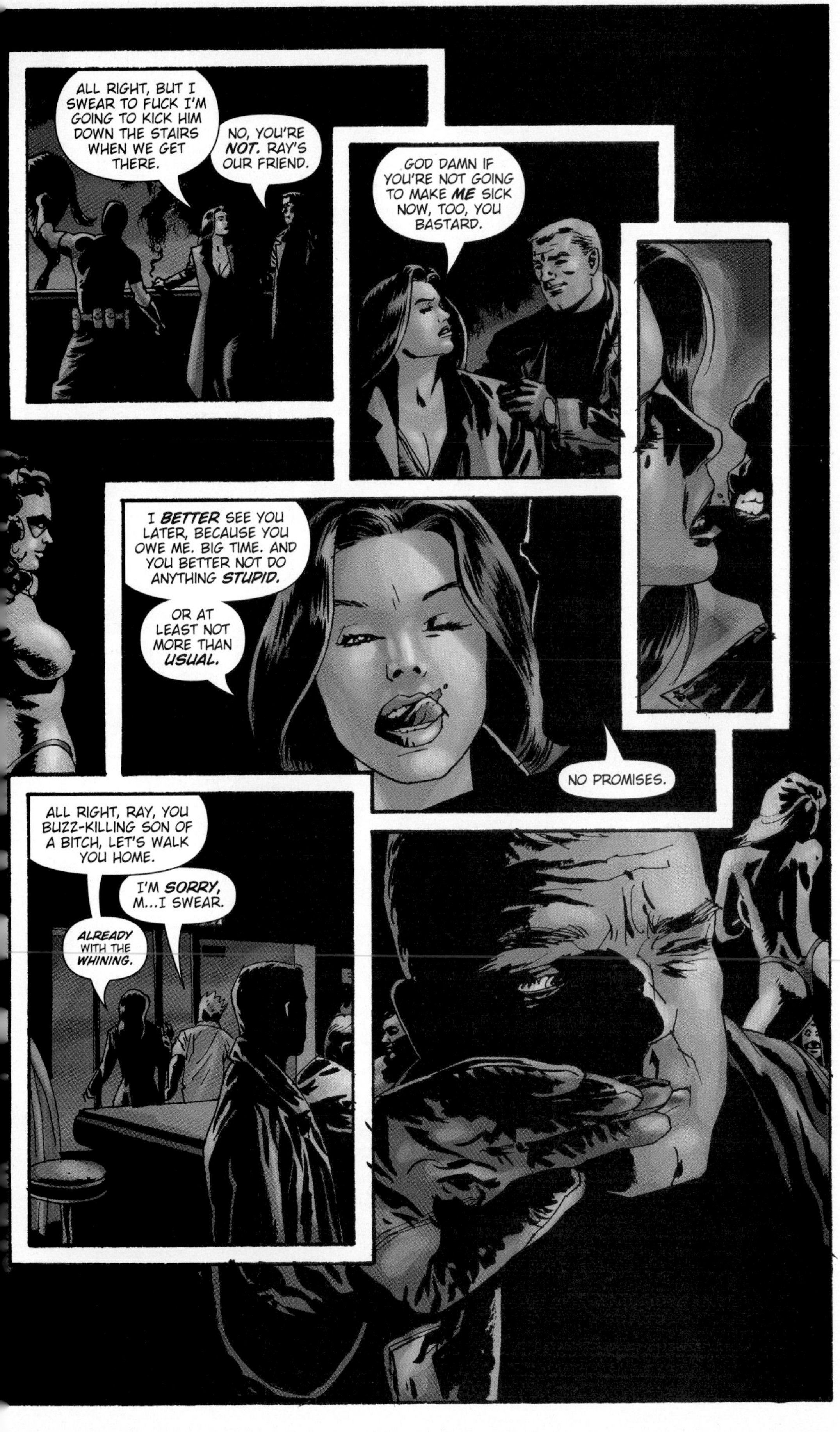
ALL RIGHT, BUT I SWEAR TO FUCK I'M GOING TO KICK HIM DOWN THE STAIRS WHEN WE GET THERE.
NO, YOU'RE NOT. RAY'S OUR FRIEND.
GOD DAMN IF YOU'RE NOT GOING TO MAKE ME SICK NOW, TOO, YOU BASTARD.
I BETTER SEE YOU LATER, BECAUSE YOU OWE ME. BIG TIME. AND YOU BETTER NOT DO ANYTHING STUPID.
OR AT LEAST NOT MORE THAN USUAL.
NO PROMISES.
ALL RIGHT, RAY, YOU BUZZ-KILLING SON OF A BITCH, LET'S WALK YOU HOME.
I'M SORRY, M...I SWEAR.
ALREADY WITH THE WHINING.

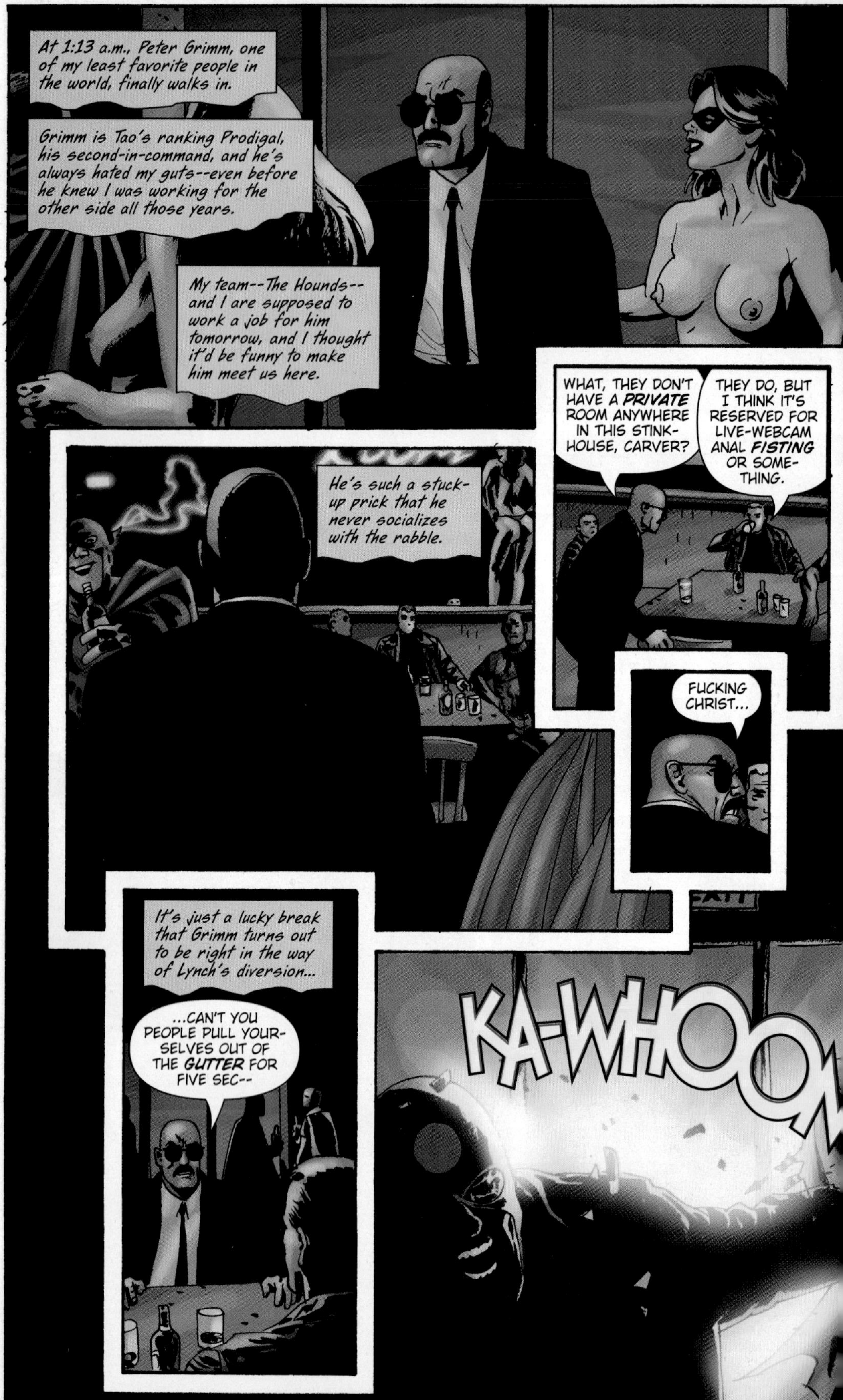

At 1:13 a.m., Peter Grimm, one of my least favorite people in the world, finally walks in.
Grimm is Tao's ranking Prodigal, his second-in-command, and he's always hated my guts--even before he knew I was working for the other side all those years.
My team--The Hounds--and I are supposed to work a job for him tomorrow, and I thought it'd be funny to make him meet us here.
He's such a stuck-up prick that he never socializes with the rabble.
WHAT, THEY DON'T HAVE A PRIVATE ROOM ANYWHERE IN THIS STINK-HOUSE, CARVER?
THEY DO, BUT I THINK IT'S RESERVED FOR LIVE-WEBCAM ANAL FISTING OR SOME-THING.
FUCKING CHRIST...
It's just a lucky break that Grimm turns out to be right in the way of Lynch's diversion...
...CAN'T YOU PEOPLE PULL YOUR-SELVES OUT OF THE GUTTER FOR FIVE SEC--
KA-WHOO

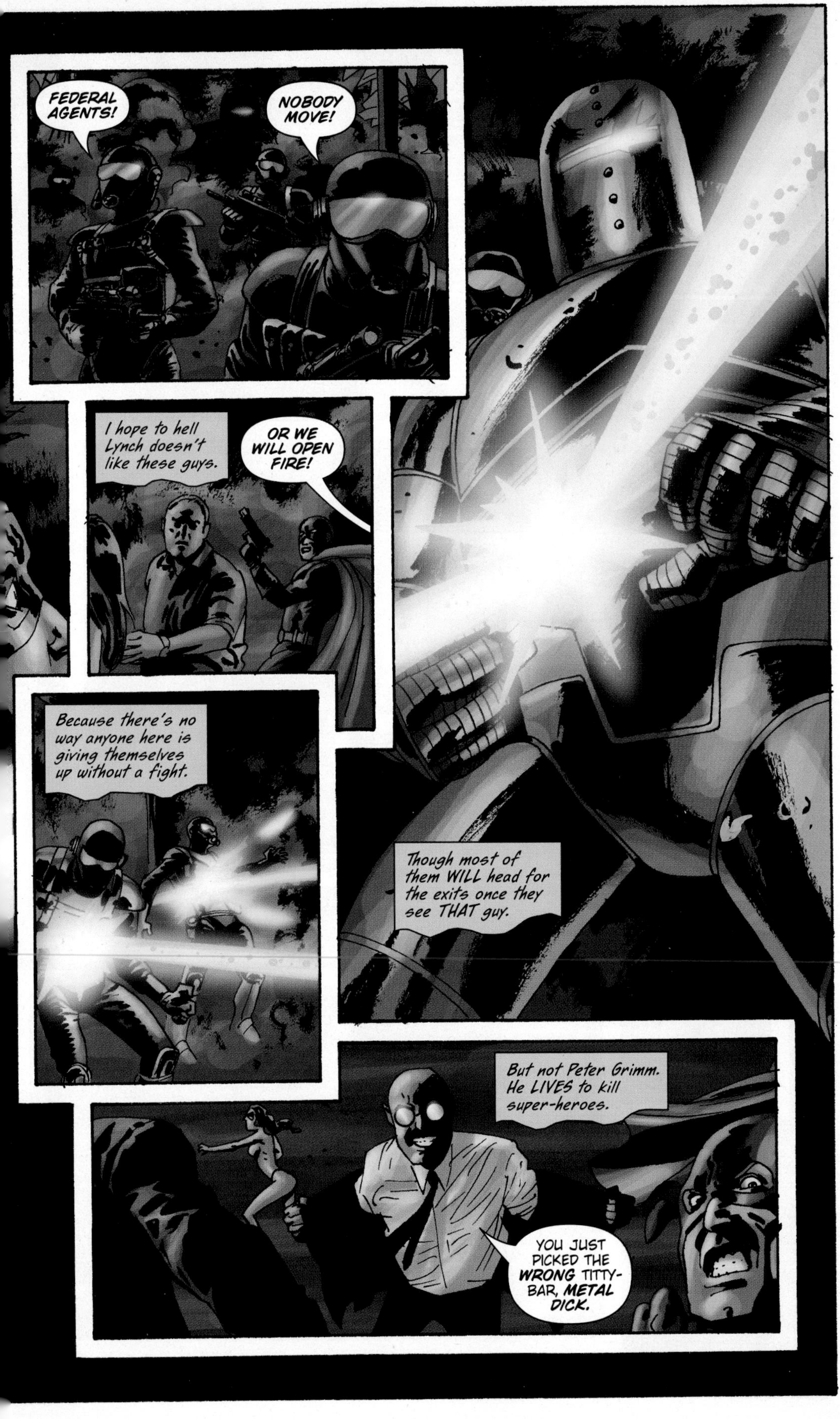
FEDERAL AGENTS!
NOBODY MOVE!
I hope to hell Lynch doesn't like these guys.
OR WE WILL OPEN FIRE!
Because there's no way anyone here is giving themselves up without a fight.
Though most of them WILL head for the exits once they see THAT guy.
But not Peter Grimm. He LIVES to kill super-heroes.
YOU JUST PICKED THE WRONG TITTY-BAR, METAL DICK.

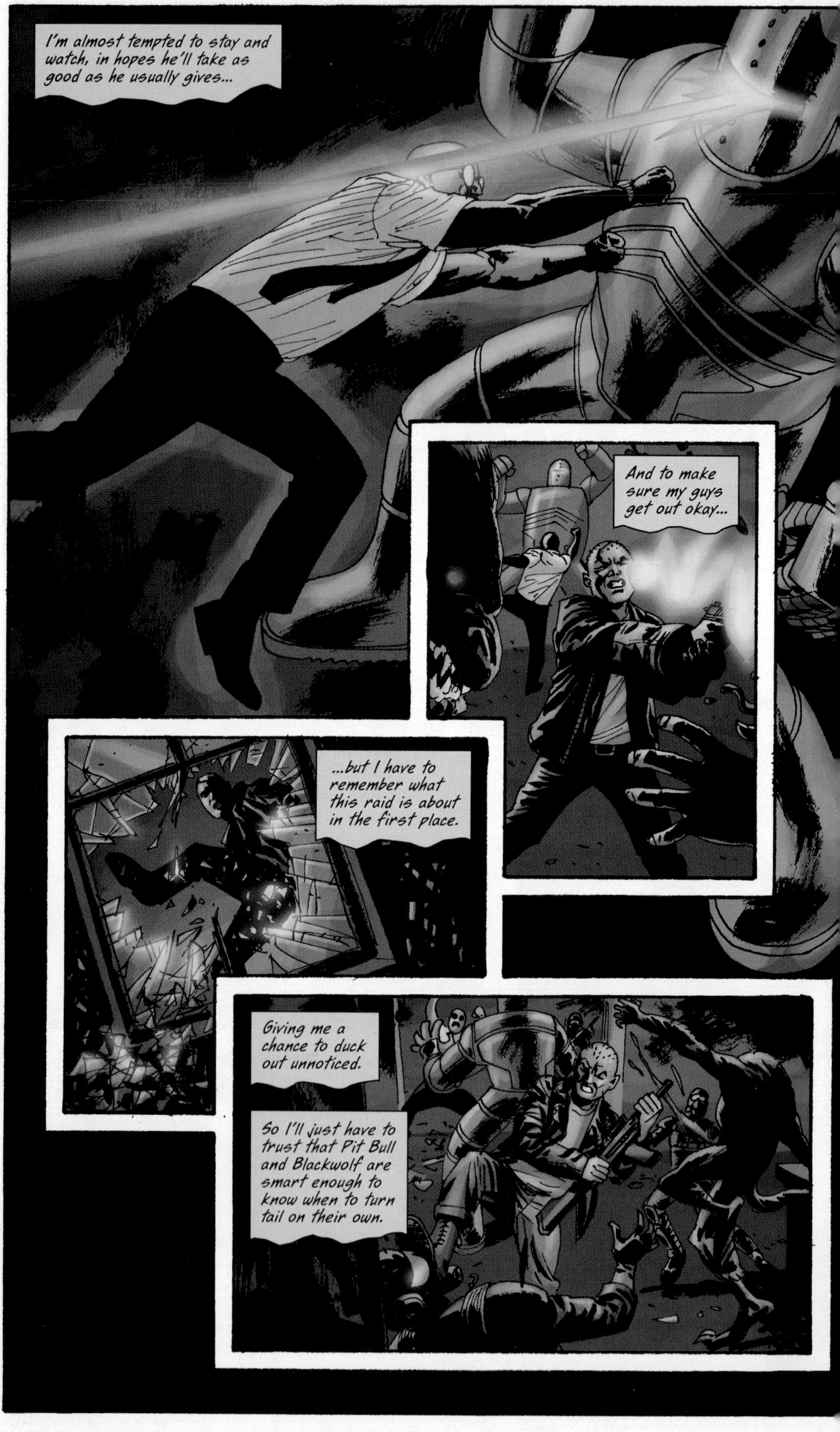
I'm almost tempted to stay and watch, in hopes he'll take as good as he usually gives...
And to make sure my guys get out okay...
...but I have to remember what this raid is about in the first place.
Giving me a chance to duck out unnoticed.
So I'll just have to trust that Pit Bull and Blackwolf are smart enough to know when to turn tail on their own.

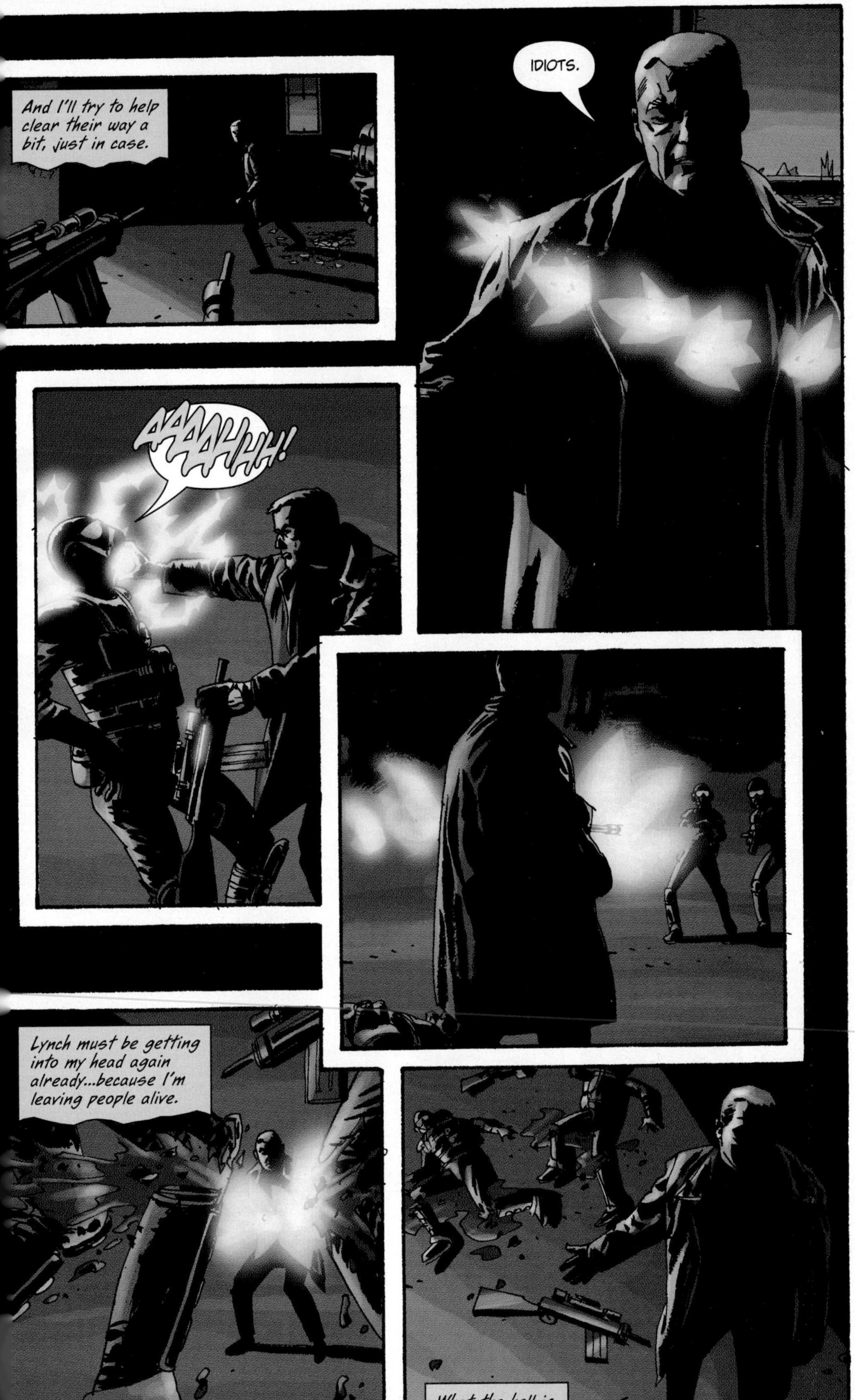
And I'll try to help clear their way a bit, just in case.
IDIOTS.
AAAAHHH!
Lynch must be getting into my head again already...because I'm leaving people alive.
What the hell is going to become of me?

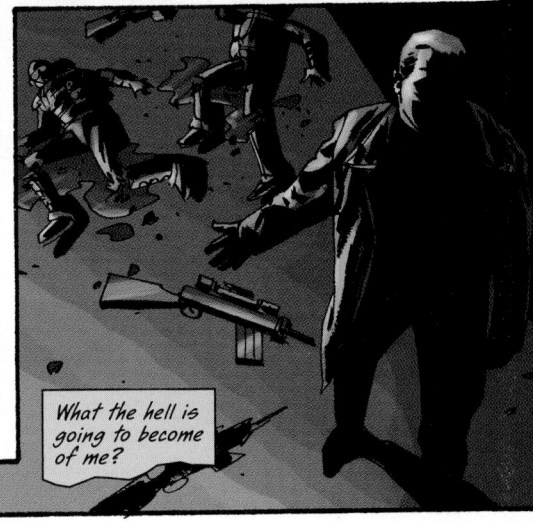

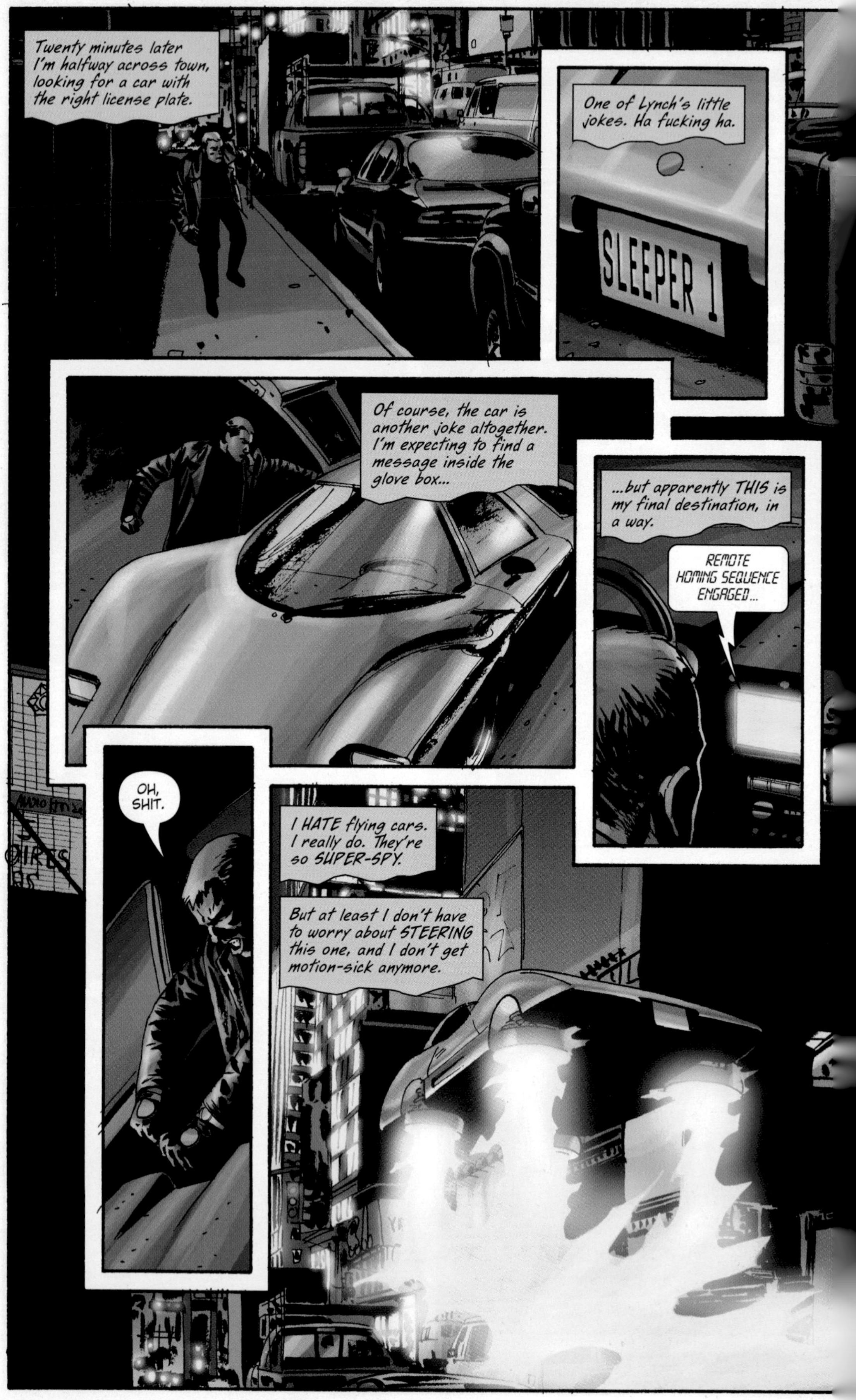

Twenty minutes later I'm halfway across town, looking for a car with the right license plate.
One of Lynch's little jokes. Ha fucking ha.
SLEEPER 1
Of course, the car is another joke altogether. I'm expecting to find a message inside the glove box...
...but apparently THIS is my final destination, in a way.
REMOTE HOMING SEQUENCE ENGAGED...
OH, SHIT.
I HATE flying cars. I really do. They're so SUPER-SPY.
But at least I don't have to worry about STEERING this one, and I don't get motion-sick anymore.

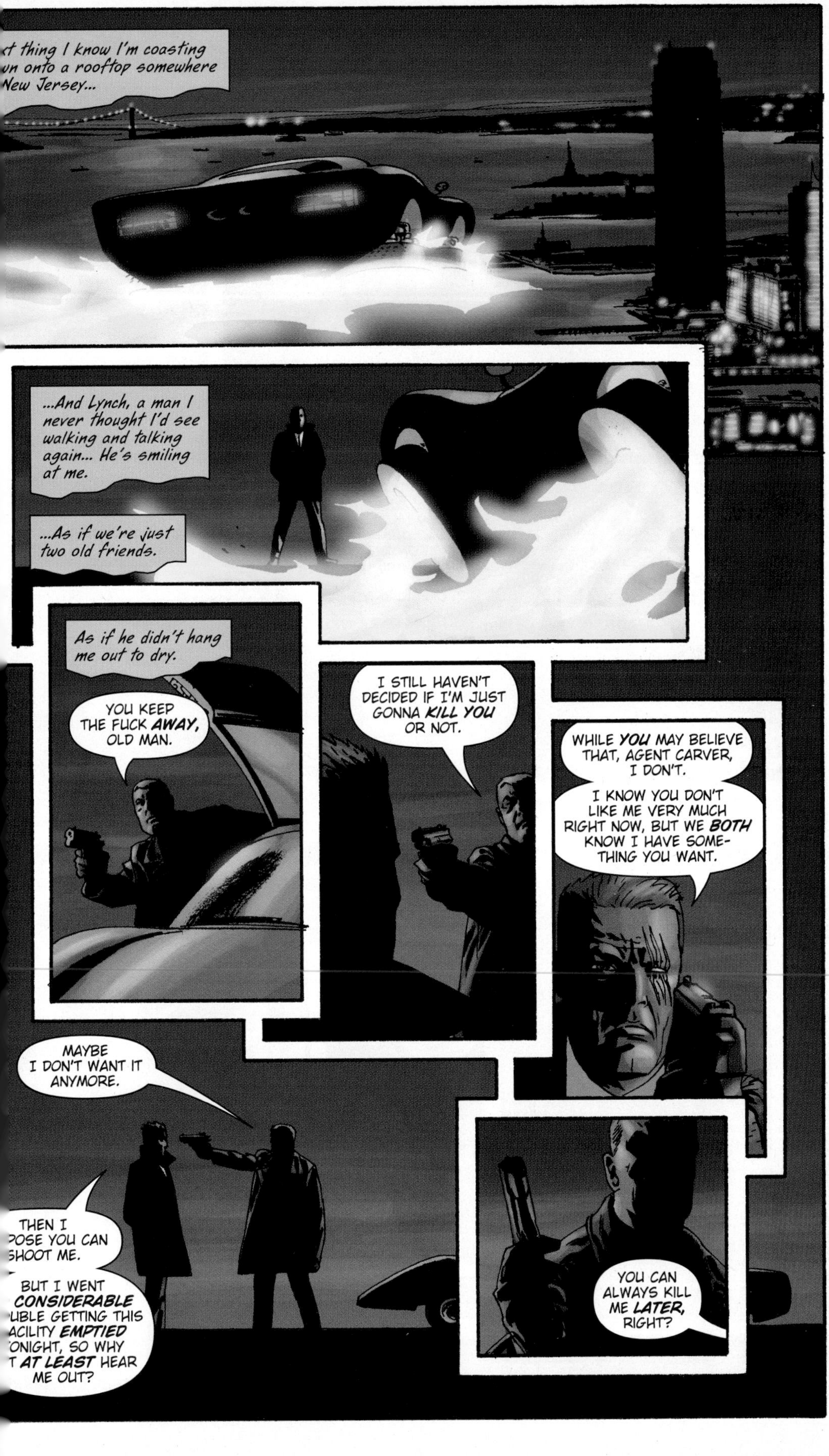

xt thing I know I'm coasting
un onto a rooftop somewhere
New Jersey...
...And Lynch, a man I never thought I'd see walking and talking again... He's smiling at me.
...As if we're just two old friends.
As if he didn't hang me out to dry.
YOU KEEP THE FUCK AWAY, OLD MAN.
I STILL HAVEN'T DECIDED IF I'M JUST GONNA KILL YOU OR NOT.
WHILE YOU MAY BELIEVE THAT, AGENT CARVER, I DON'T.
I KNOW YOU DON'T LIKE ME VERY MUCH RIGHT NOW, BUT WE BOTH KNOW I HAVE SOMETHING YOU WANT.
MAYBE I DON'T WANT IT ANYMORE.
THEN I
POSE YOU CAN
SHOOT ME.
BUT I WENT
CONSIDERABLE
UBLE GETTING THIS
ACILITY EMPTIED
TONIGHT, SO WHY
T AT LEAST HEAR
ME OUT?
YOU CAN ALWAYS KILL ME LATER, RIGHT?

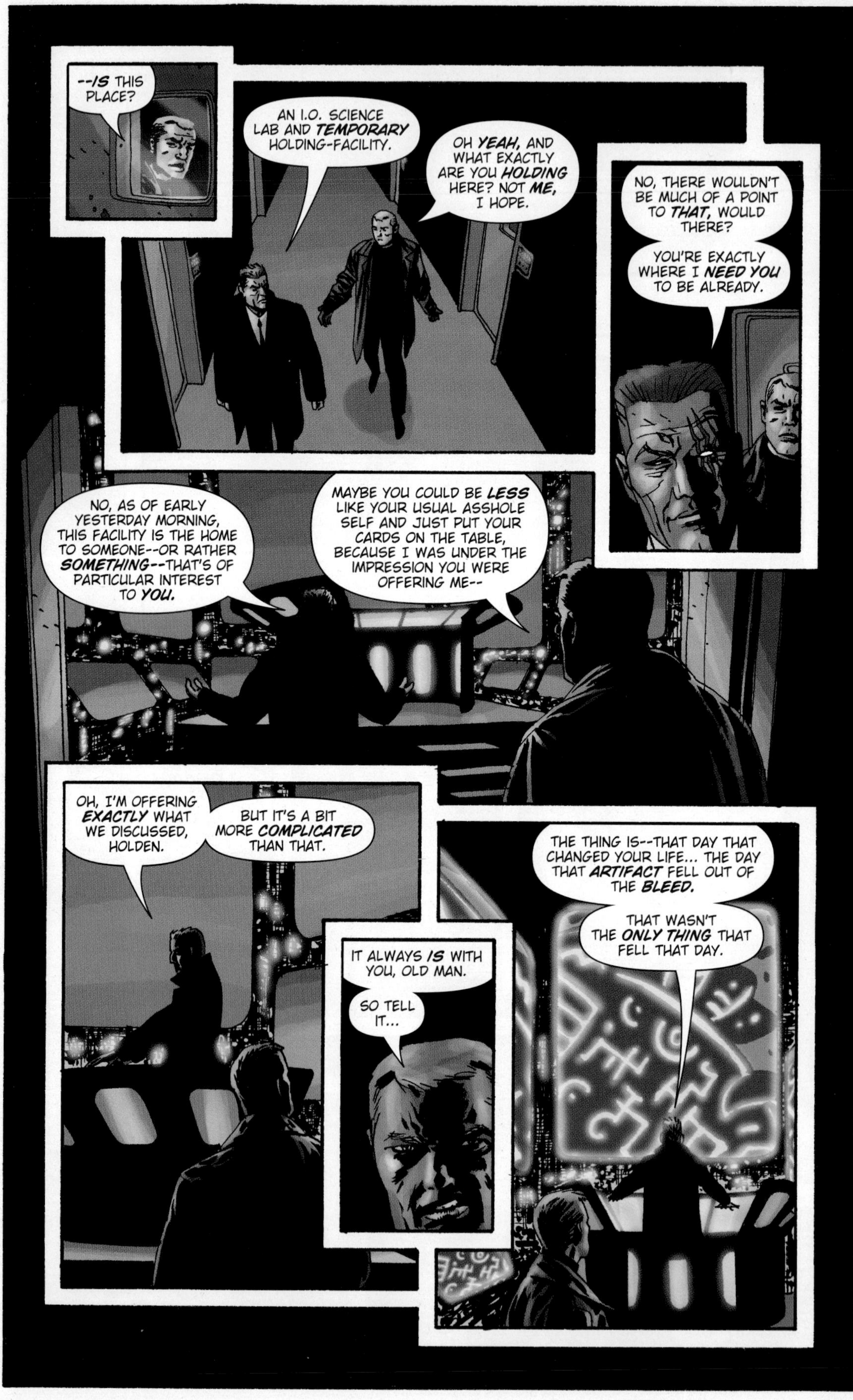
--IS THIS PLACE?
AN I.O. SCIENCE LAB AND TEMPORARY HOLDING-FACILITY.
OH YEAH, AND WHAT EXACTLY ARE YOU HOLDING HERE? NOT ME, I HOPE.
NO, THERE WOULDN'T BE MUCH OF A POINT TO THAT, WOULD THERE?
YOU'RE EXACTLY WHERE I NEED YOU TO BE ALREADY.
NO, AS OF EARLY YESTERDAY MORNING, THIS FACILITY IS THE HOME TO SOMEONE--OR RATHER SOMETHING--THAT'S OF PARTICULAR INTEREST TO YOU.
MAYBE YOU COULD BE LESS LIKE YOUR USUAL ASSHOLE SELF AND JUST PUT YOUR CARDS ON THE TABLE, BECAUSE I WAS UNDER THE IMPRESSION YOU WERE OFFERING ME--
OH, I'M OFFERING EXACTLY WHAT WE DISCUSSED, HOLDEN.
BUT IT'S A BIT MORE COMPLICATED THAN THAT.
IT ALWAYS IS WITH YOU, OLD MAN.
SO TELL IT...
THE THING IS--THAT DAY THAT CHANGED YOUR LIFE... THE DAY THAT ARTIFACT FELL OUT OF THE BLEED.
THAT WASN'T THE ONLY THING THAT FELL THAT DAY.

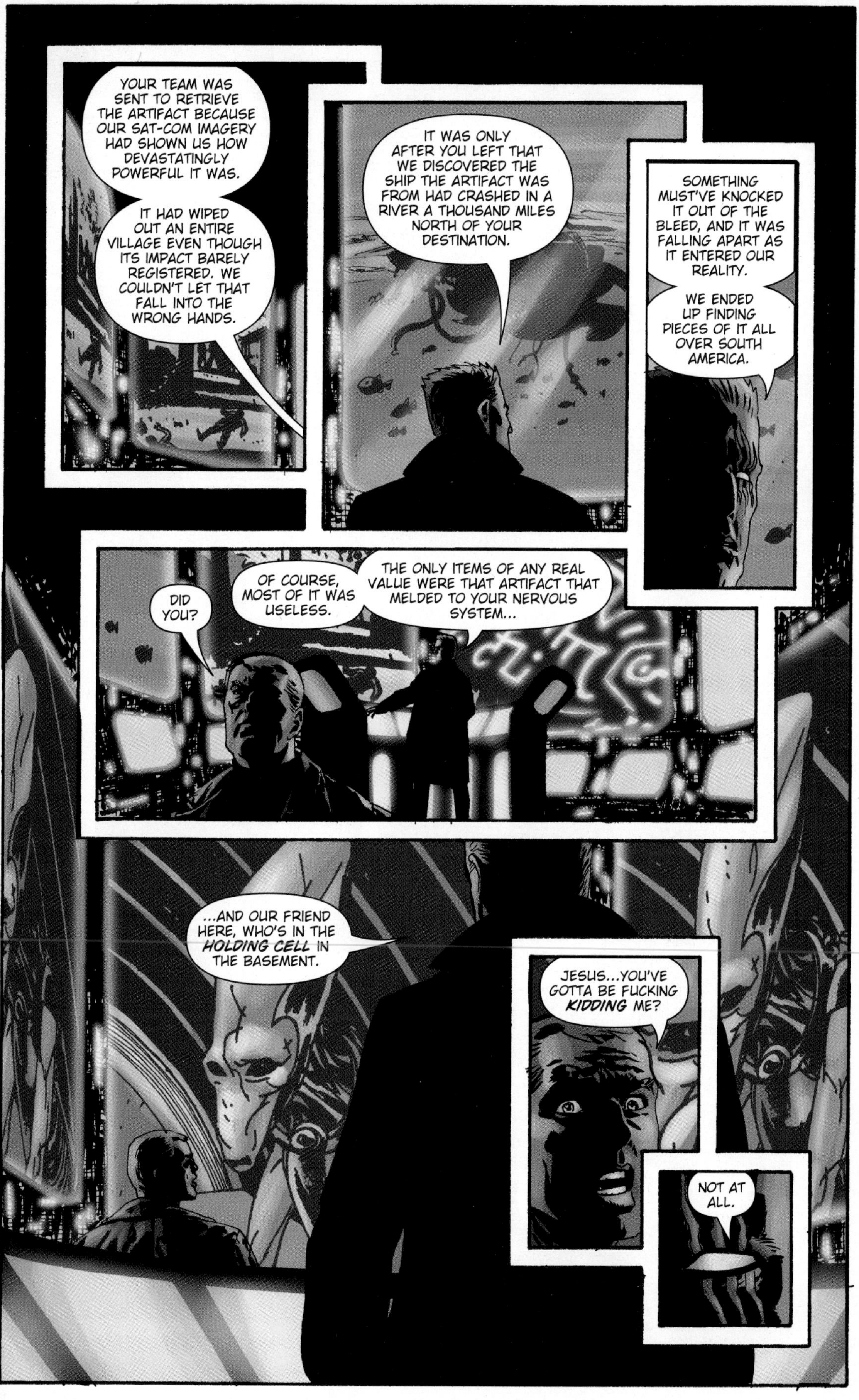
YOUR TEAM WAS SENT TO RETRIEVE THE ARTIFACT BECAUSE OUR SAT-COM IMAGERY HAD SHOWN US HOW DEVASTATINGLY POWERFUL IT WAS.
IT HAD WIPED OUT AN ENTIRE VILLAGE EVEN THOUGH ITS IMPACT BARELY REGISTERED. WE COULDN'T LET THAT FALL INTO THE WRONG HANDS.
IT WAS ONLY AFTER YOU LEFT THAT WE DISCOVERED THE SHIP THE ARTIFACT WAS FROM HAD CRASHED IN A RIVER A THOUSAND MILES NORTH OF YOUR DESTINATION.
SOMETHING MUST'VE KNOCKED IT OUT OF THE BLEED, AND IT WAS FALLING APART AS IT ENTERED OUR REALITY.
WE ENDED UP FINDING PIECES OF IT ALL OVER SOUTH AMERICA.
DID YOU?
OF COURSE, MOST OF IT WAS USELESS.
THE ONLY ITEMS OF ANY REAL VALUE WERE THAT ARTIFACT THAT MELDED TO YOUR NERVOUS SYSTEM...
...AND OUR FRIEND HERE, WHO'S IN THE *HOLDING CELL* IN THE BASEMENT.
JESUS...YOU'VE GOTTA BE FUCKING *KIDDING* ME?
NOT AT ALL.

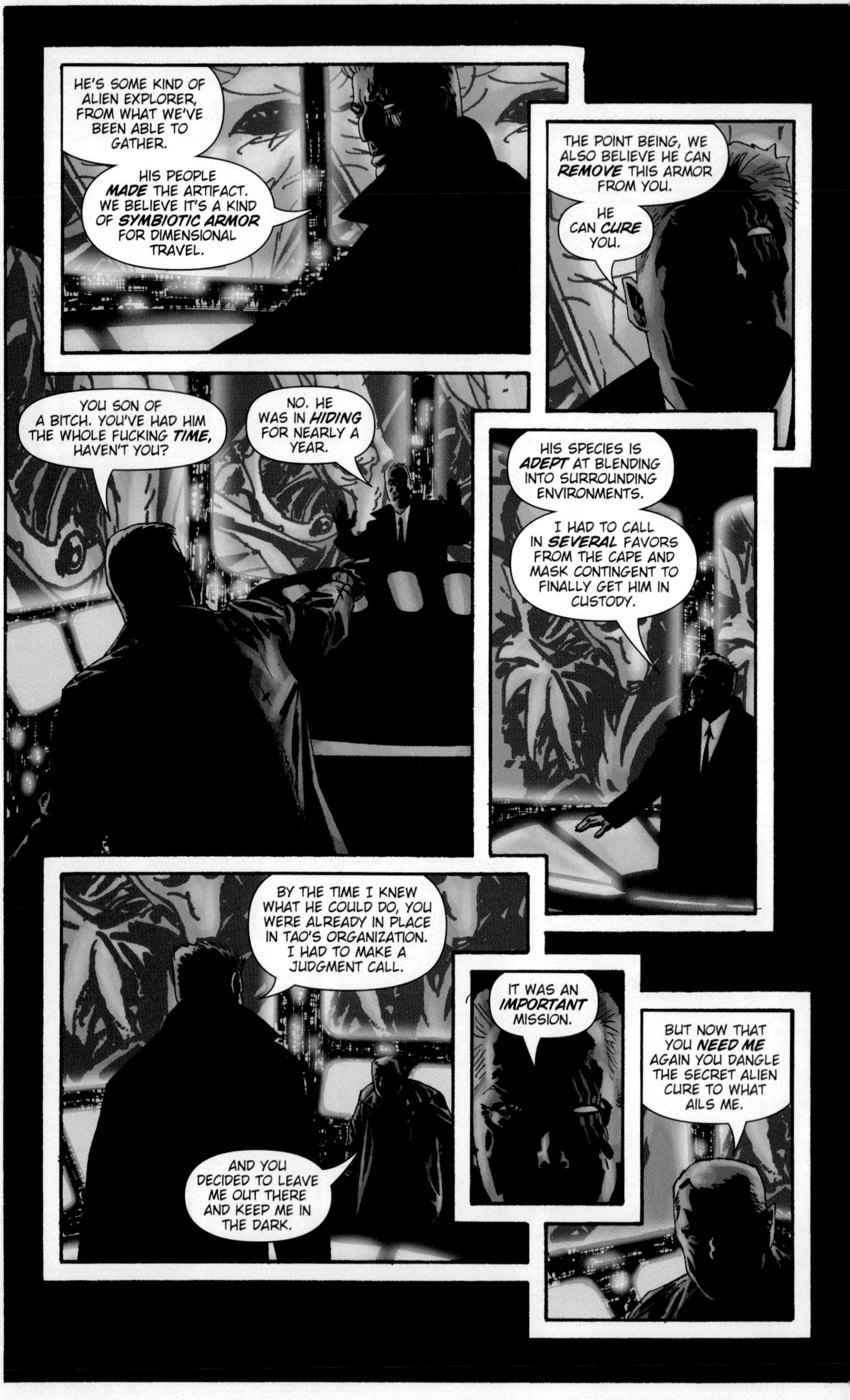
HE'S SOME KIND OF ALIEN EXPLORER, FROM WHAT WE'VE BEEN ABLE TO GATHER.
HIS PEOPLE MADE THE ARTIFACT. WE BELIEVE IT'S A KIND OF SYMBIOTIC ARMOR FOR DIMENSIONAL TRAVEL.
THE POINT BEING, WE ALSO BELIEVE HE CAN REMOVE THIS ARMOR FROM YOU.
HE CAN CURE YOU.
YOU SON OF A BITCH. YOU'VE HAD HIM THE WHOLE FUCKING TIME, HAVEN'T YOU?
NO. HE WAS IN HIDING FOR NEARLY A YEAR.
HIS SPECIES IS ADEPT AT BLENDING INTO SURROUNDING ENVIRONMENTS.
I HAD TO CALL IN SEVERAL FAVORS FROM THE CAPE AND MASK CONTINGENT TO FINALLY GET HIM IN CUSTODY.
BY THE TIME I KNEW WHAT HE COULD DO, YOU WERE ALREADY IN PLACE IN TAO'S ORGANIZATION. I HAD TO MAKE A JUDGMENT CALL.
AND YOU DECIDED TO LEAVE ME OUT THERE AND KEEP ME IN THE DARK.
IT WAS AN IMPORTANT MISSION.
BUT NOW THAT YOU NEED ME AGAIN YOU DANGLE THE SECRET ALIEN CURE TO WHAT AILS ME.

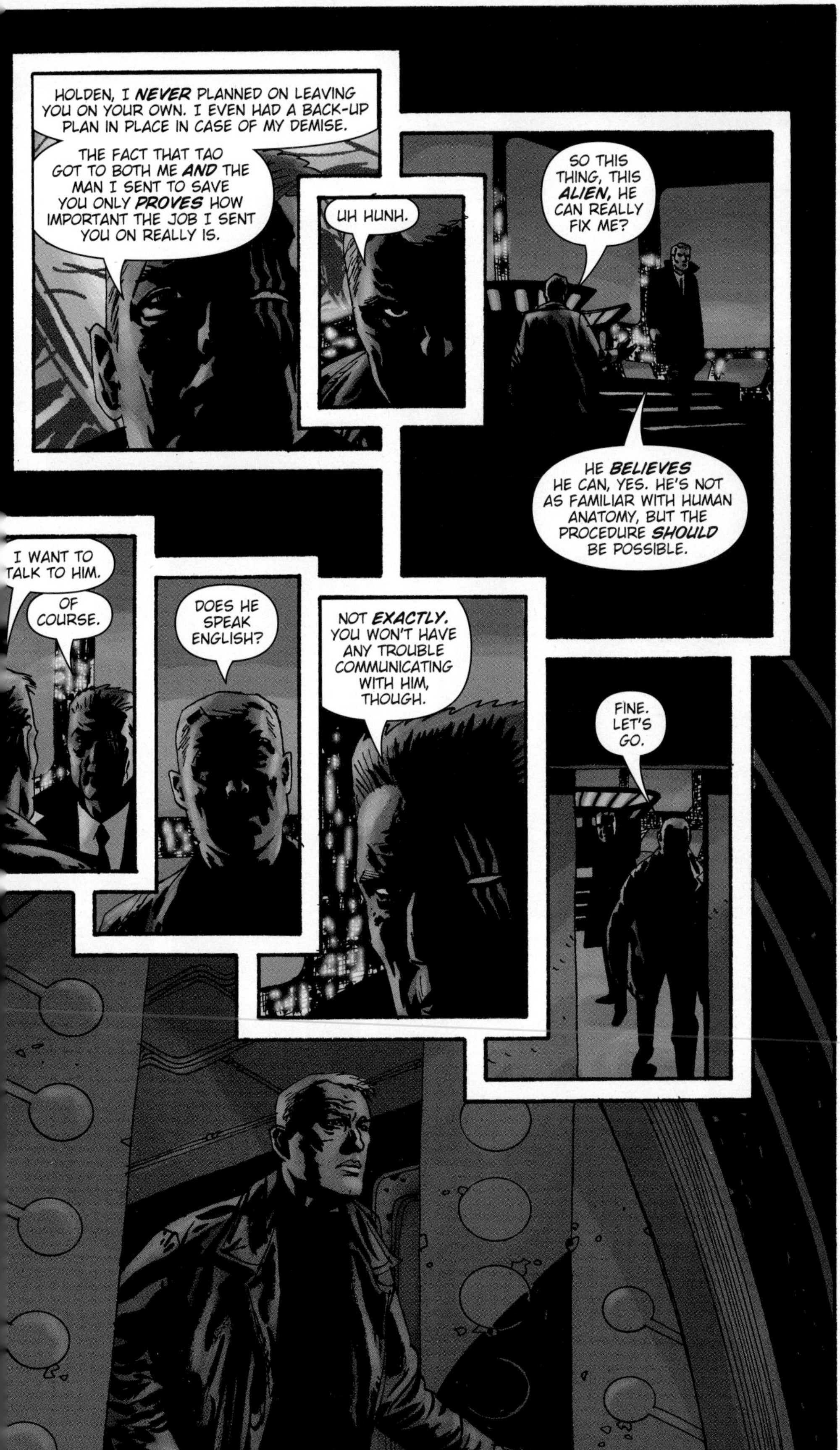
HOLDEN, I NEVER PLANNED ON LEAVING YOU ON YOUR OWN. I EVEN HAD A BACK-UP PLAN IN PLACE IN CASE OF MY DEMISE.
THE FACT THAT TAO GOT TO BOTH ME AND THE MAN I SENT TO SAVE YOU ONLY PROVES HOW IMPORTANT THE JOB I SENT YOU ON REALLY IS.
UH HUNH.
SO THIS THING, THIS ALIEN, HE CAN REALLY FIX ME?
HE BELIEVES HE CAN, YES. HE'S NOT AS FAMILIAR WITH HUMAN ANATOMY, BUT THE PROCEDURE SHOULD BE POSSIBLE.
I WANT TO TALK TO HIM.
OF COURSE.
DOES HE SPEAK ENGLISH?
NOT EXACTLY. YOU WON'T HAVE ANY TROUBLE COMMUNICATING WITH HIM, THOUGH.
FINE. LET'S GO.

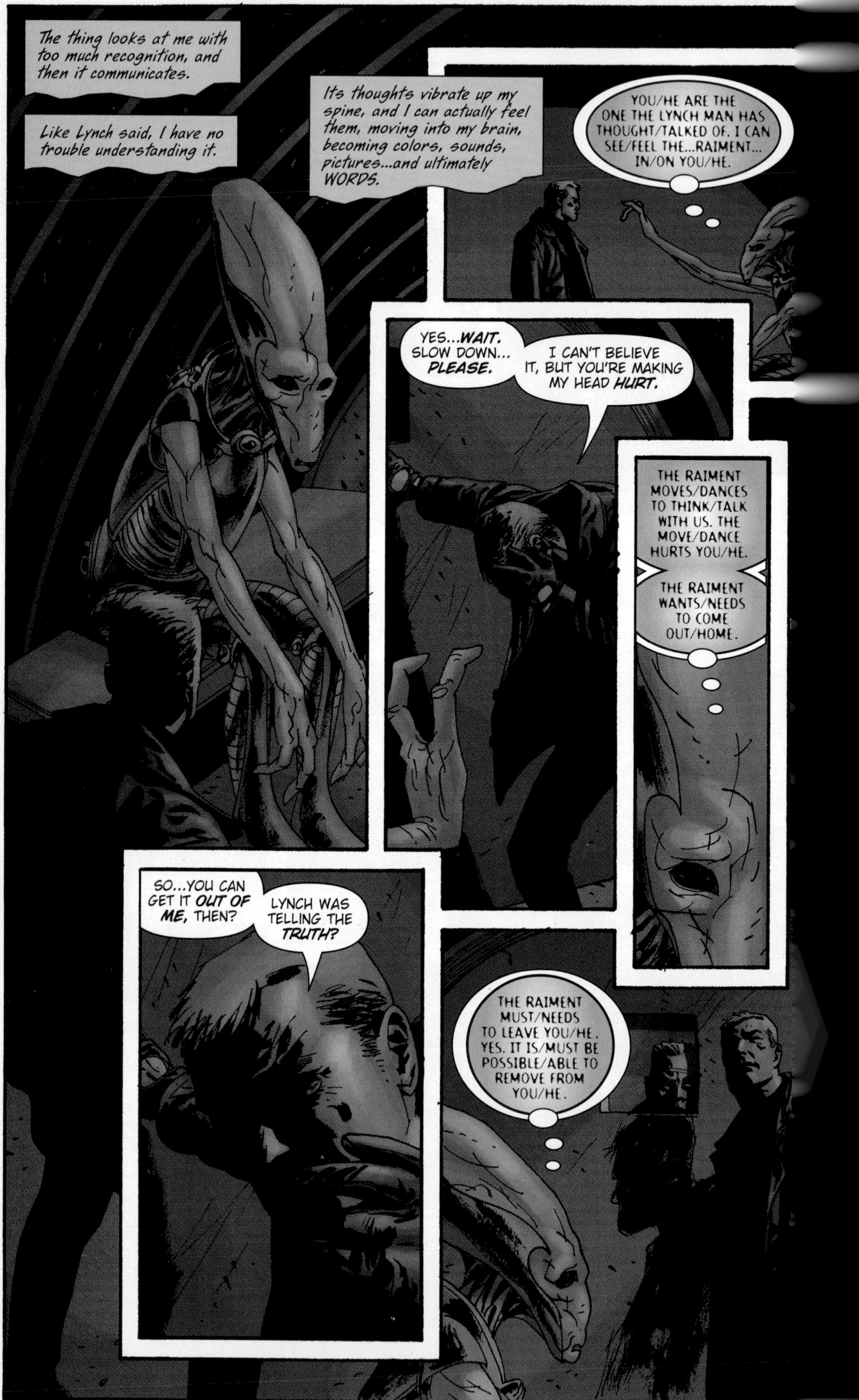
The thing looks at me with too much recognition, and then it communicates.
Like Lynch said, I have no trouble understanding it.
Its thoughts vibrate up my spine, and I can actually feel them, moving into my brain, becoming colors, sounds, pictures...and ultimately WORDS.
YOU/HE ARE THE ONE THE LYNCH MAN HAS THOUGHT/TALKED OF. I CAN SEE/FEEL THE...RAIMENT... IN/ON YOU/HE.
YES...WAIT. SLOW DOWN... PLEASE.
I CAN'T BELIEVE IT, BUT YOU'RE MAKING MY HEAD HURT.
THE RAIMENT MOVES/DANCES TO THINK/TALK WITH US. THE MOVE/DANCE HURTS YOU/HE.
THE RAIMENT WANTS/NEEDS TO COME OUT/HOME.
SO...YOU CAN GET IT OUT OF ME, THEN?
LYNCH WAS TELLING THE TRUTH?
THE RAIMENT MUST/NEEDS TO LEAVE YOU/HE. YES. IT IS/MUST BE POSSIBLE/ABLE TO REMOVE FROM YOU/HE.

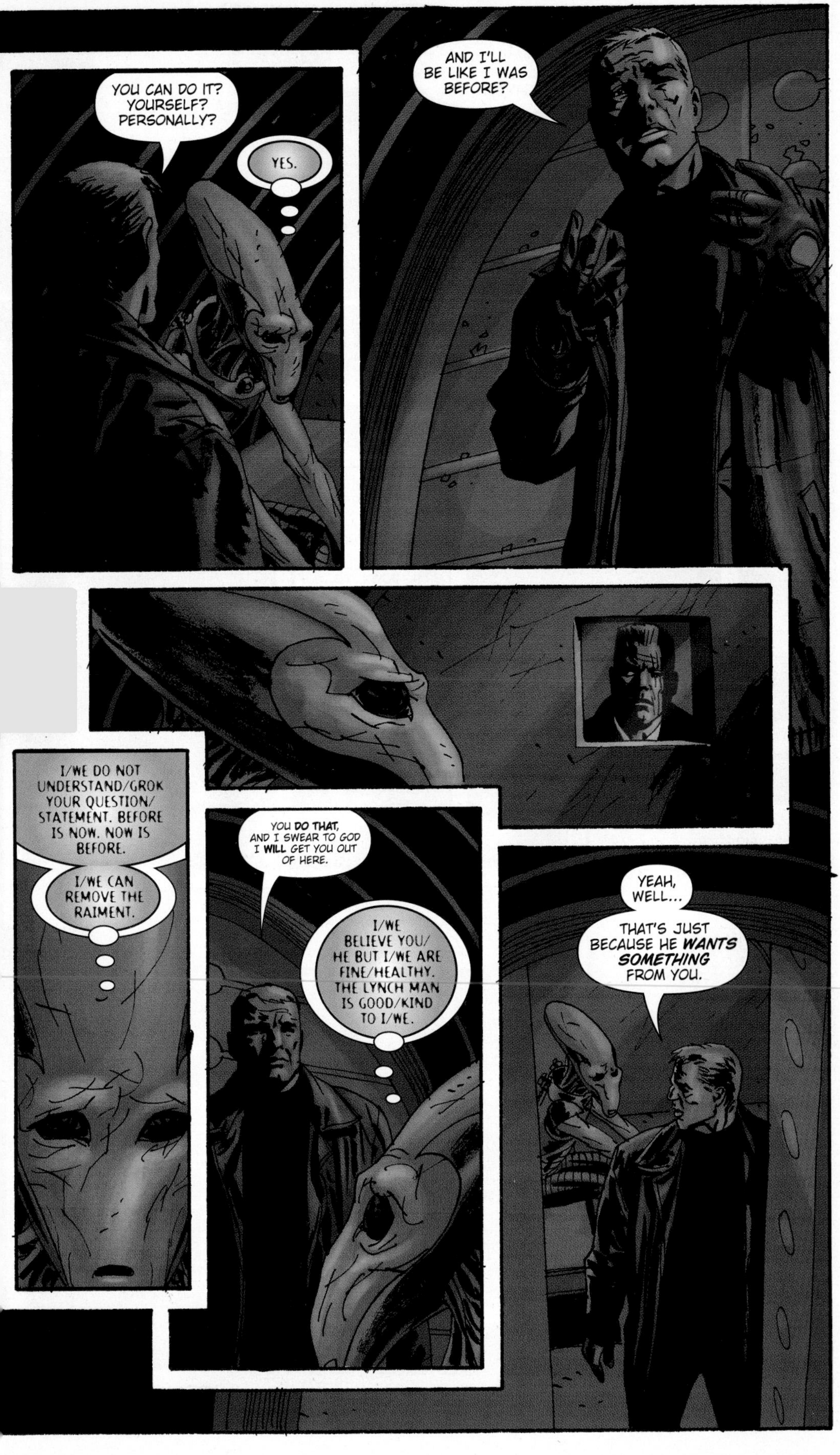
YOU CAN DO IT? YOURSELF? PERSONALLY?
YES.
AND I'LL BE LIKE I WAS BEFORE?
I/WE DO NOT UNDERSTAND/GROK YOUR QUESTION/ STATEMENT. BEFORE IS NOW. NOW IS BEFORE.
I/WE CAN REMOVE THE RAIMENT.
YOU DO THAT, AND I SWEAR TO GOD I WILL GET YOU OUT OF HERE.
I/WE BELIEVE YOU/ HE BUT I/WE ARE FINE/HEALTHY. THE LYNCH MAN IS GOOD/KIND TO I/WE.
YEAH, WELL...
THAT'S JUST BECAUSE HE WANTS SOMETHING FROM YOU.

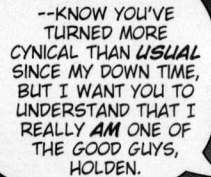

--KNOW YOU'VE TURNED MORE CYNICAL THAN *USUAL* SINCE MY DOWN TIME, BUT I WANT YOU TO UNDERSTAND THAT I REALLY *AM* ONE OF THE GOOD GUYS, HOLDEN.

I'M FIGHTING TO MAINTAIN SOME SEMBLANCE OF *ORDER* IN THIS WORLD. SOME SENSE OF *JUSTICE*. YOU USED TO BE *PART* OF THAT FIGHT.

I WAS...BUT AFTER A WHILE, YOU HAVE TO WONDER IF THE ENDS *REALLY DO* JUSTIFY THE MEANS, LYNCH.

I MEAN, IT'S NOT AS IF THIS WORLD YOU'VE HELPED SHAPE IS ANYTHING TO BE *PROUD OF.*

WELL...REGARDLESS OF YOUR *FEELINGS*, WE NEED ONE ANOTHER, AGENT CARVER.

YOU CAN HELP ME BRING DOWN TAO, AND I CAN CURE YOU.

THAT'S NOT *GOOD ENOUGH.* IF YOU WANT ME, I'VE GOT SOME *OTHER* DEMANDS, TOO.

I'M LISTENING.

FIRST OFF, YOU STAY THE FUCK AWAY FROM TRIPLE-X RAY. *AND* I WANT HIM *PARDONED* ONCE WE GET TAO.

AND I WANT A NEW *LIFE*, ON SOME *TROPICAL ISLAND* SOMEWHERE, AWAY FROM ALL THIS BULLSHIT...WITH ENOUGH MONEY TO NOT WORRY ABOUT MONEY EVER AGAIN.

DONE. ALL OF IT.

RIGHT. AND THERE'S JUST *ONE MORE* THING...

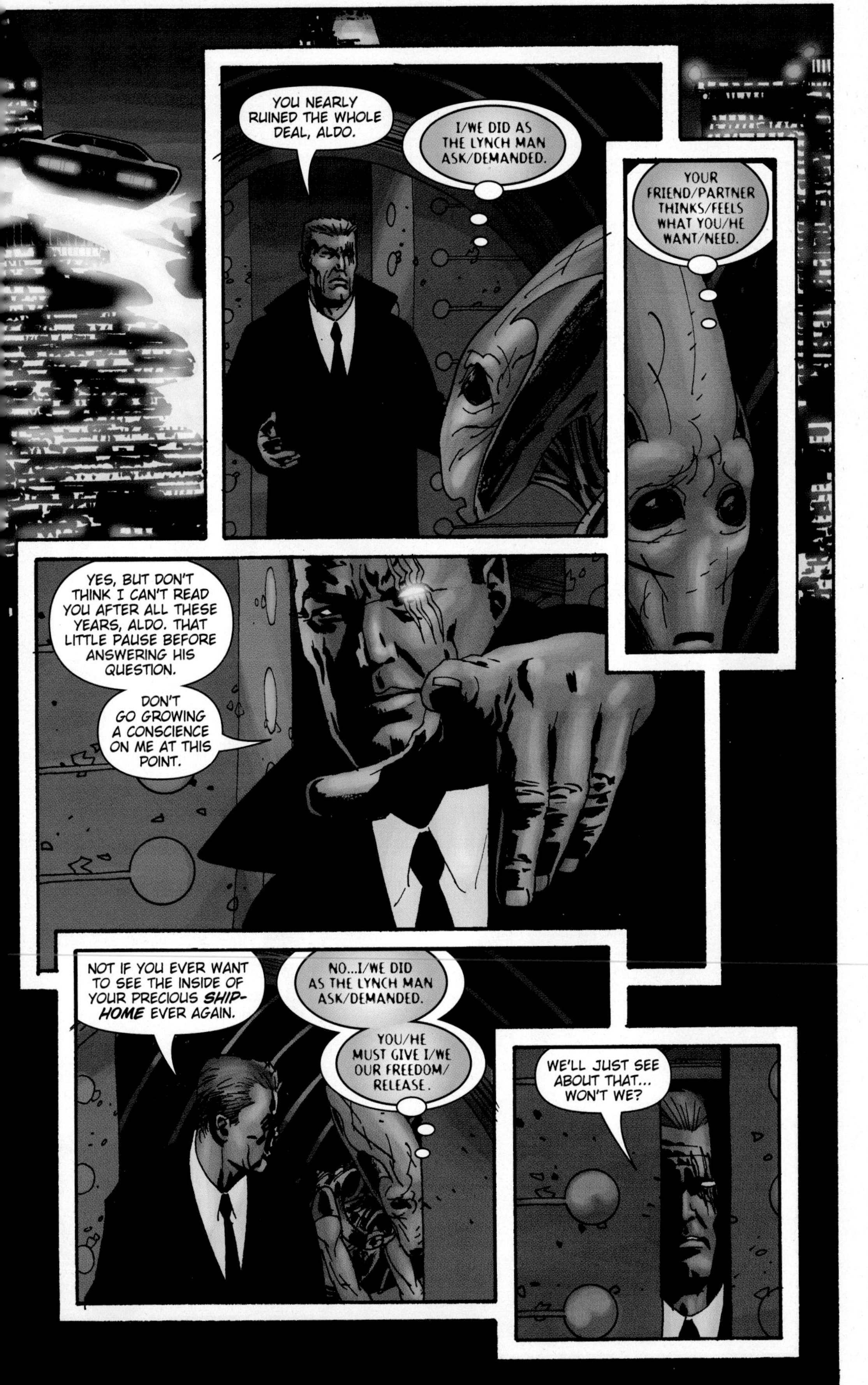
YOU NEARLY RUINED THE WHOLE DEAL, ALDO.
I/WE DID AS THE LYNCH MAN ASK/DEMANDED.
YOUR FRIEND/PARTNER THINKS/FEELS WHAT YOU/HE WANT/NEED.
YES, BUT DON'T THINK I CAN'T READ YOU AFTER ALL THESE YEARS, ALDO. THAT LITTLE PAUSE BEFORE ANSWERING HIS QUESTION.
DON'T GO GROWING A CONSCIENCE ON ME AT THIS POINT.
NOT IF YOU EVER WANT TO SEE THE INSIDE OF YOUR PRECIOUS *SHIP-HOME* EVER AGAIN.
NO...I/WE DID AS THE LYNCH MAN ASK/DEMANDED.
YOU/HE MUST GIVE I/WE OUR FREEDOM/RELEASE.
WE'LL JUST SEE ABOUT THAT... WON'T WE?

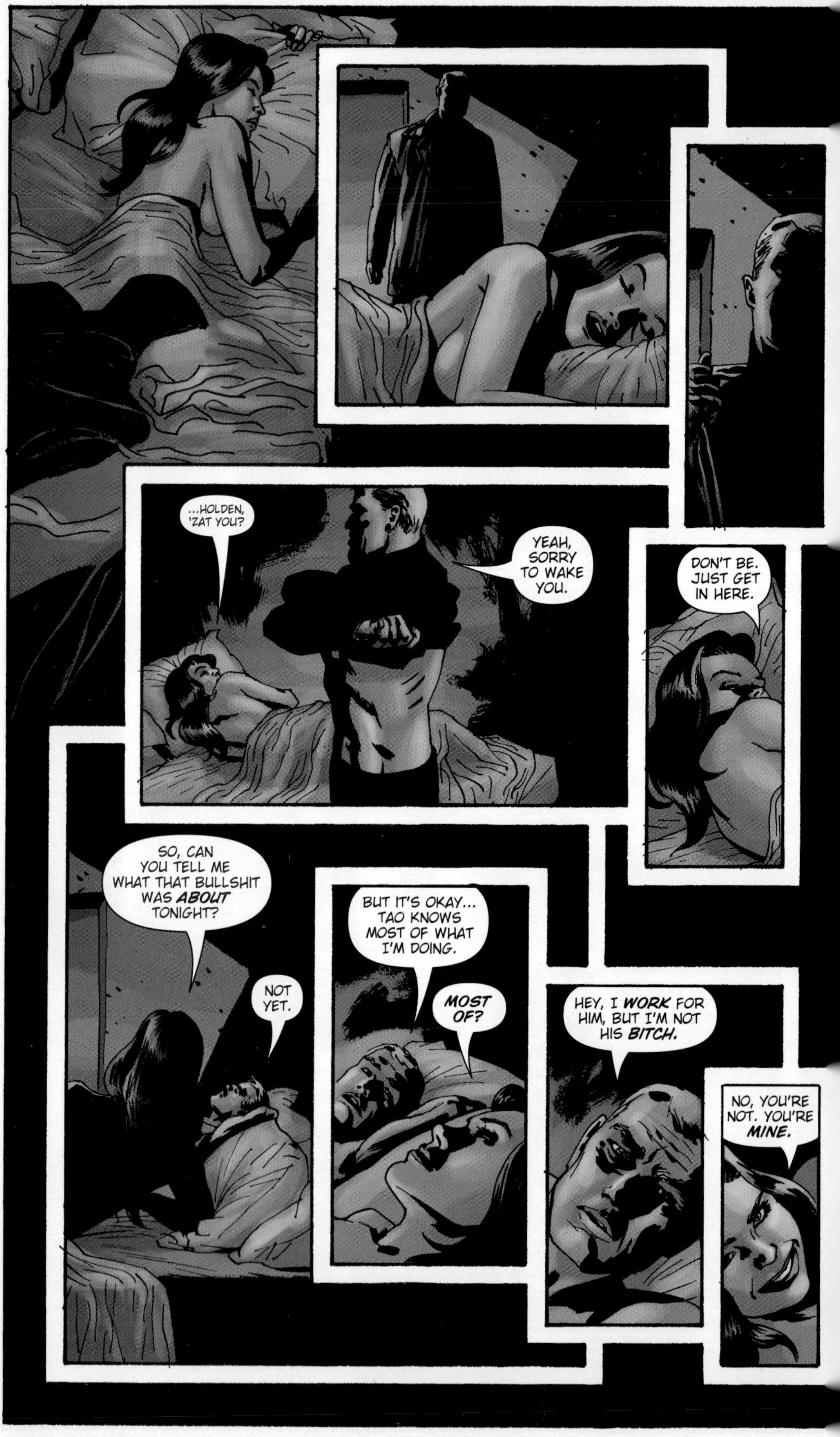
...HOLDEN, 'ZAT YOU?
YEAH, SORRY TO WAKE YOU.
DON'T BE. JUST GET IN HERE.
SO, CAN YOU TELL ME WHAT THAT BULLSHIT WAS ABOUT TONIGHT?
NOT YET.
BUT IT'S OKAY... TAO KNOWS MOST OF WHAT I'M DOING.
MOST OF?
HEY, I WORK FOR HIM, BUT I'M NOT HIS BITCH.
NO, YOU'RE NOT. YOU'RE MINE.

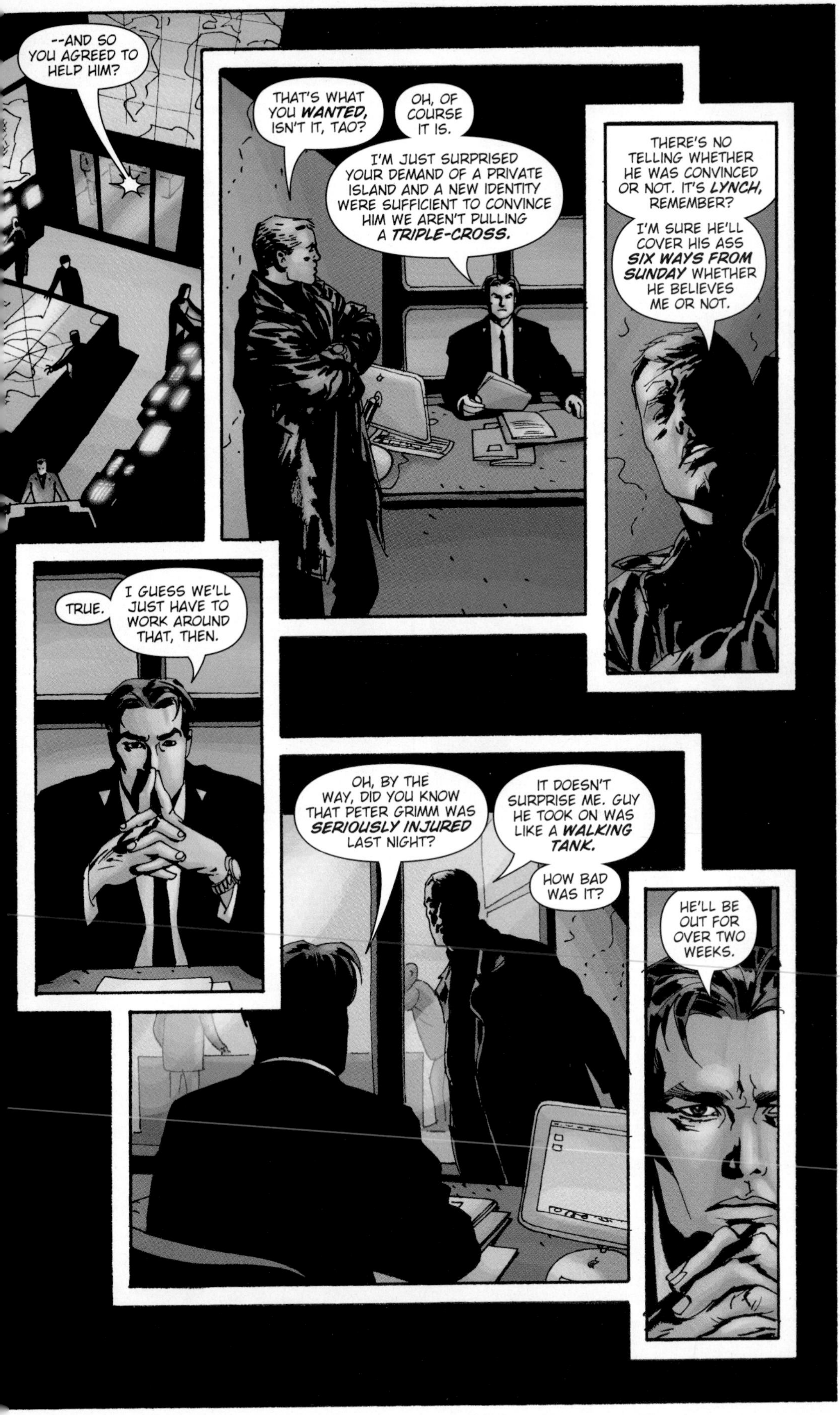
--AND SO YOU AGREED TO HELP HIM?
THAT'S WHAT YOU WANTED, ISN'T IT, TAO?
OH, OF COURSE IT IS.
I'M JUST SURPRISED YOUR DEMAND OF A PRIVATE ISLAND AND A NEW IDENTITY WERE SUFFICIENT TO CONVINCE HIM WE AREN'T PULLING A TRIPLE-CROSS.
THERE'S NO TELLING WHETHER HE WAS CONVINCED OR NOT. IT'S LYNCH, REMEMBER?
I'M SURE HE'LL COVER HIS ASS SIX WAYS FROM SUNDAY WHETHER HE BELIEVES ME OR NOT.
TRUE.
I GUESS WE'LL JUST HAVE TO WORK AROUND THAT, THEN.
OH, BY THE WAY, DID YOU KNOW THAT PETER GRIMM WAS SERIOUSLY INJURED LAST NIGHT?
IT DOESN'T SURPRISE ME. GUY HE TOOK ON WAS LIKE A WALKING TANK.
HOW BAD WAS IT?
HE'LL BE OUT FOR OVER TWO WEEKS.

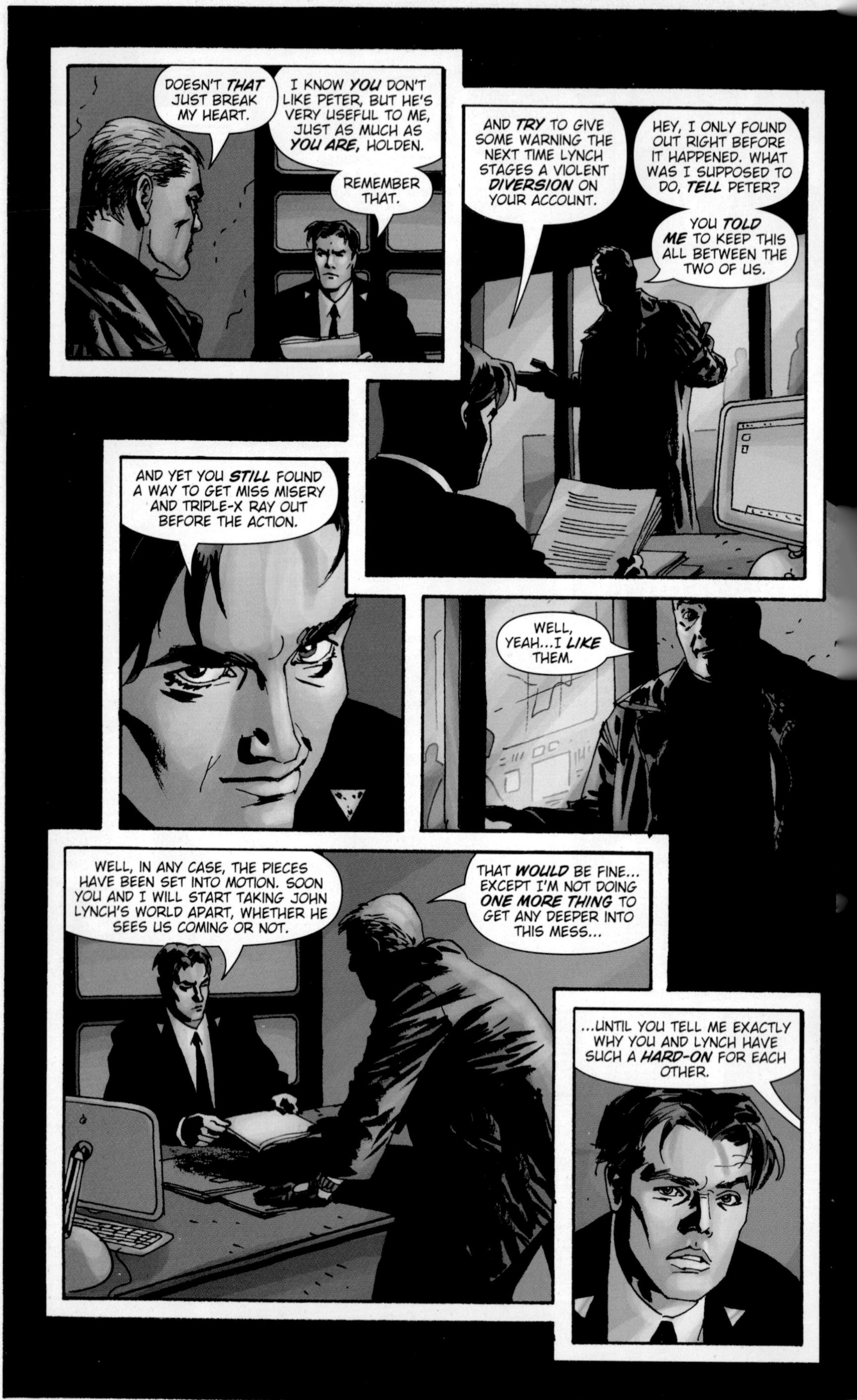
DOESN'T THAT JUST BREAK MY HEART.
I KNOW YOU DON'T LIKE PETER, BUT HE'S VERY USEFUL TO ME, JUST AS MUCH AS YOU ARE, HOLDEN.
REMEMBER THAT.
AND TRY TO GIVE SOME WARNING THE NEXT TIME LYNCH STAGES A VIOLENT DIVERSION ON YOUR ACCOUNT.
HEY, I ONLY FOUND OUT RIGHT BEFORE IT HAPPENED. WHAT WAS I SUPPOSED TO DO, TELL PETER?
YOU TOLD ME TO KEEP THIS ALL BETWEEN THE TWO OF US.
AND YET YOU STILL FOUND A WAY TO GET MISS MISERY AND TRIPLE-X RAY OUT BEFORE THE ACTION.
WELL, YEAH...I LIKE THEM.
WELL, IN ANY CASE, THE PIECES HAVE BEEN SET INTO MOTION. SOON YOU AND I WILL START TAKING JOHN LYNCH'S WORLD APART, WHETHER HE SEES US COMING OR NOT.
THAT WOULD BE FINE... EXCEPT I'M NOT DOING ONE MORE THING TO GET ANY DEEPER INTO THIS MESS...
...UNTIL YOU TELL ME EXACTLY WHY YOU AND LYNCH HAVE SUCH A HARD-ON FOR EACH OTHER.

chapter seventeen

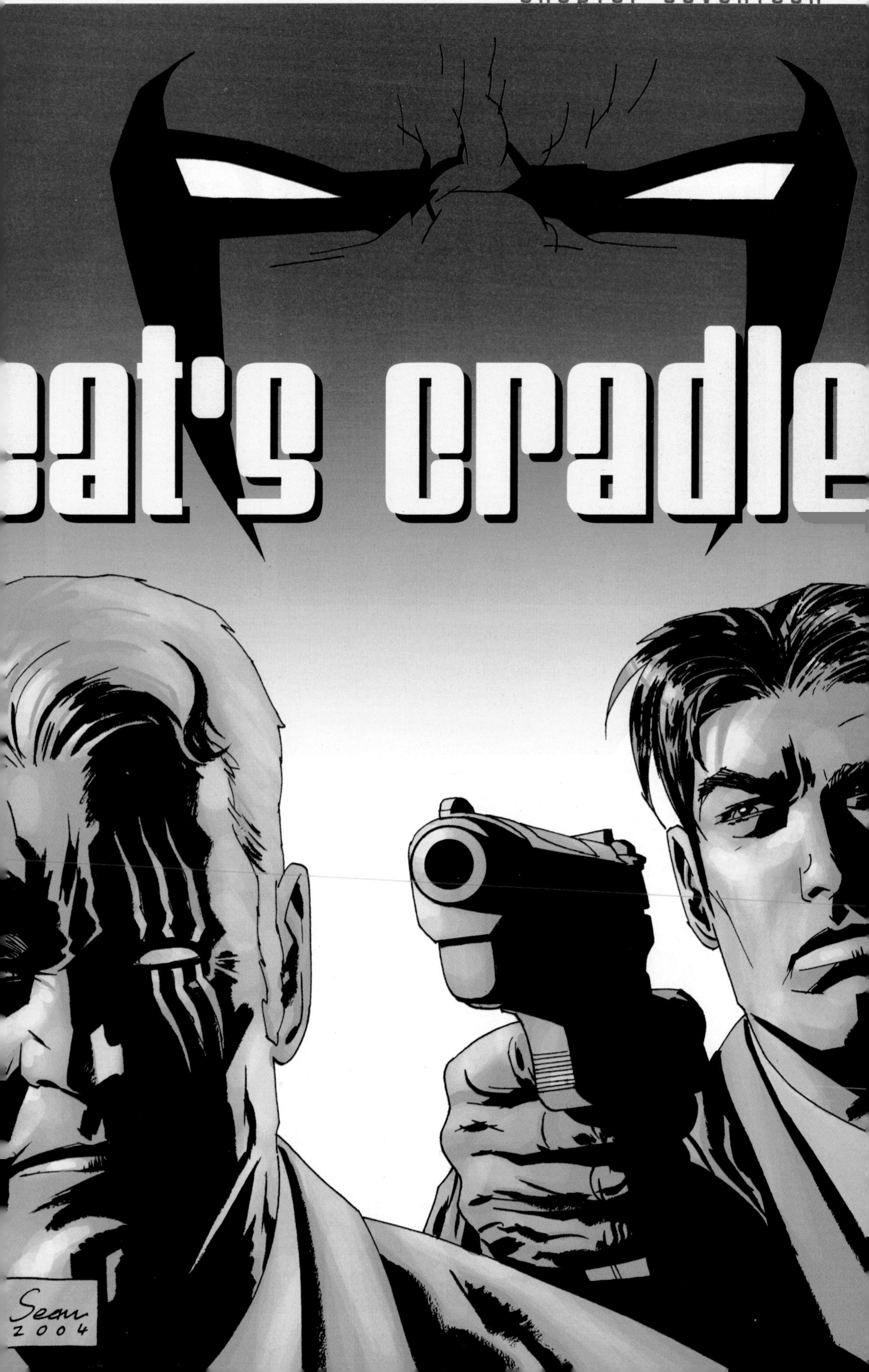
cat's cradle
Sean 2004

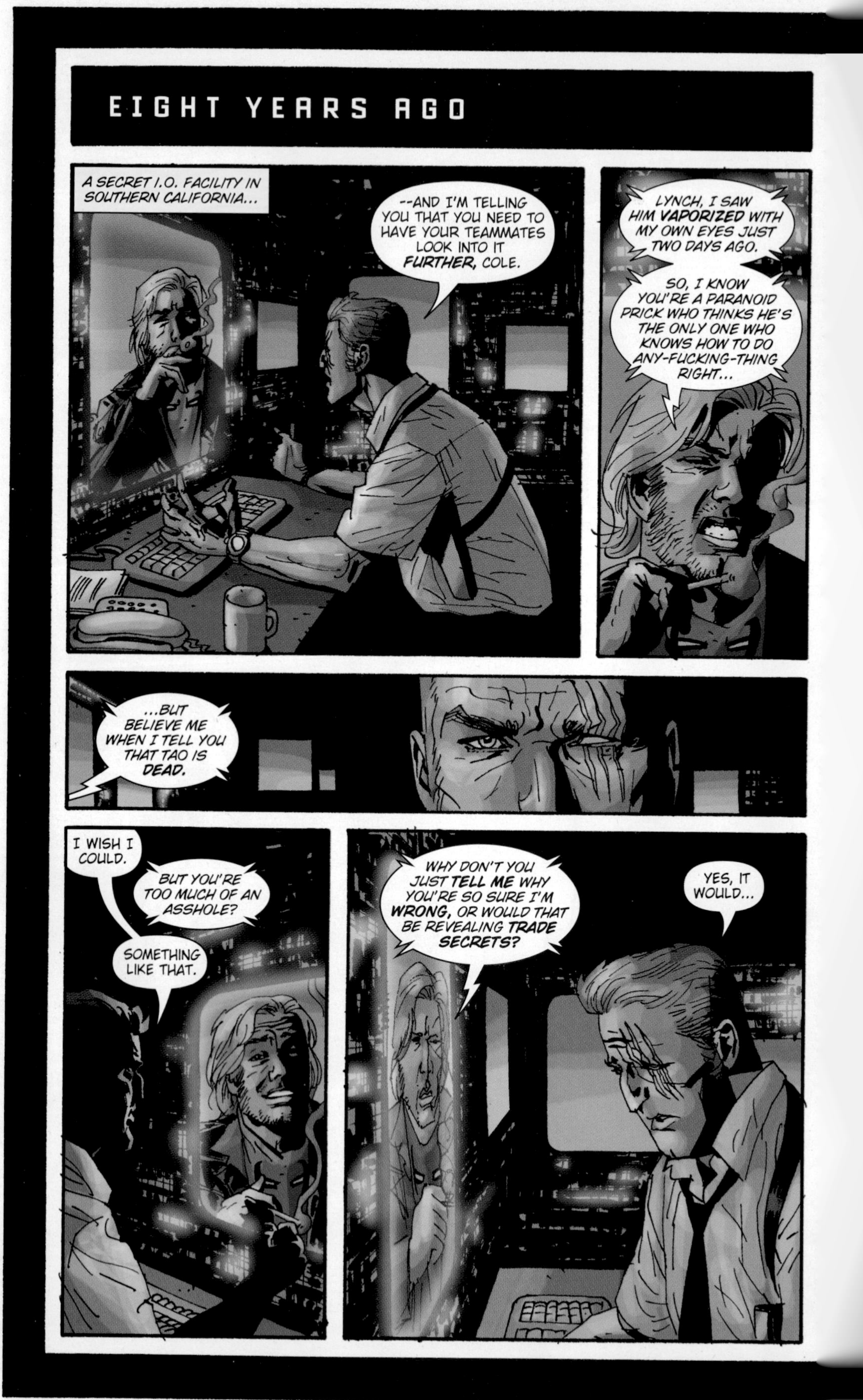
EIGHT YEARS AGO
A SECRET I.O. FACILITY IN SOUTHERN CALIFORNIA...
--AND I'M TELLING YOU THAT YOU NEED TO HAVE YOUR TEAMMATES LOOK INTO IT FURTHER, COLE.
LYNCH, I SAW HIM VAPORIZED WITH MY OWN EYES JUST TWO DAYS AGO.
SO, I KNOW YOU'RE A PARANOID PRICK WHO THINKS HE'S THE ONLY ONE WHO KNOWS HOW TO DO ANY-FUCKING-THING RIGHT...
...BUT BELIEVE ME WHEN I TELL YOU THAT TAO IS DEAD.
I WISH I COULD.
BUT YOU'RE TOO MUCH OF AN ASSHOLE?
SOMETHING LIKE THAT.
WHY DON'T YOU JUST TELL ME WHY YOU'RE SO SURE I'M WRONG, OR WOULD THAT BE REVEALING TRADE SECRETS?
YES, IT WOULD...

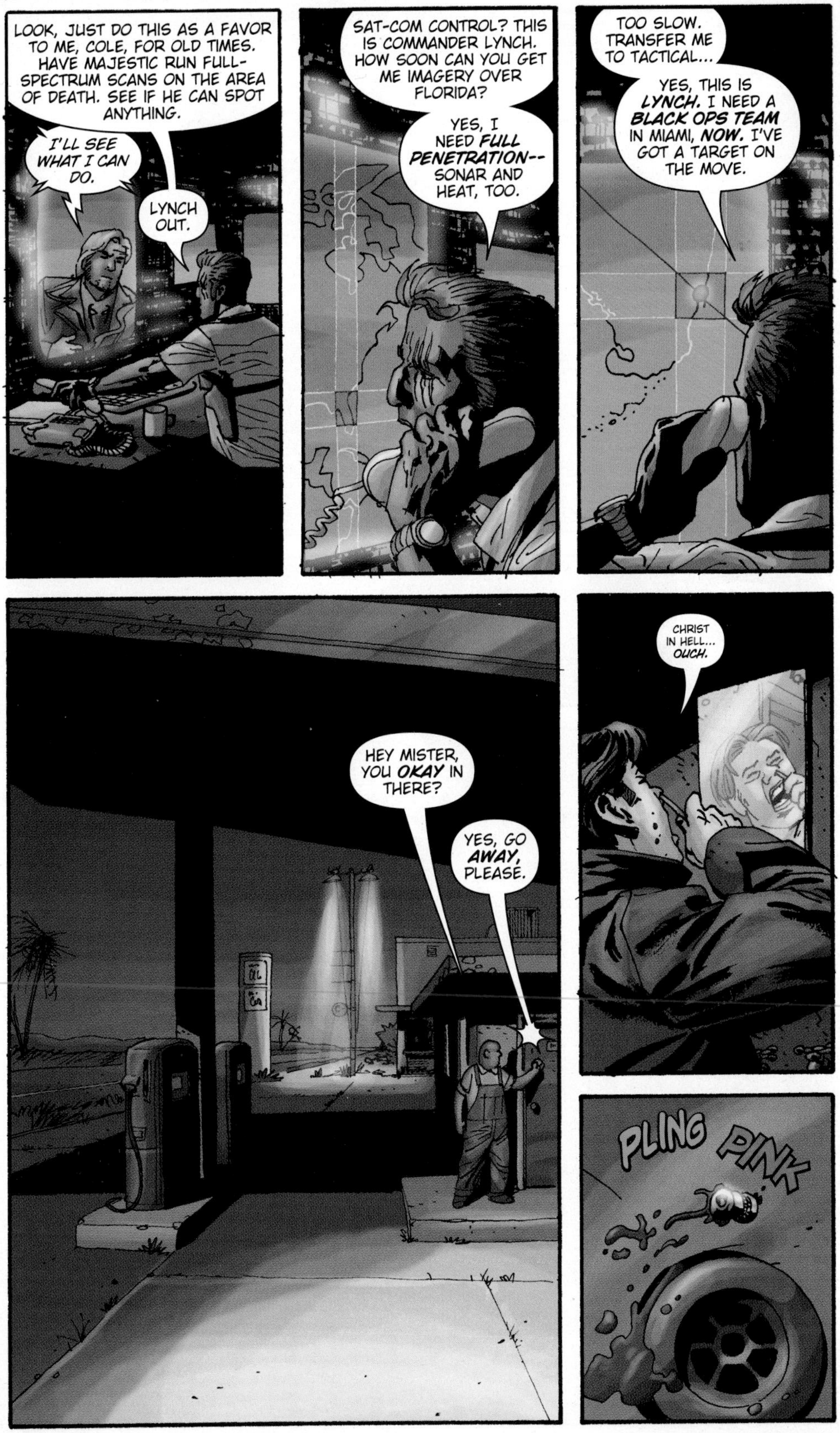
LOOK, JUST DO THIS AS A FAVOR TO ME, COLE, FOR OLD TIMES. HAVE MAJESTIC RUN FULL-SPECTRUM SCANS ON THE AREA OF DEATH. SEE IF HE CAN SPOT ANYTHING.
I'LL SEE WHAT I CAN DO.
LYNCH OUT.
SAT-COM CONTROL? THIS IS COMMANDER LYNCH. HOW SOON CAN YOU GET ME IMAGERY OVER FLORIDA?
YES, I NEED FULL PENETRATION-- SONAR AND HEAT, TOO.
TOO SLOW. TRANSFER ME TO TACTICAL...
YES, THIS IS LYNCH. I NEED A BLACK OPS TEAM IN MIAMI, NOW. I'VE GOT A TARGET ON THE MOVE.
HEY MISTER, YOU OKAY IN THERE?
YES, GO AWAY, PLEASE.
CHRIST IN HELL... OUCH.
PLING
PINK

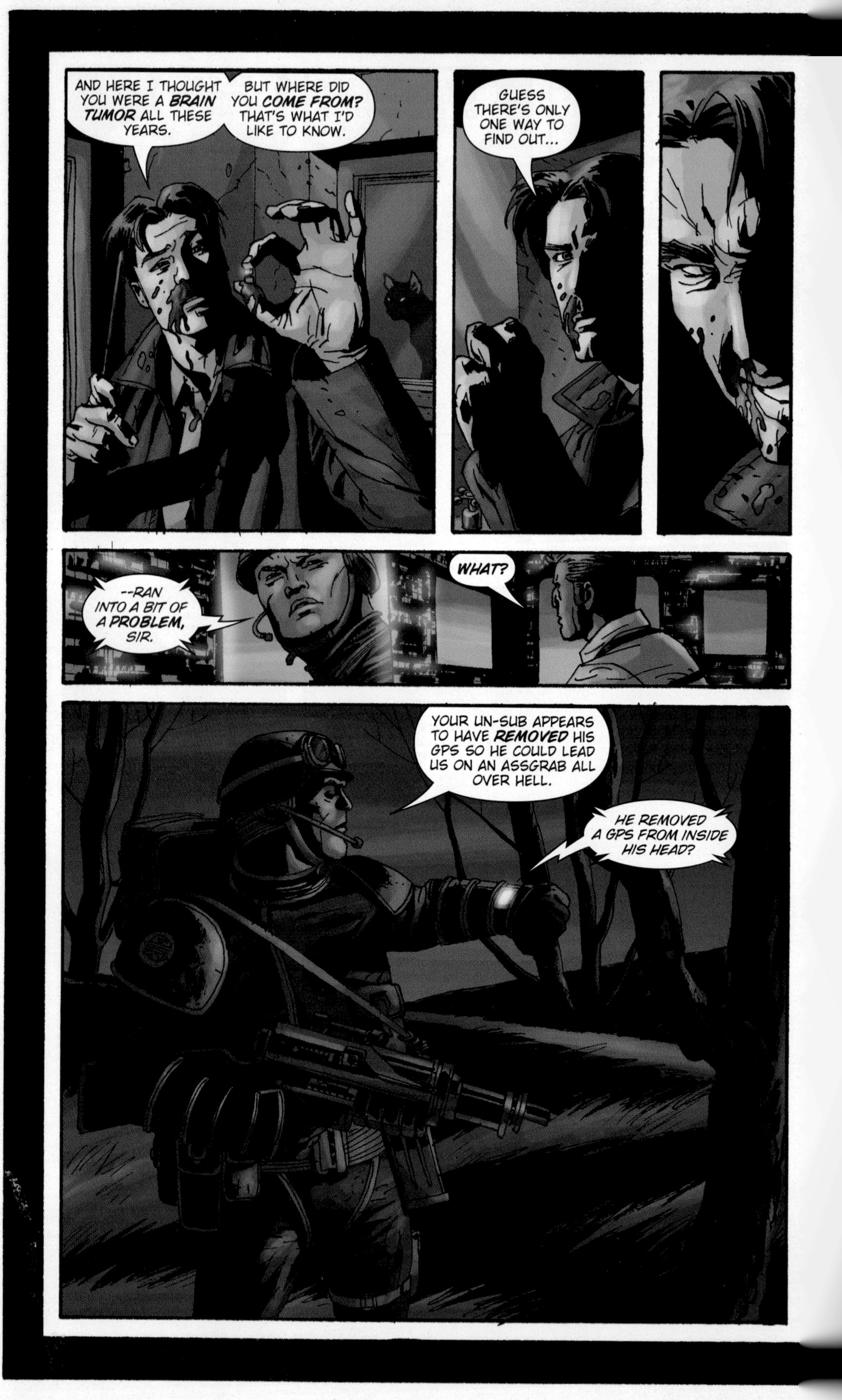
AND HERE I THOUGHT YOU WERE A BRAIN TUMOR ALL THESE YEARS.
BUT WHERE DID YOU COME FROM? THAT'S WHAT I'D LIKE TO KNOW.
GUESS THERE'S ONLY ONE WAY TO FIND OUT...
--RAN INTO A BIT OF A PROBLEM, SIR.
WHAT?
YOUR UN-SUB APPEARS TO HAVE REMOVED HIS GPS SO HE COULD LEAD US ON AN ASSGRAB ALL OVER HELL.
HE REMOVED A GPS FROM INSIDE HIS HEAD?

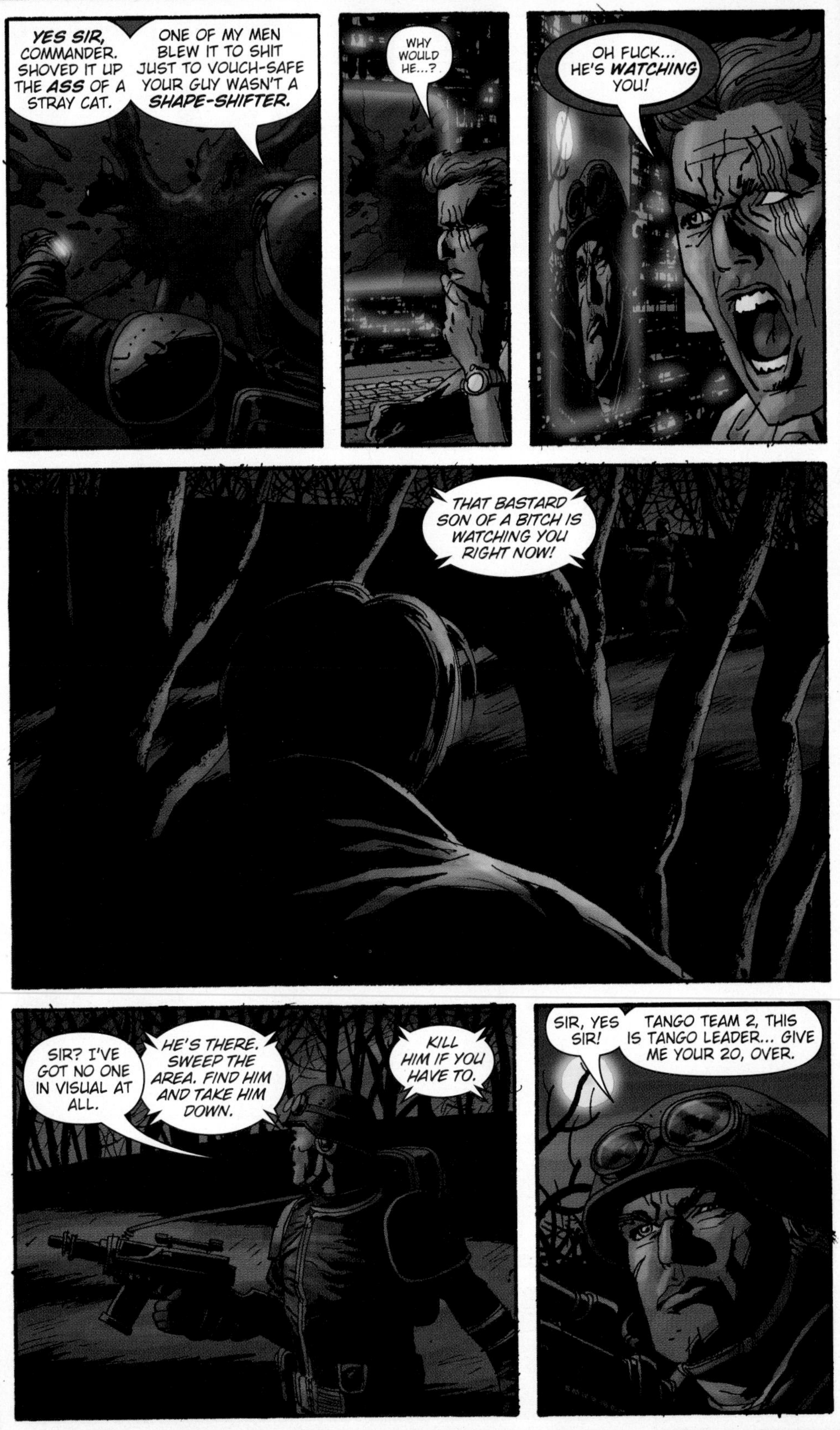
YES SIR, COMMANDER. SHOVED IT UP THE ASS OF A STRAY CAT.
ONE OF MY MEN BLEW IT TO SHIT JUST TO VOUCH-SAFE YOUR GUY WASN'T A SHAPE-SHIFTER.
WHY WOULD HE...?
OH FUCK... HE'S WATCHING YOU!
THAT BASTARD SON OF A BITCH IS WATCHING YOU RIGHT NOW!
SIR? I'VE GOT NO ONE IN VISUAL AT ALL.
HE'S THERE. SWEEP THE AREA. FIND HIM AND TAKE HIM DOWN.
KILL HIM IF YOU HAVE TO.
SIR, YES SIR!
TANGO TEAM 2, THIS IS TANGO LEADER... GIVE ME YOUR 20, OVER.

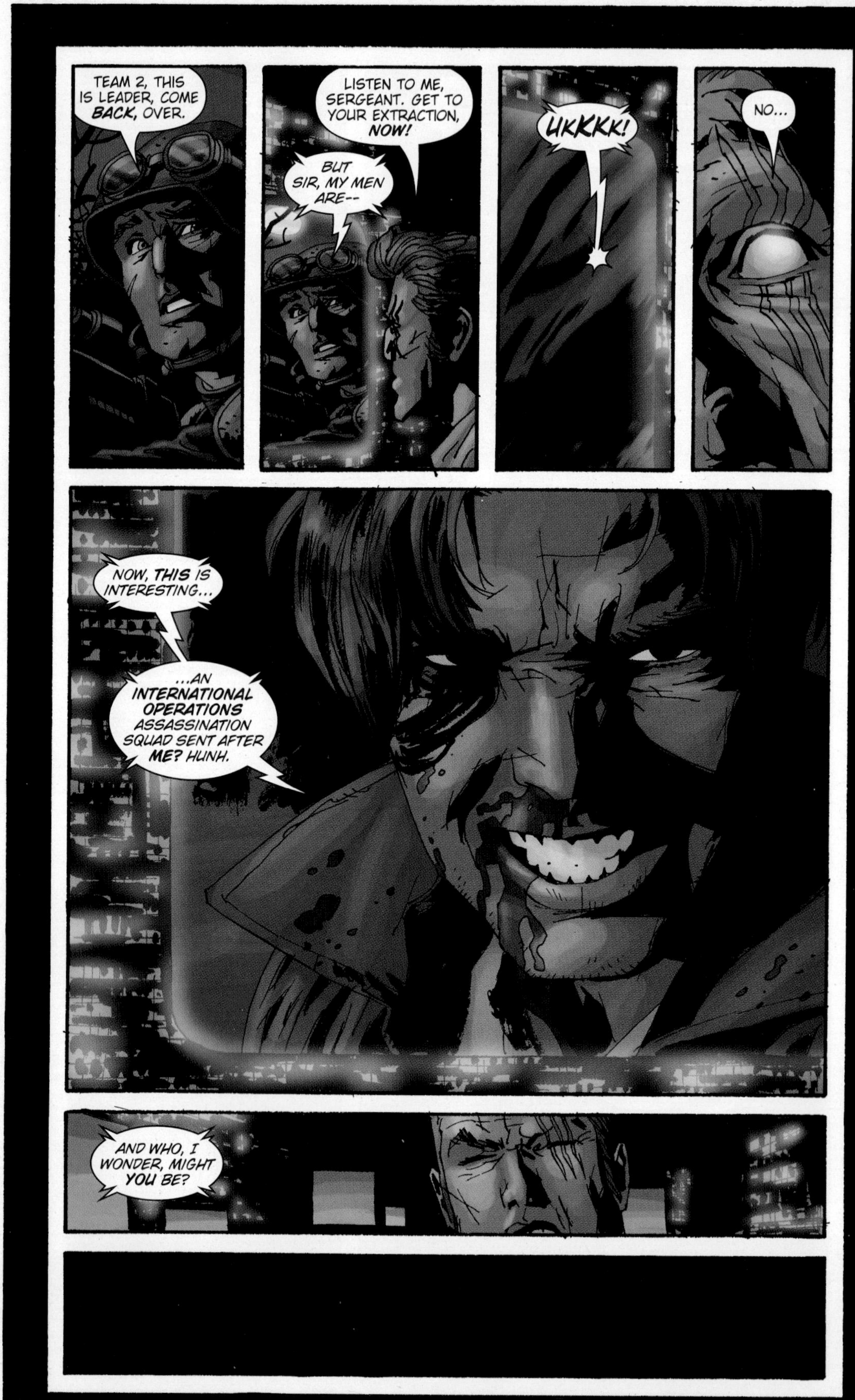
TEAM 2, THIS IS LEADER, COME BACK, OVER.
LISTEN TO ME, SERGEANT. GET TO YOUR EXTRACTION, NOW!
BUT SIR, MY MEN ARE--
UKKKK!
NO...
NOW, THIS IS INTERESTING...
...AN INTERNATIONAL OPERATIONS ASSASSINATION SQUAD SENT AFTER ME? HUNH.
AND WHO, I WONDER, MIGHT YOU BE?

--TARGET IS KNOWN AS T.A.O.--OR, THE *TACTICALLY AUGMENTED* ORGANISM.

UNTIL A WEEK AGO, WHEN HE SENT A *LETTER* TO AN OLD GIRLFRIEND, MOST OF THE WORLD THOUGHT HE WAS DEAD.

MOST OF THE WORLD.

BUT NOT *ME.*

THE *EXTENT* OF HIS POWERS ISN'T KNOWN, BUT MOST ARE *MENTAL.* YOU'LL BE EQUIPPED WITH SONIC BLOCKERS, SO IF HE TALKS YOU'LL HEAR NOTHING BUT STATIC.

BUT EVEN IF HE CAN'T GET INSIDE YOUR HEAD, THE MAN IS *DANGEROUS.*

WE'VE HAD *TWO* CHANCES TO CATCH HIM IN THE PAST FEW YEARS, BUT HE'S SLIPPED THROUGH OUR FINGERS BOTH TIMES.

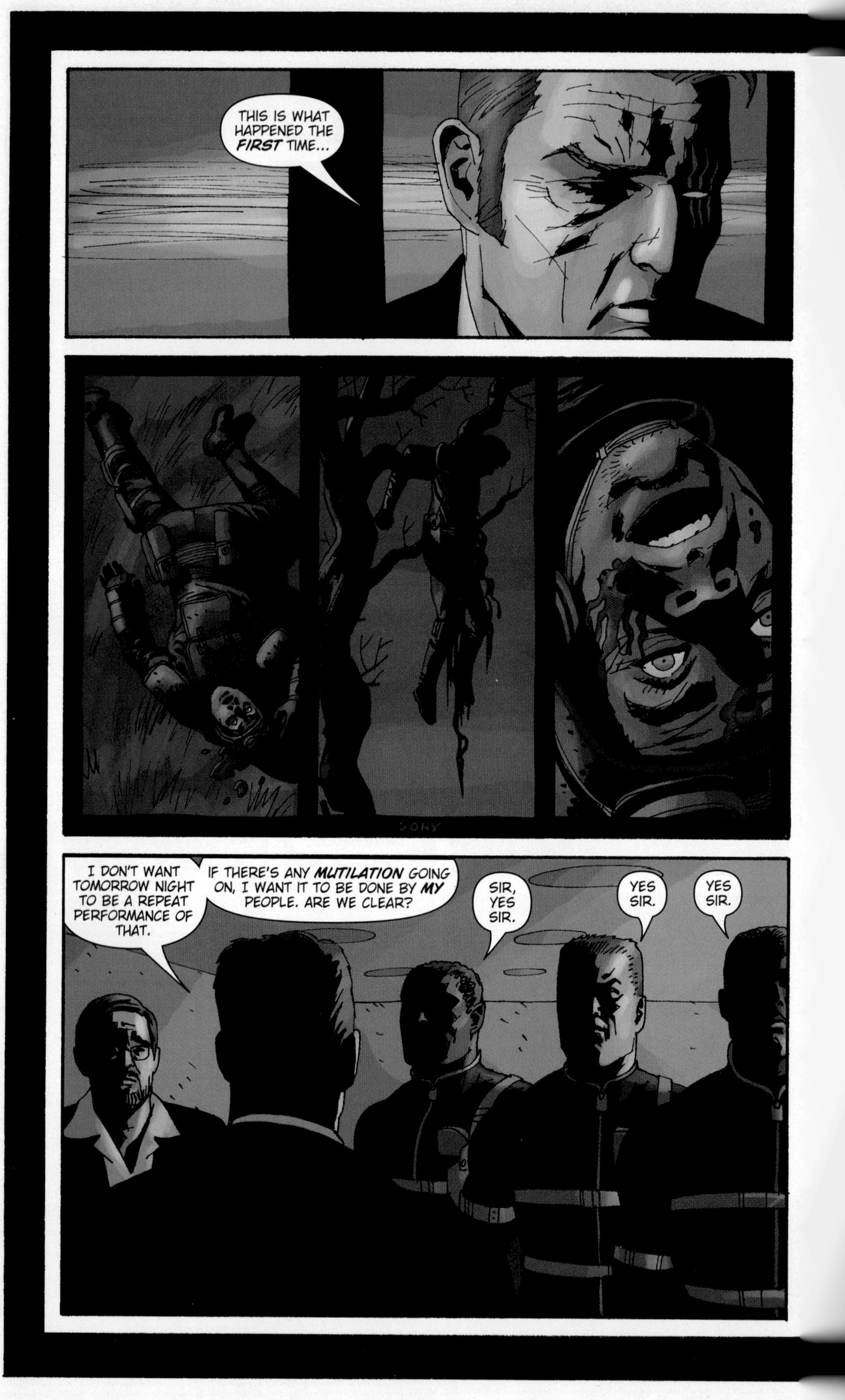
THIS IS WHAT HAPPENED THE *FIRST* TIME...
I DON'T WANT TOMORROW NIGHT TO BE A REPEAT PERFORMANCE OF THAT.
IF THERE'S ANY *MUTILATION* GOING ON, I WANT IT TO BE DONE BY *MY* PEOPLE. ARE WE CLEAR?
SIR, YES SIR.
YES SIR.
YES SIR.

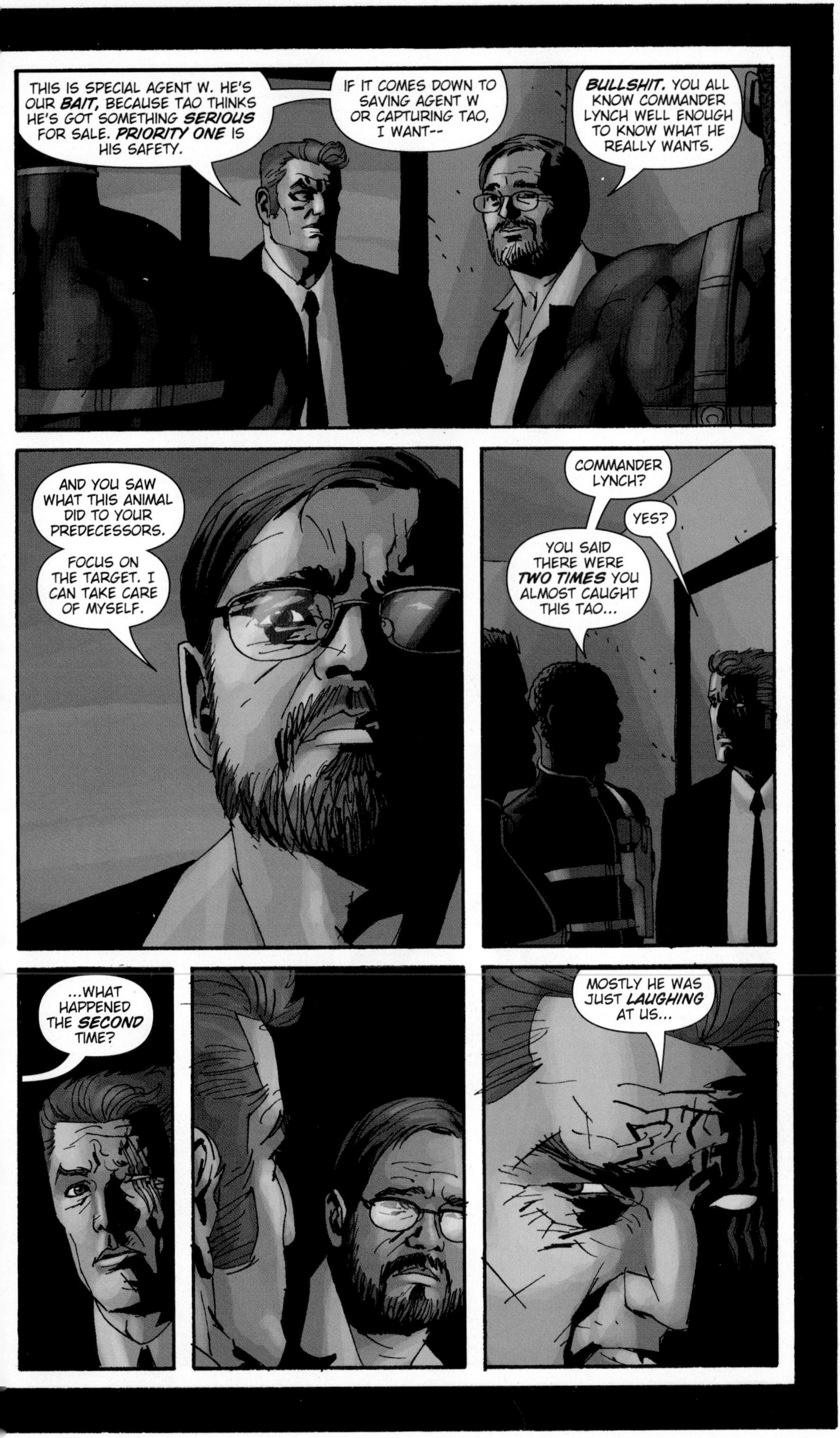
THIS IS SPECIAL AGENT W. HE'S OUR BAIT, BECAUSE TAO THINKS HE'S GOT SOMETHING SERIOUS FOR SALE. PRIORITY ONE IS HIS SAFETY.
IF IT COMES DOWN TO SAVING AGENT W OR CAPTURING TAO, I WANT--
BULLSHIT. YOU ALL KNOW COMMANDER LYNCH WELL ENOUGH TO KNOW WHAT HE REALLY WANTS.
AND YOU SAW WHAT THIS ANIMAL DID TO YOUR PREDECESSORS.
FOCUS ON THE TARGET. I CAN TAKE CARE OF MYSELF.
COMMANDER LYNCH?
YES?
YOU SAID THERE WERE TWO TIMES YOU ALMOST CAUGHT THIS TAO...
...WHAT HAPPENED THE SECOND TIME?
MOSTLY HE WAS JUST LAUGHING AT US...

THE BRITISH LIBRARY, ST. PANCRAS, LONDON. NINE AND A HALF MONTHS EARLIER...
THE BRITISH LIBRARY
MOVE FAST AND MOVE SILENT.
BRAVO TEAM LEADER TO COMMAND--WE'RE IN AND APPROACHING FAST.
ANY ADDITIONAL DATA ON WHAT *LEVEL* OUR TARGET IS ON?
I'M *MOBILE* AT THE MOMENT, SO THE ANSWER IS NO, BUT THE GODDAMN LIBRARY ISN'T EVEN OPEN TO THE *PUBLIC* YET, BRAVO LEADER.
HE *SHOULDN'T* BE HARD TO *FIND.*
WE'RE ON IT, SIR.

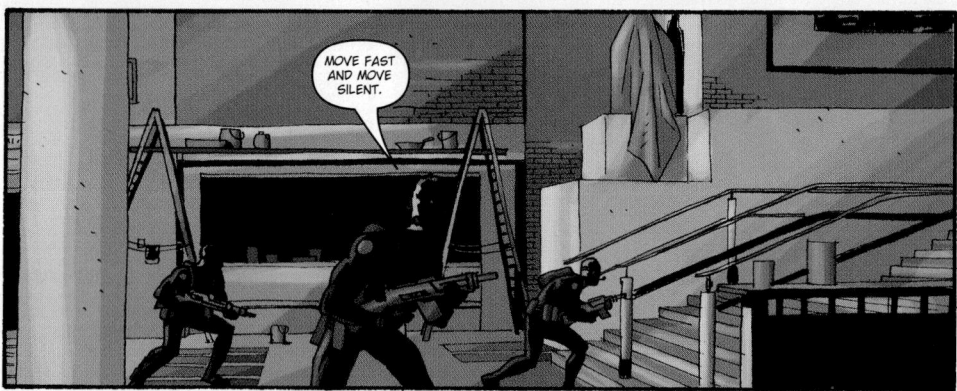

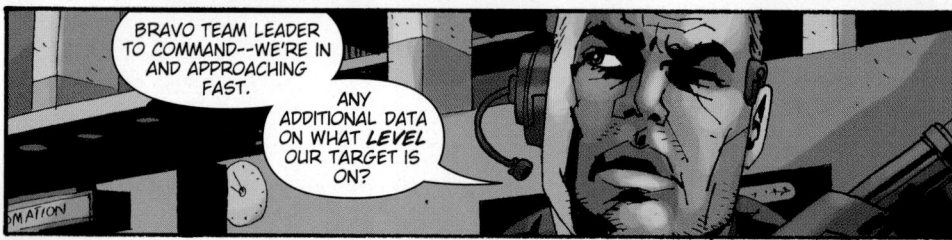

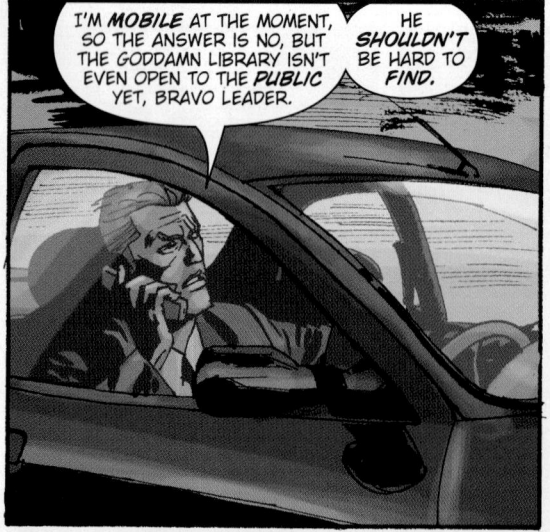

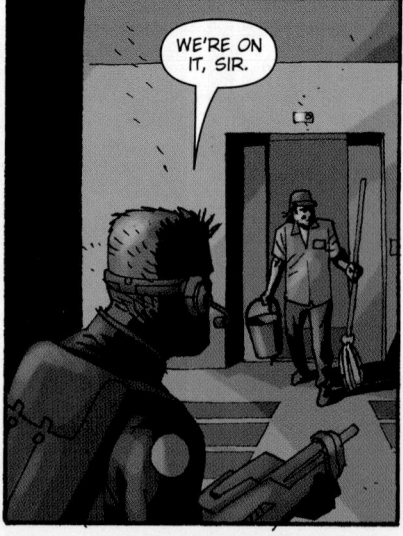

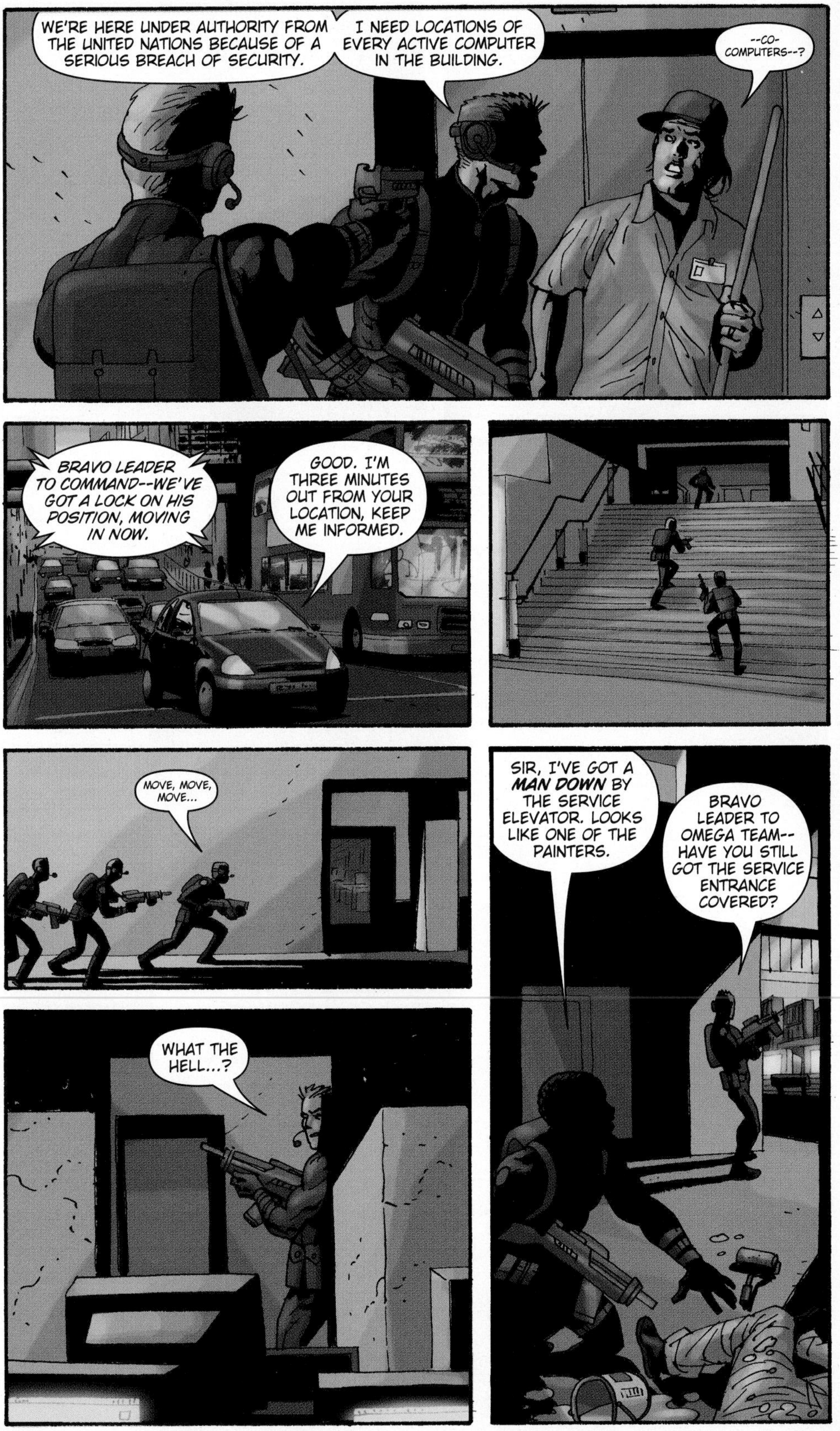
WE'RE HERE UNDER AUTHORITY FROM THE UNITED NATIONS BECAUSE OF A SERIOUS BREACH OF SECURITY.
I NEED LOCATIONS OF EVERY ACTIVE COMPUTER IN THE BUILDING.
--CO-COMPUTERS--?
BRAVO LEADER TO COMMAND--WE'VE GOT A LOCK ON HIS POSITION, MOVING IN NOW.
GOOD. I'M THREE MINUTES OUT FROM YOUR LOCATION, KEEP ME INFORMED.
MOVE, MOVE, MOVE...
SIR, I'VE GOT A MAN DOWN BY THE SERVICE ELEVATOR. LOOKS LIKE ONE OF THE PAINTERS.
BRAVO LEADER TO OMEGA TEAM--HAVE YOU STILL GOT THE SERVICE ENTRANCE COVERED?
WHAT THE HELL...?

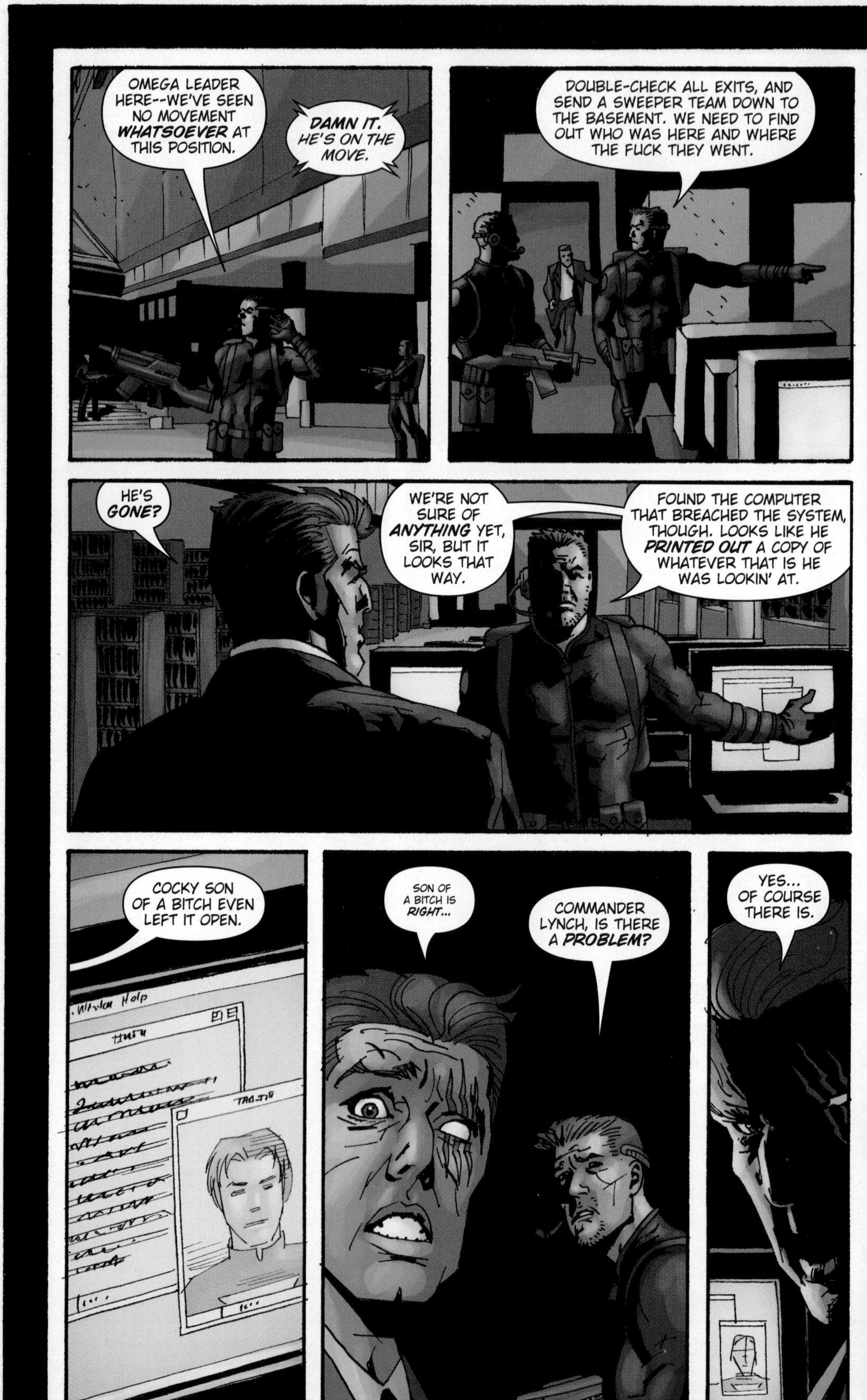

OMEGA LEADER HERE--WE'VE SEEN NO MOVEMENT WHATSOEVER AT THIS POSITION.
DAMN IT. HE'S ON THE MOVE.
DOUBLE-CHECK ALL EXITS, AND SEND A SWEEPER TEAM DOWN TO THE BASEMENT. WE NEED TO FIND OUT WHO WAS HERE AND WHERE THE FUCK THEY WENT.
HE'S GONE?
WE'RE NOT SURE OF ANYTHING YET, SIR, BUT IT LOOKS THAT WAY.
FOUND THE COMPUTER THAT BREACHED THE SYSTEM, THOUGH. LOOKS LIKE HE PRINTED OUT A COPY OF WHATEVER THAT IS HE WAS LOOKIN' AT.
COCKY SON OF A BITCH EVEN LEFT IT OPEN.
SON OF A BITCH IS RIGHT...
COMMANDER LYNCH, IS THERE A PROBLEM?
YES... OF COURSE THERE IS.

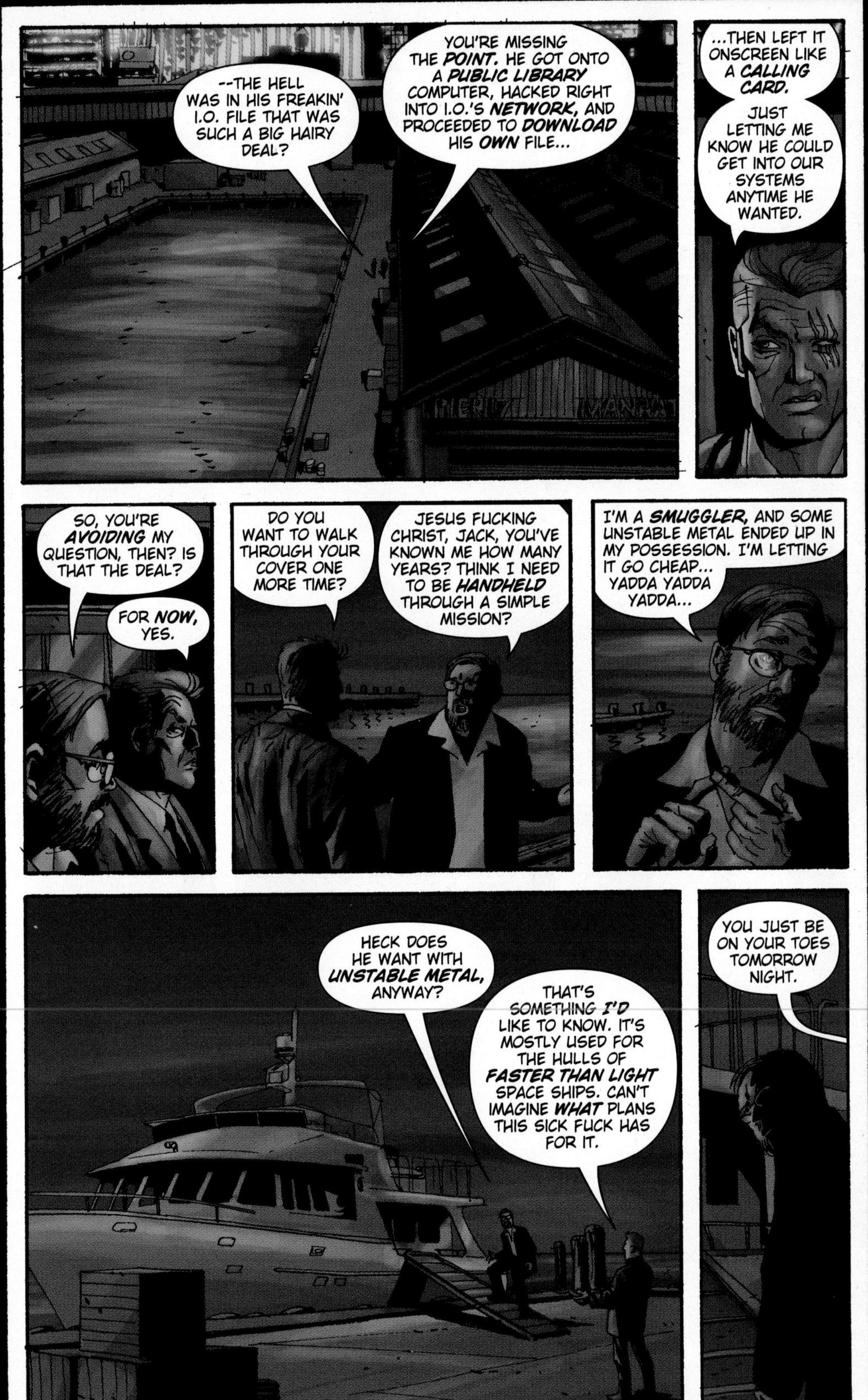
--THE HELL WAS IN HIS FREAKIN' I.O. FILE THAT WAS SUCH A BIG HAIRY DEAL?
YOU'RE MISSING THE POINT. HE GOT ONTO A PUBLIC LIBRARY COMPUTER, HACKED RIGHT INTO I.O.'S NETWORK, AND PROCEEDED TO DOWNLOAD HIS OWN FILE...
...THEN LEFT IT ONSCREEN LIKE A CALLING CARD.
JUST LETTING ME KNOW HE COULD GET INTO OUR SYSTEMS ANYTIME HE WANTED.
SO, YOU'RE AVOIDING MY QUESTION, THEN? IS THAT THE DEAL?
FOR NOW, YES.
DO YOU WANT TO WALK THROUGH YOUR COVER ONE MORE TIME?
JESUS FUCKING CHRIST, JACK, YOU'VE KNOWN ME HOW MANY YEARS? THINK I NEED TO BE HANDHELD THROUGH A SIMPLE MISSION?
I'M A SMUGGLER, AND SOME UNSTABLE METAL ENDED UP IN MY POSSESSION. I'M LETTING IT GO CHEAP... YADDA YADDA YADDA...
HECK DOES HE WANT WITH UNSTABLE METAL, ANYWAY?
THAT'S SOMETHING I'D LIKE TO KNOW. IT'S MOSTLY USED FOR THE HULLS OF FASTER THAN LIGHT SPACE SHIPS. CAN'T IMAGINE WHAT PLANS THIS SICK FUCK HAS FOR IT.
YOU JUST BE ON YOUR TOES TOMORROW NIGHT.

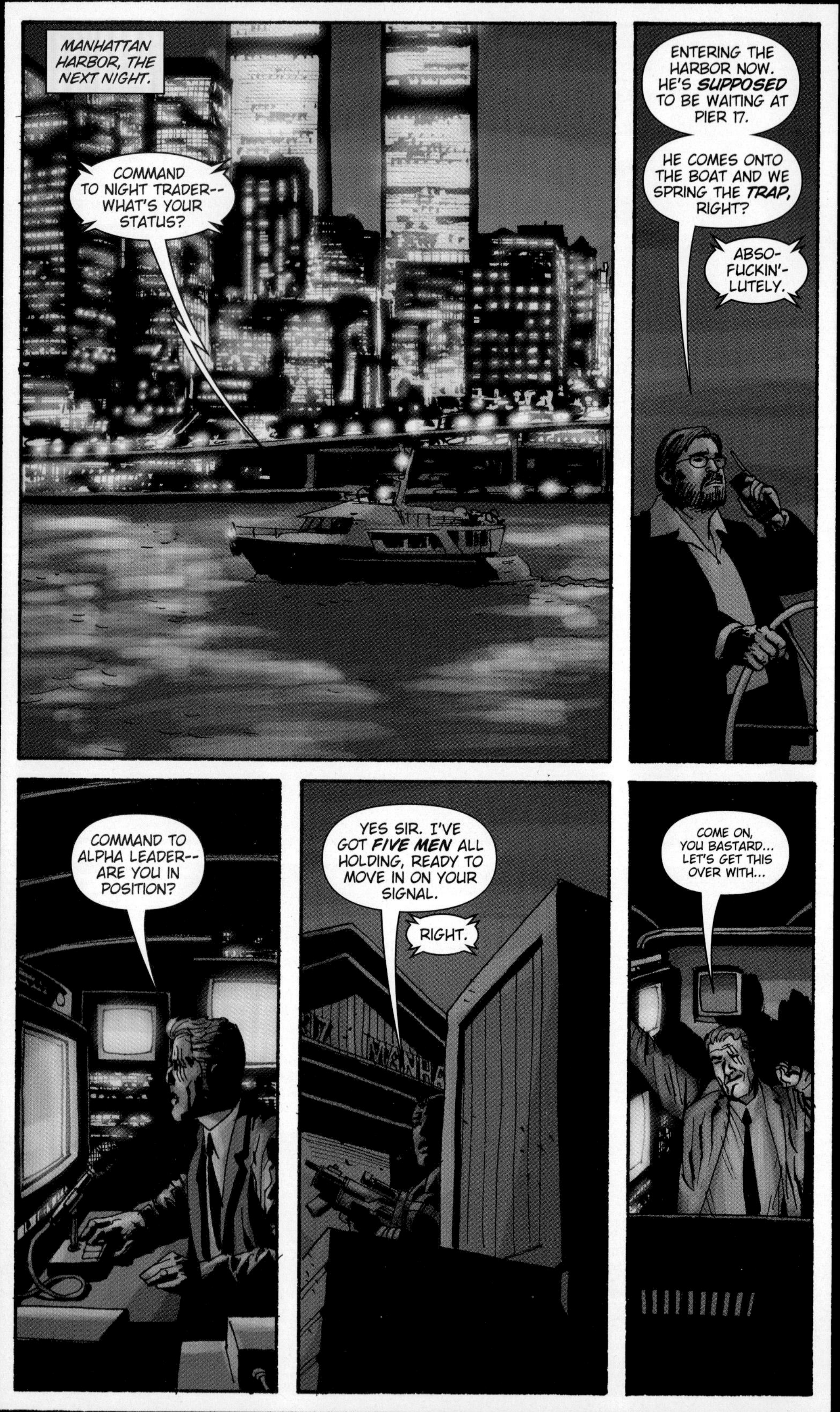
MANHATTAN HARBOR, THE NEXT NIGHT.
COMMAND TO NIGHT TRADER-- WHAT'S YOUR STATUS?
ENTERING THE HARBOR NOW. HE'S **SUPPOSED** TO BE WAITING AT PIER 17.
HE COMES ONTO THE BOAT AND WE SPRING THE **TRAP,** RIGHT?
ABSO-FUCKIN'-LUTELY.
COMMAND TO ALPHA LEADER-- ARE YOU IN POSITION?
YES SIR. I'VE GOT **FIVE MEN** ALL HOLDING, READY TO MOVE IN ON YOUR SIGNAL.
RIGHT.
COME ON, YOU BASTARD... LET'S GET THIS OVER WITH...

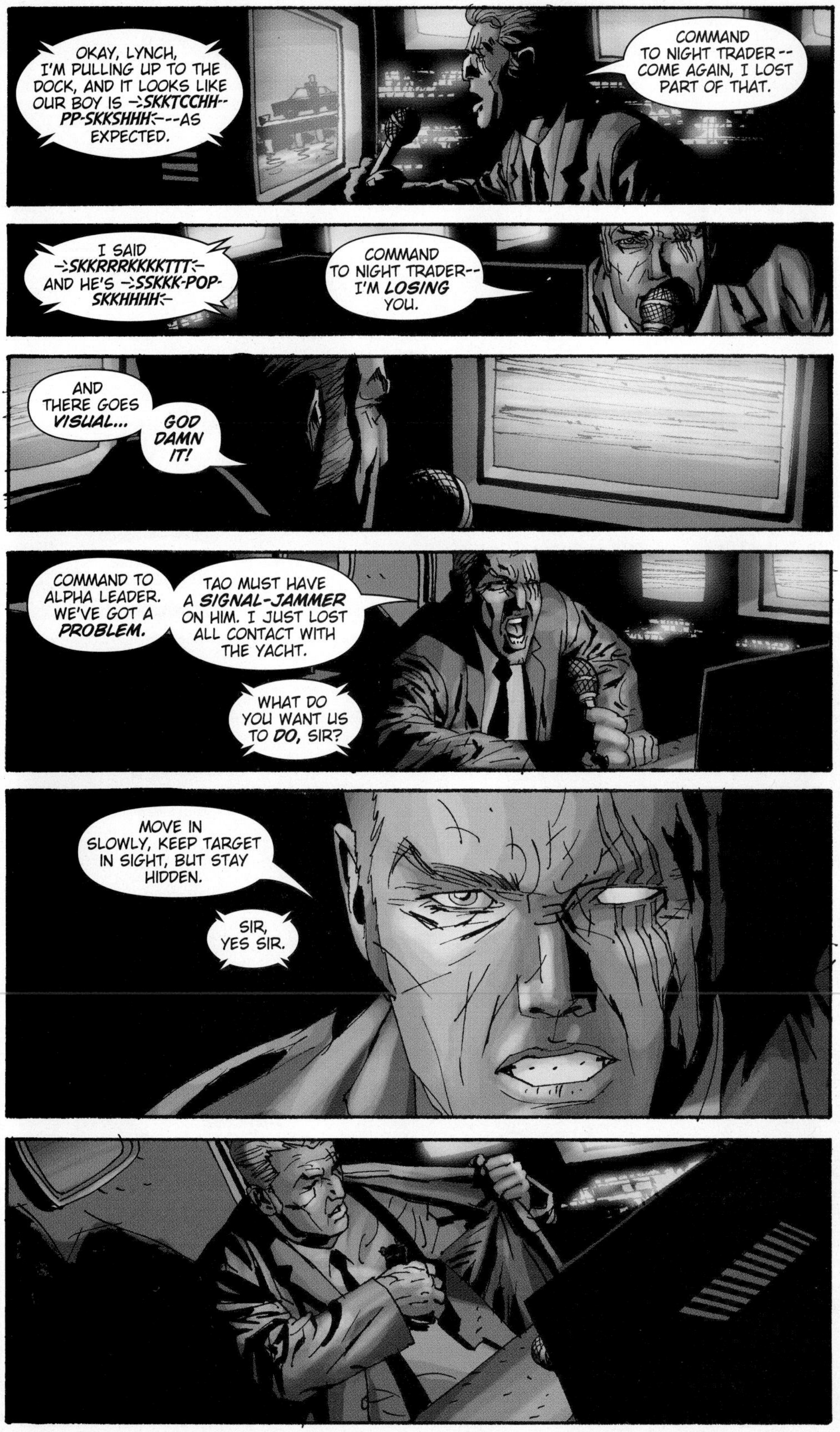
OKAY, LYNCH, I'M PULLING UP TO THE DOCK, AND IT LOOKS LIKE OUR BOY IS -SKKTCCHH-PP-SKKSHHH---AS EXPECTED.
COMMAND TO NIGHT TRADER-- COME AGAIN, I LOST PART OF THAT.
I SAID -SKKRRRKKKKTTT- AND HE'S -SSKKK-POP-SKKHHHH-
COMMAND TO NIGHT TRADER-- I'M LOSING YOU.
AND THERE GOES VISUAL...
GOD DAMN IT!
COMMAND TO ALPHA LEADER. WE'VE GOT A PROBLEM.
TAO MUST HAVE A SIGNAL-JAMMER ON HIM. I JUST LOST ALL CONTACT WITH THE YACHT.
WHAT DO YOU WANT US TO DO, SIR?
MOVE IN SLOWLY, KEEP TARGET IN SIGHT, BUT STAY HIDDEN.
SIR, YES SIR.

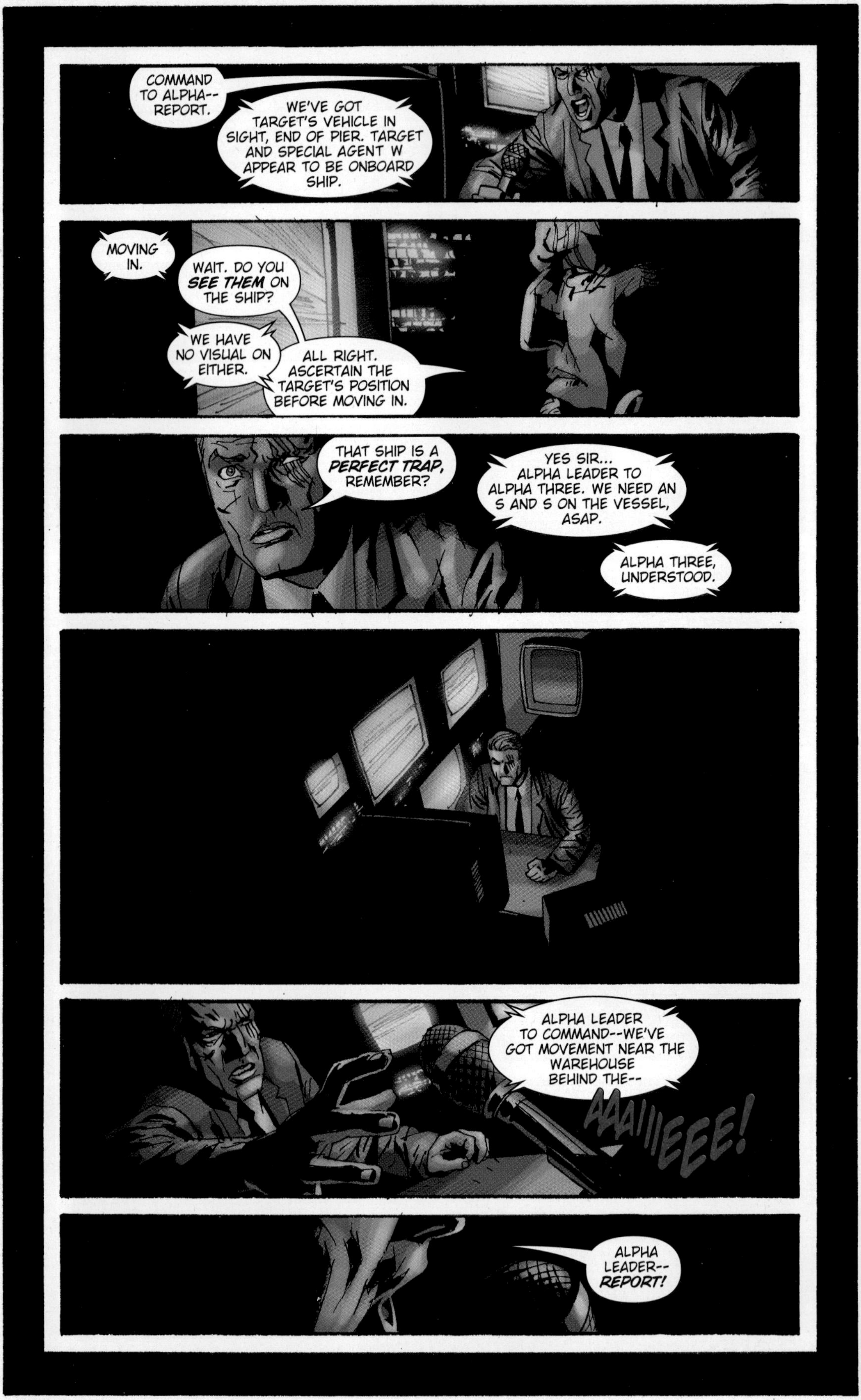
COMMAND TO ALPHA-- REPORT.
WE'VE GOT TARGET'S VEHICLE IN SIGHT, END OF PIER. TARGET AND SPECIAL AGENT W APPEAR TO BE ONBOARD SHIP.
MOVING IN.
WAIT. DO YOU **SEE THEM** ON THE SHIP?
WE HAVE NO VISUAL ON EITHER.
ALL RIGHT. ASCERTAIN THE TARGET'S POSITION BEFORE MOVING IN.
THAT SHIP IS A **PERFECT TRAP,** REMEMBER?
YES SIR... ALPHA LEADER TO ALPHA THREE. WE NEED AN S AND S ON THE VESSEL, ASAP.
ALPHA THREE, UNDERSTOOD.
ALPHA LEADER TO COMMAND--WE'VE GOT MOVEMENT NEAR THE WAREHOUSE BEHIND THE--
AAAIIIIEEE!
ALPHA LEADER-- **REPORT!**

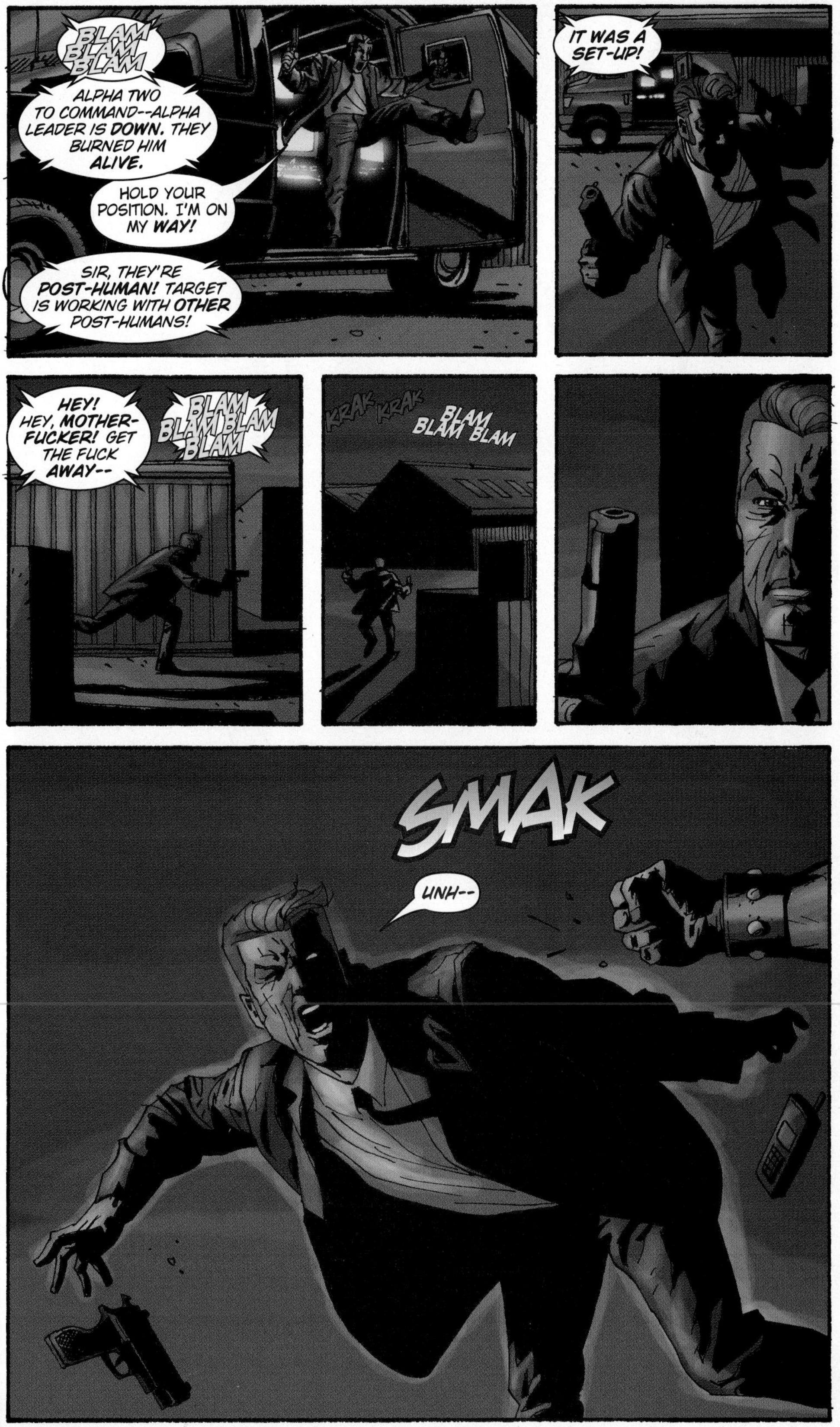

BLAM BLAM BLAM
ALPHA TWO TO COMMAND--ALPHA LEADER IS DOWN. THEY BURNED HIM ALIVE.
HOLD YOUR POSITION. I'M ON MY WAY!
SIR, THEY'RE POST-HUMAN! TARGET IS WORKING WITH OTHER POST-HUMANS!
IT WAS A SET-UP!
HEY! HEY, MOTHER-FUCKER! GET THE FUCK AWAY--
BLAM BLAM BLAM BLAM
KRAK KRAK
BLAM BLAM BLAM
SMAK
UNH--

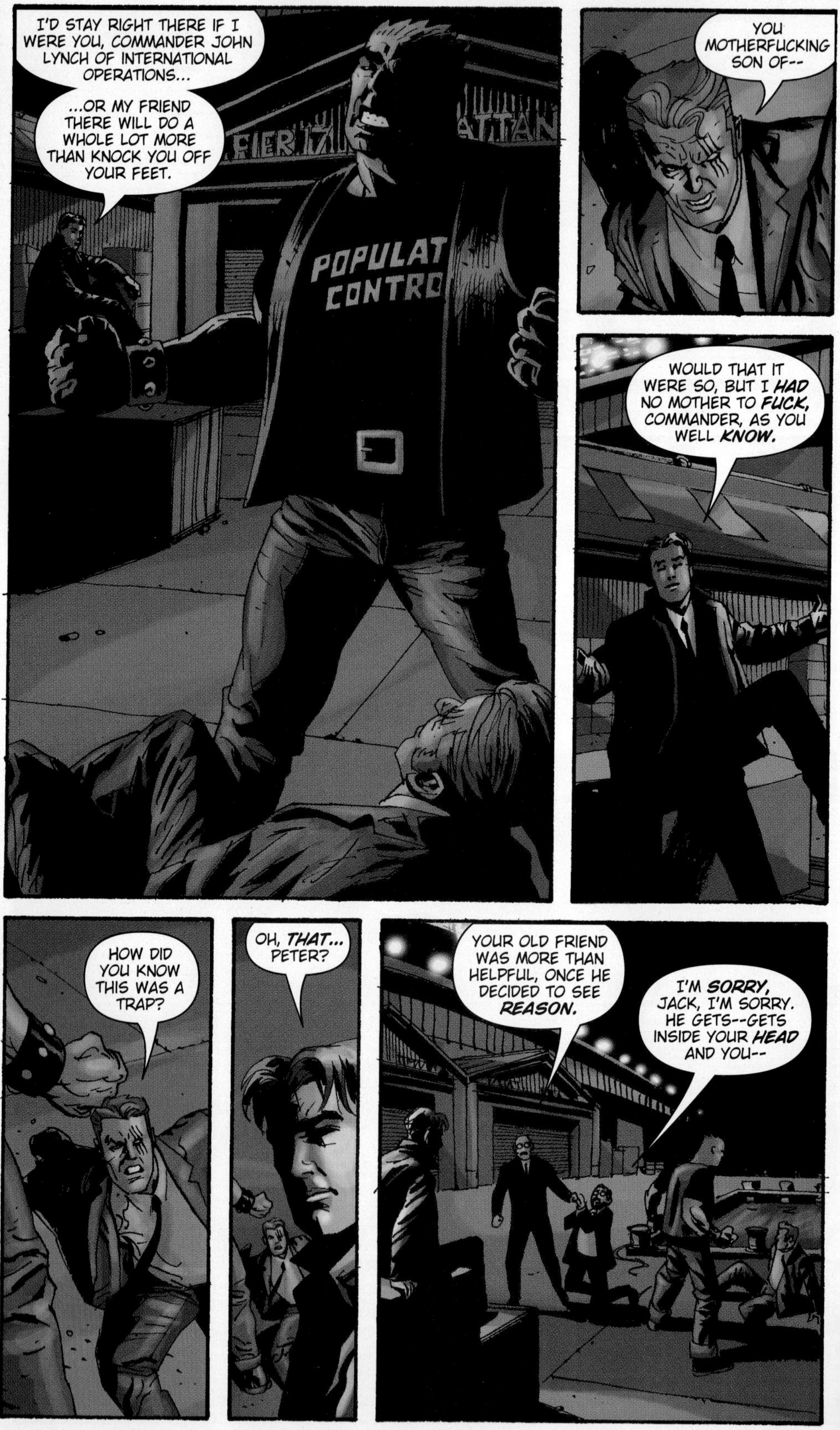
I'D STAY RIGHT THERE IF I WERE YOU, COMMANDER JOHN LYNCH OF INTERNATIONAL OPERATIONS...
...OR MY FRIEND THERE WILL DO A WHOLE LOT MORE THAN KNOCK YOU OFF YOUR FEET.
PIER 17
POPULAT CONTRO
YOU MOTHERFUCKING SON OF--
WOULD THAT IT WERE SO, BUT I HAD NO MOTHER TO FUCK, COMMANDER, AS YOU WELL KNOW.
HOW DID YOU KNOW THIS WAS A TRAP?
OH, THAT... PETER?
YOUR OLD FRIEND WAS MORE THAN HELPFUL, ONCE HE DECIDED TO SEE REASON.
I'M SORRY, JACK, I'M SORRY. HE GETS--GETS INSIDE YOUR HEAD AND YOU--

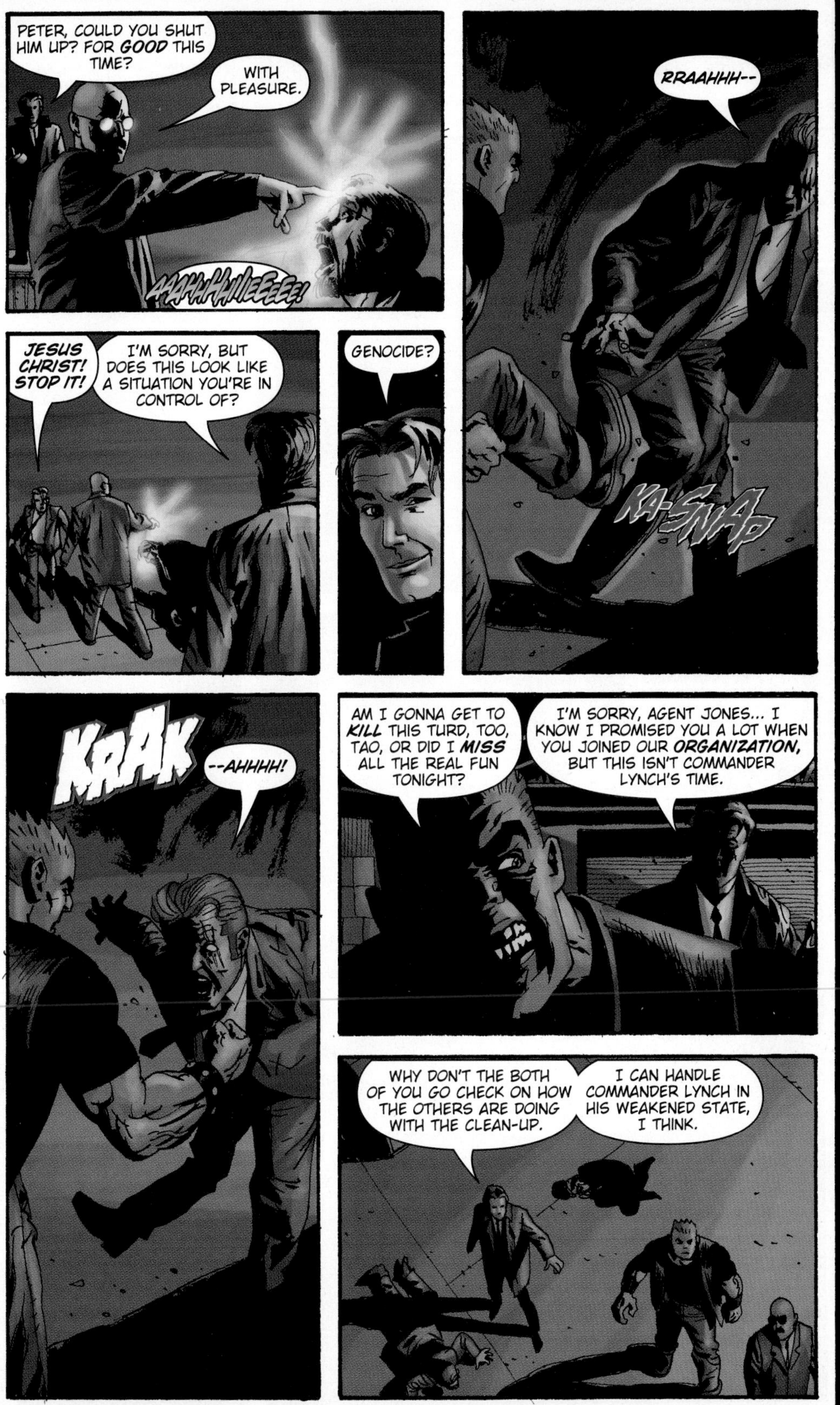
PETER, COULD YOU SHUT HIM UP? FOR GOOD THIS TIME?
WITH PLEASURE.
AAAHHHHIIEEEEE!
RRAAHHH--
KA-SNAP
JESUS CHRIST! STOP IT!
I'M SORRY, BUT DOES THIS LOOK LIKE A SITUATION YOU'RE IN CONTROL OF?
GENOCIDE?
KRAK
--AHHHH!
AM I GONNA GET TO KILL THIS TURD, TOO, TAO, OR DID I MISS ALL THE REAL FUN TONIGHT?
I'M SORRY, AGENT JONES... I KNOW I PROMISED YOU A LOT WHEN YOU JOINED OUR ORGANIZATION, BUT THIS ISN'T COMMANDER LYNCH'S TIME.
WHY DON'T THE BOTH OF YOU GO CHECK ON HOW THE OTHERS ARE DOING WITH THE CLEAN-UP.
I CAN HANDLE COMMANDER LYNCH IN HIS WEAKENED STATE, I THINK.

I WOULDN'T BE... SO SURE... ABOUT THAT...

OH, I KNOW YOU'RE TOUGH, OLD MAN... BUT I'VE SEEN WHAT GENOCIDE'S FISTS DO TO PEOPLE. HE'S BULLETPROOF, DID YOU KNOW?

LIKE GETTING HIT BY A SMALL BOULDER.

...WHAT THE FUCK DO... YOU WANT?

I SHOULD THINK THAT WOULD BE OBVIOUS TO YOU.

...SPELL IT OUT FOR ME...ANYWAY.

WELL, OBVIOUSLY, I'VE BEEN WANTING TO MEET YOU EVER SINCE I FOUND OUT THE TRUTH.

YOU SEE, I WAS QUITE CONFUSED ABOUT WHY I.O. WOULD HAVE ANY INTEREST IN ME, AND THOUGH I DIDN'T PUT TOO MUCH THOUGHT INTO IT AT FIRST...

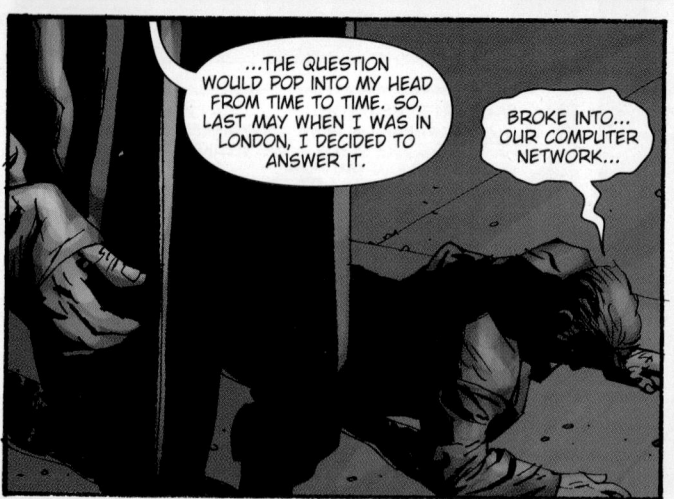

...THE QUESTION WOULD POP INTO MY HEAD FROM TIME TO TIME. SO, LAST MAY WHEN I WAS IN LONDON, I DECIDED TO ANSWER IT.

BROKE INTO... OUR COMPUTER NETWORK...

YES, I DID, AND IMAGINE MY TOTAL LACK OF SURPRISE TO FIND OUT THAT OPTIGEN, THE LAB THAT GREW ME IN A TEST TUBE, WAS SECRETLY DOING WORK FOR I.O.

WHICH EXPLAINS THE TRACKING DEVICE PLANTED IN MY SINUSES.

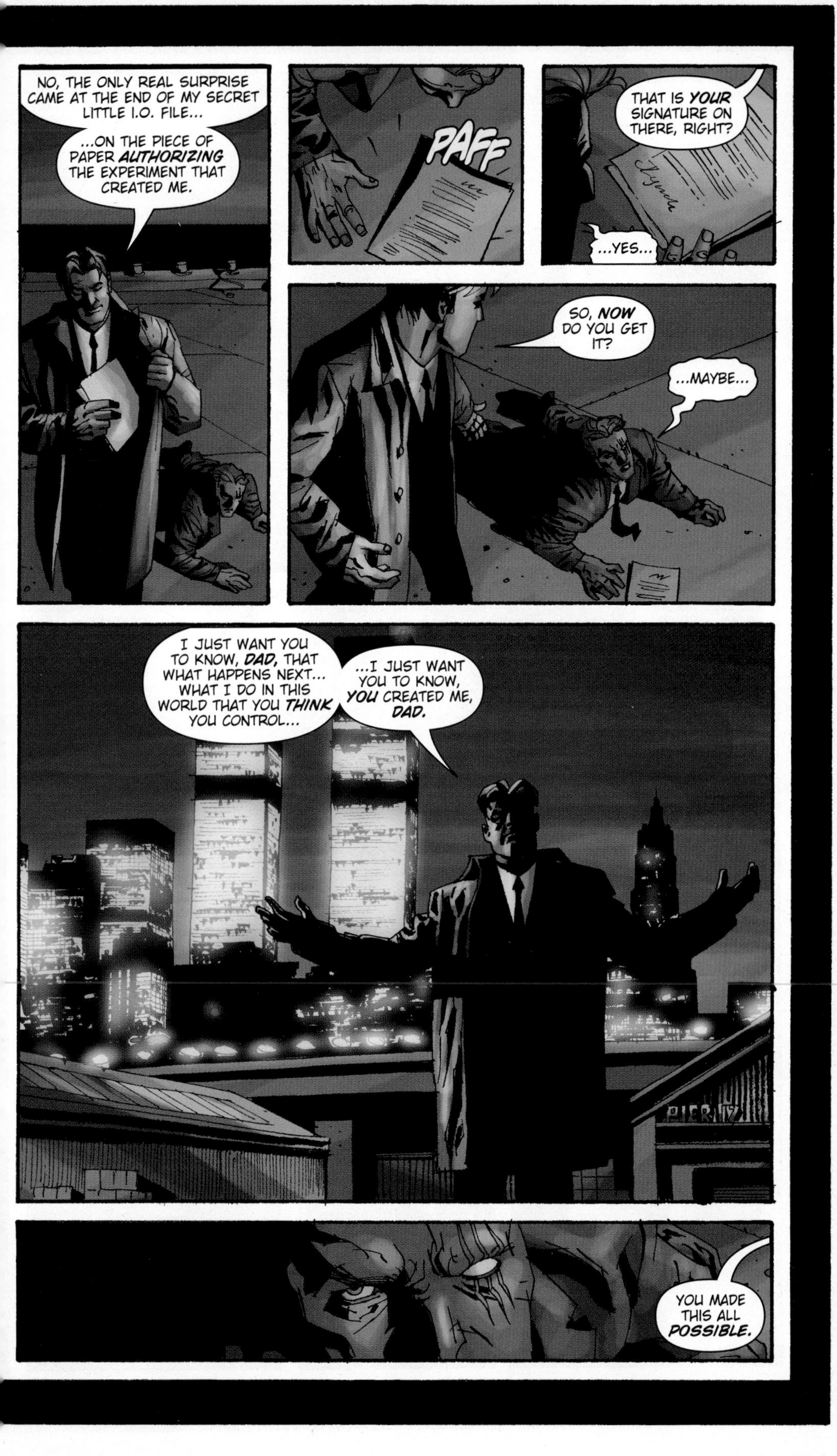
NO, THE ONLY REAL SURPRISE CAME AT THE END OF MY SECRET LITTLE I.O. FILE...
...ON THE PIECE OF PAPER AUTHORIZING THE EXPERIMENT THAT CREATED ME.
PAFF
THAT IS YOUR SIGNATURE ON THERE, RIGHT?
...YES...
SO, NOW DO YOU GET IT?
...MAYBE...
I JUST WANT YOU TO KNOW, DAD, THAT WHAT HAPPENS NEXT... WHAT I DO IN THIS WORLD THAT YOU THINK YOU CONTROL...
...I JUST WANT YOU TO KNOW, YOU CREATED ME, DAD.
PIER 17
YOU MADE THIS ALL POSSIBLE.

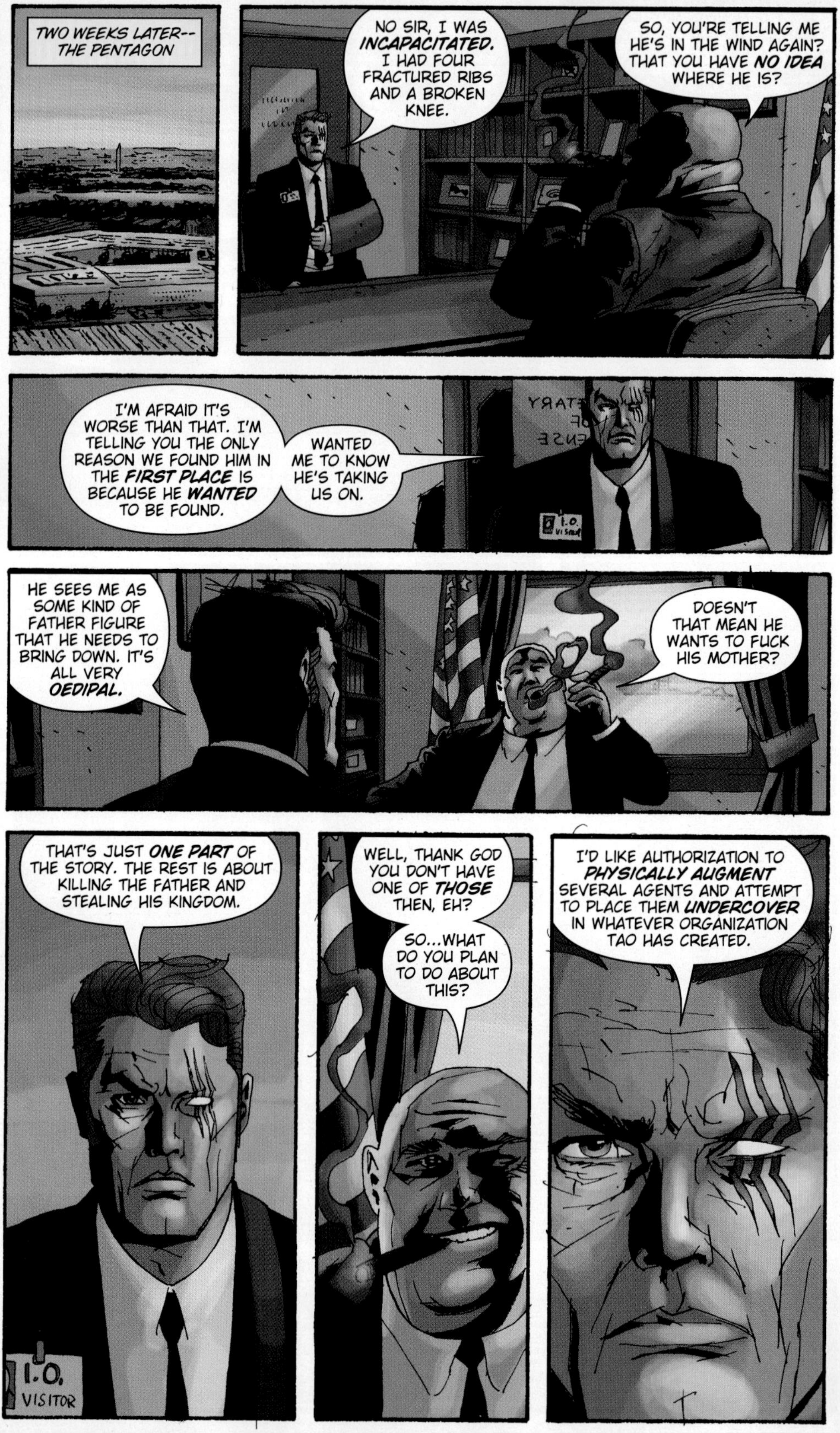

TWO WEEKS LATER-- THE PENTAGON
NO SIR, I WAS INCAPACITATED. I HAD FOUR FRACTURED RIBS AND A BROKEN KNEE.
SO, YOU'RE TELLING ME HE'S IN THE WIND AGAIN? THAT YOU HAVE NO IDEA WHERE HE IS?
I'M AFRAID IT'S WORSE THAN THAT. I'M TELLING YOU THE ONLY REASON WE FOUND HIM IN THE FIRST PLACE IS BECAUSE HE WANTED TO BE FOUND.
WANTED ME TO KNOW HE'S TAKING US ON.
HE SEES ME AS SOME KIND OF FATHER FIGURE THAT HE NEEDS TO BRING DOWN. IT'S ALL VERY OEDIPAL.
DOESN'T THAT MEAN HE WANTS TO FUCK HIS MOTHER?
THAT'S JUST ONE PART OF THE STORY. THE REST IS ABOUT KILLING THE FATHER AND STEALING HIS KINGDOM.
I.O. VISITOR
WELL, THANK GOD YOU DON'T HAVE ONE OF THOSE THEN, EH?
SO...WHAT DO YOU PLAN TO DO ABOUT THIS?
I'D LIKE AUTHORIZATION TO PHYSICALLY AUGMENT SEVERAL AGENTS AND ATTEMPT TO PLACE THEM UNDERCOVER IN WHATEVER ORGANIZATION TAO HAS CREATED.

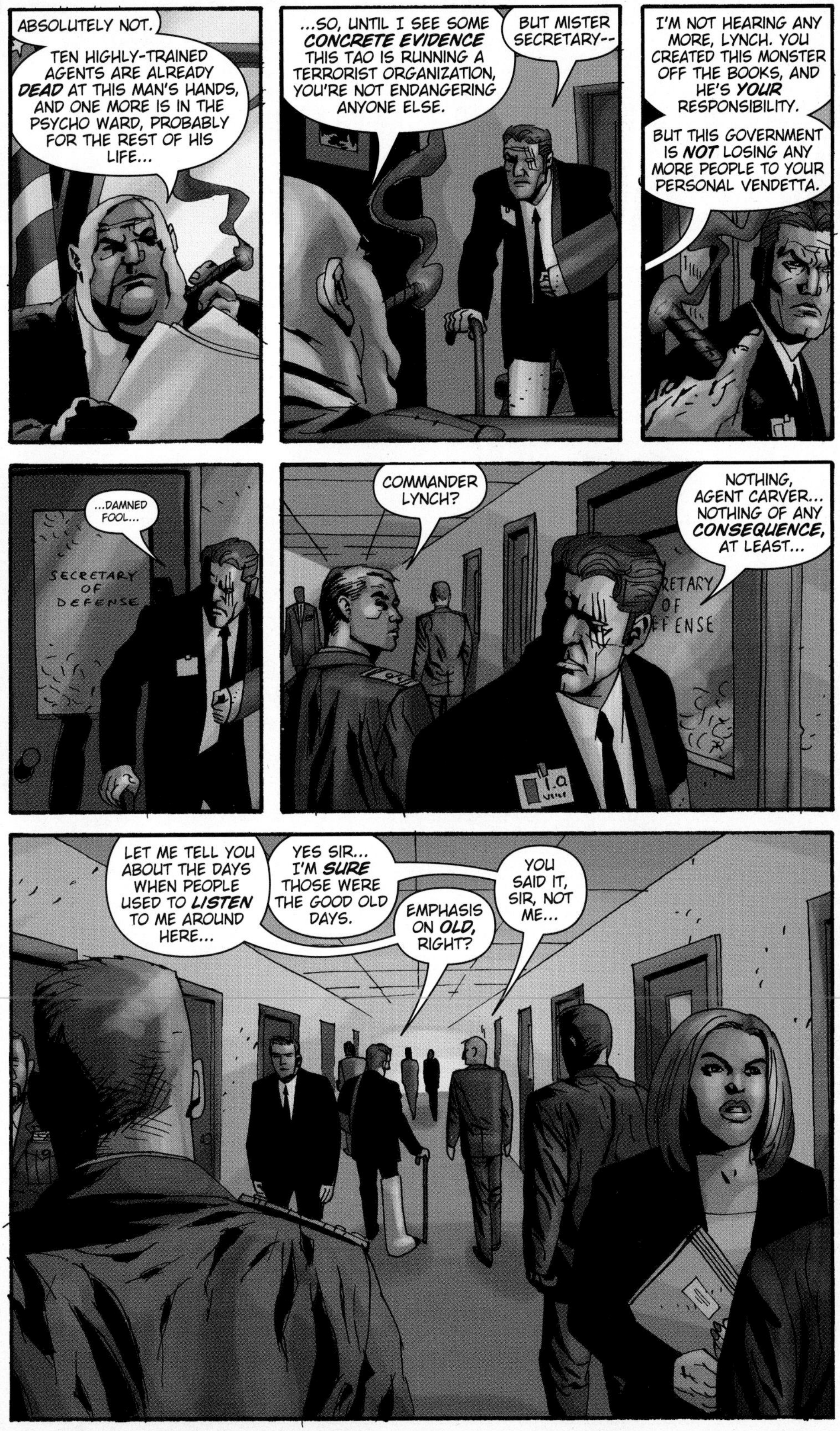

ABSOLUTELY NOT.
TEN HIGHLY-TRAINED AGENTS ARE ALREADY DEAD AT THIS MAN'S HANDS, AND ONE MORE IS IN THE PSYCHO WARD, PROBABLY FOR THE REST OF HIS LIFE...
...SO, UNTIL I SEE SOME CONCRETE EVIDENCE THIS TAO IS RUNNING A TERRORIST ORGANIZATION, YOU'RE NOT ENDANGERING ANYONE ELSE.
BUT MISTER SECRETARY--
I'M NOT HEARING ANY MORE, LYNCH. YOU CREATED THIS MONSTER OFF THE BOOKS, AND HE'S YOUR RESPONSIBILITY.
BUT THIS GOVERNMENT IS NOT LOSING ANY MORE PEOPLE TO YOUR PERSONAL VENDETTA.
...DAMNED FOOL...
SECRETARY OF DEFENSE
COMMANDER LYNCH?
NOTHING, AGENT CARVER... NOTHING OF ANY CONSEQUENCE, AT LEAST...
LET ME TELL YOU ABOUT THE DAYS WHEN PEOPLE USED TO LISTEN TO ME AROUND HERE...
YES SIR... I'M SURE THOSE WERE THE GOOD OLD DAYS.
EMPHASIS ON OLD, RIGHT?
YOU SAID IT, SIR, NOT ME...

chapter eighteen

four-sided triangl

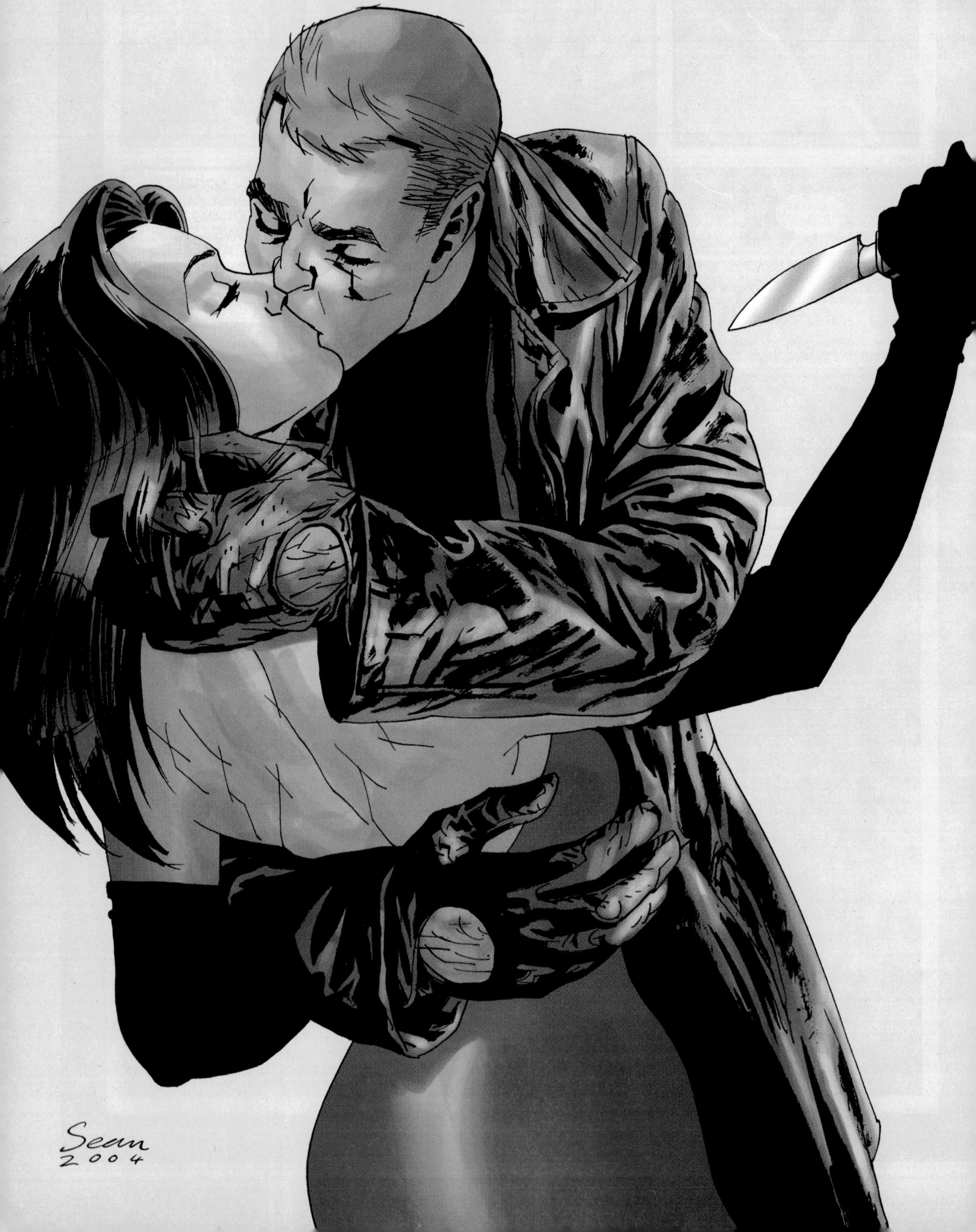
Sean
2004

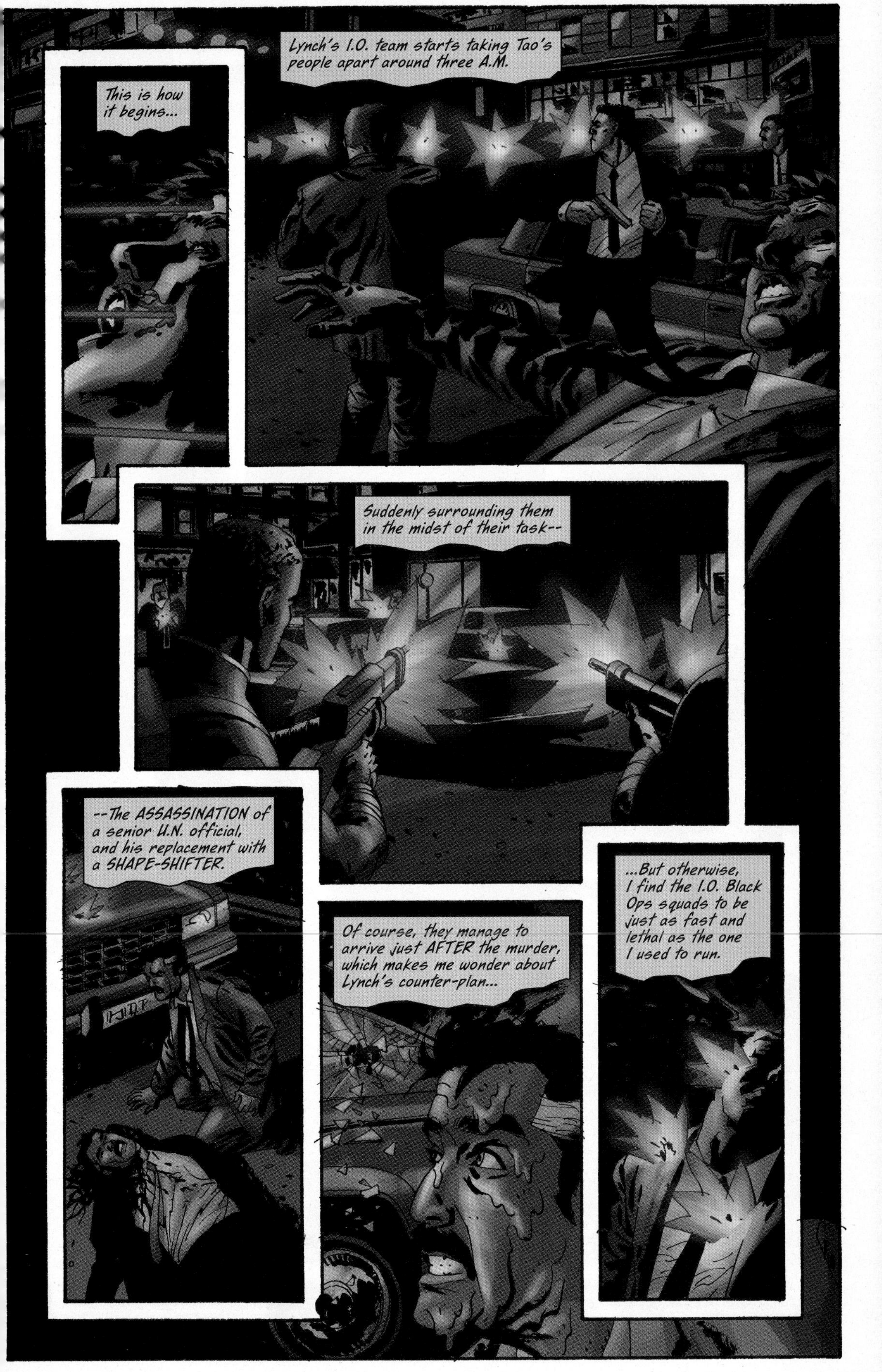
This is how it begins...
Lynch's I.O. team starts taking Tao's people apart around three A.M.
Suddenly surrounding them in the midst of their task--
--The ASSASSINATION of a senior U.N. official, and his replacement with a SHAPE-SHIFTER.
Of course, they manage to arrive just AFTER the murder, which makes me wonder about Lynch's counter-plan...
...But otherwise, I find the I.O. Black Ops squads to be just as fast and lethal as the one I used to run.

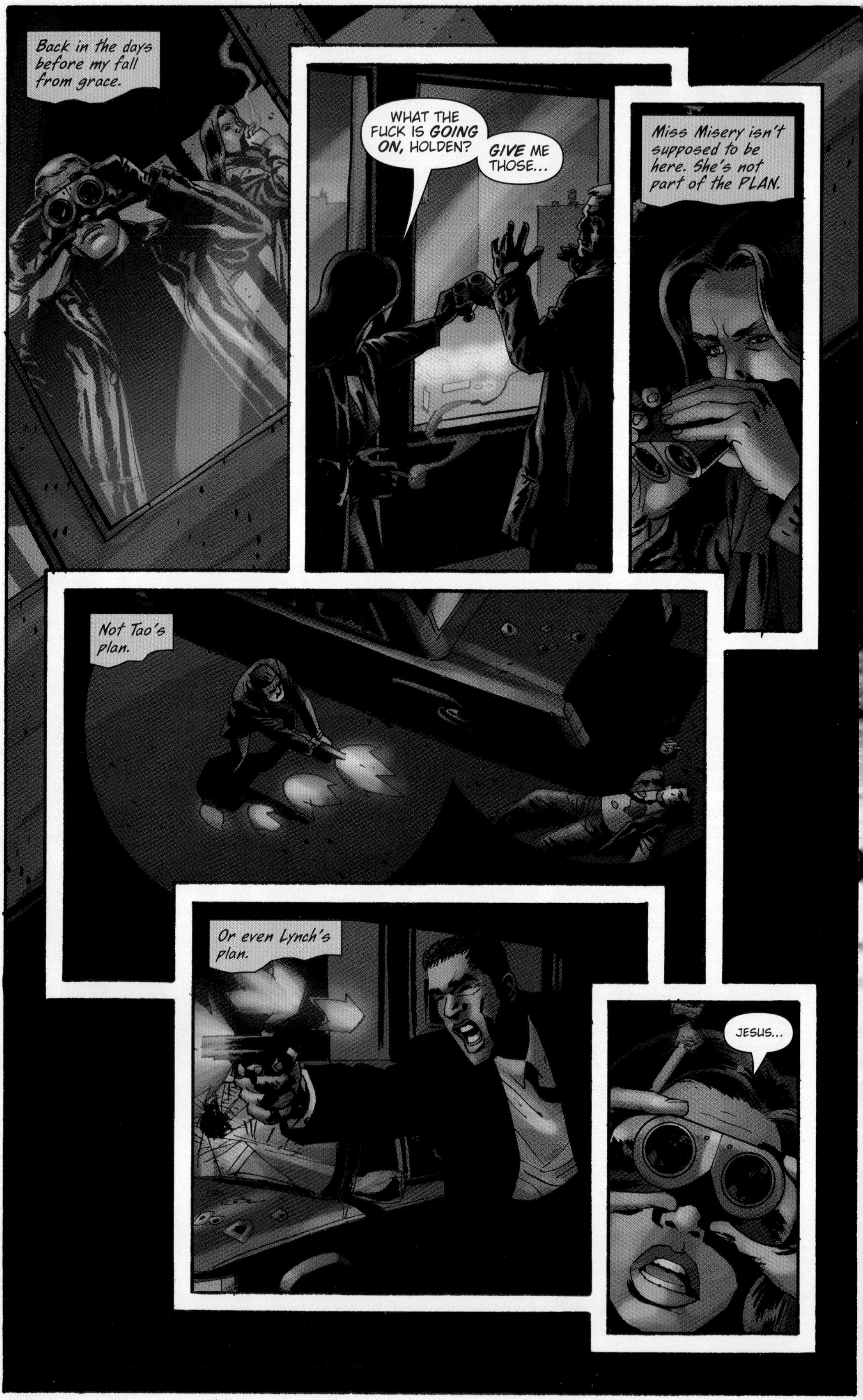
Back in the days before my fall from grace.
WHAT THE FUCK IS GOING ON, HOLDEN?
GIVE ME THOSE...
Miss Misery isn't supposed to be here. She's not part of the PLAN.
Not Tao's plan.
Or even Lynch's plan.
JESUS...

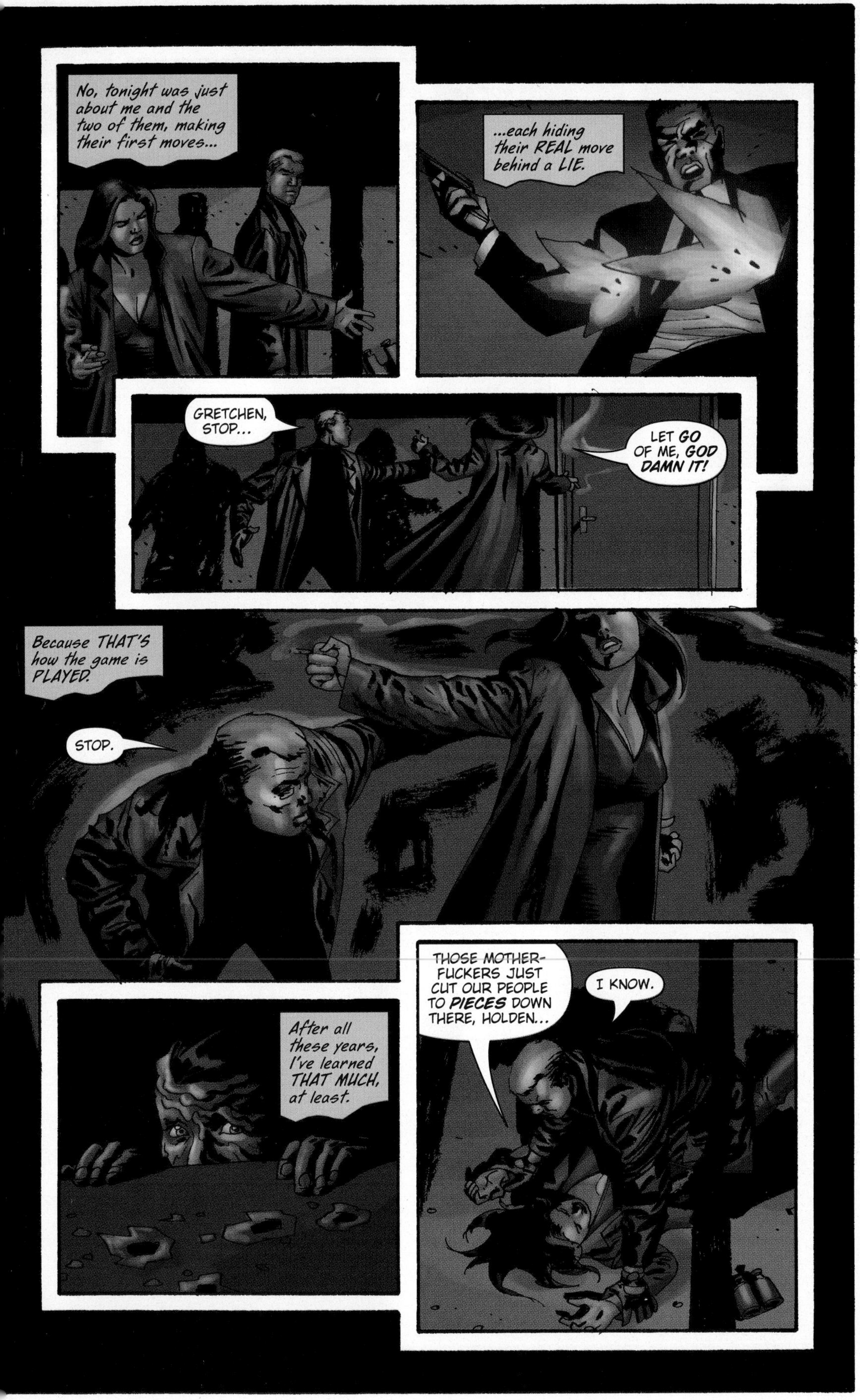
No, tonight was just about me and the two of them, making their first moves...
...each hiding their REAL move behind a LIE.
GRETCHEN, STOP...
LET GO OF ME, GOD DAMN IT!
Because THAT'S how the game is PLAYED.
STOP.
After all these years, I've learned THAT MUCH, at least.
THOSE MOTHER-FUCKERS JUST CUT OUR PEOPLE TO PIECES DOWN THERE, HOLDEN...
I KNOW.

DON'T TELL ME YOU SUDDENLY *GIVE A SHIT* IF SOME OF OUR PEOPLE GET *KILLED?*

THAT'S *NOT* THE POINT.

THE POINT IS THE *LAW* IS KILLING OUR MEN AND WE'RE NOT DOING *ANYTHING* ABOUT IT.

AND THAT *REALLY* BUGS YOU?

I CAN *ALREADY* FEEL THE BILE IN MY THROAT, YOU BASTARD.

HOLDEN, YOU BETTER TELL ME WHAT'S GOING ON HERE RIGHT *NOW...*

...OR I SWEAR TO GOD THE NEXT TIME WE FUCK I WILL *FIND A WAY* TO MAKE YOU FEEL PAIN.

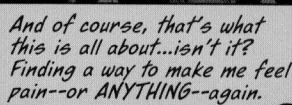

And of course, that's what this is all about...isn't it? Finding a way to make me feel pain--or ANYTHING--again.

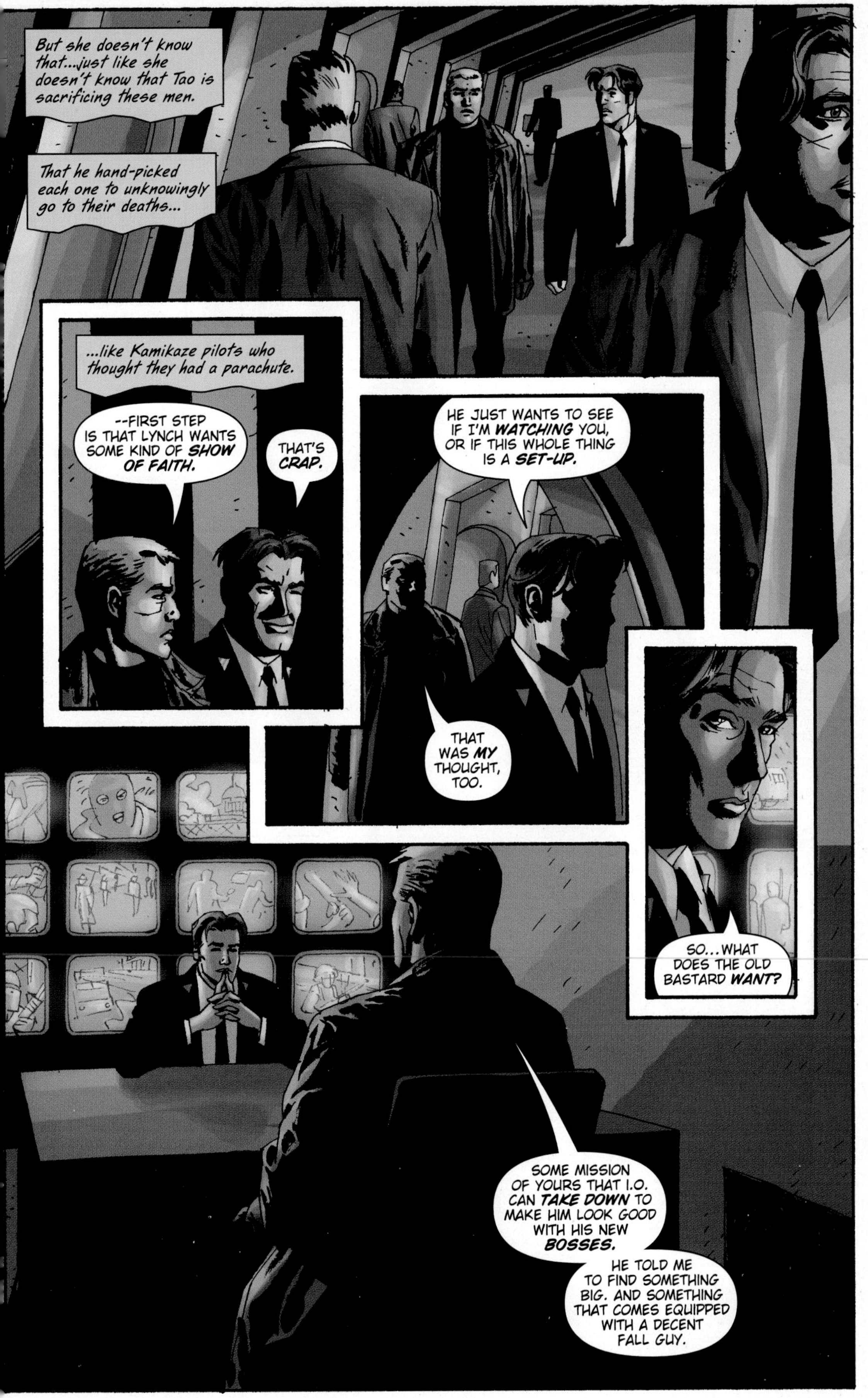
But she doesn't know that...just like she doesn't know that Tao is sacrificing these men.
That he hand-picked each one to unknowingly go to their deaths...
...like Kamikaze pilots who thought they had a parachute.
--FIRST STEP IS THAT LYNCH WANTS SOME KIND OF SHOW OF FAITH.
THAT'S CRAP.
HE JUST WANTS TO SEE IF I'M WATCHING YOU, OR IF THIS WHOLE THING IS A SET-UP.
THAT WAS MY THOUGHT, TOO.
SO...WHAT DOES THE OLD BASTARD WANT?
SOME MISSION OF YOURS THAT I.O. CAN TAKE DOWN TO MAKE HIM LOOK GOOD WITH HIS NEW BOSSES.
HE TOLD ME TO FIND SOMETHING BIG. AND SOMETHING THAT COMES EQUIPPED WITH A DECENT FALL GUY.

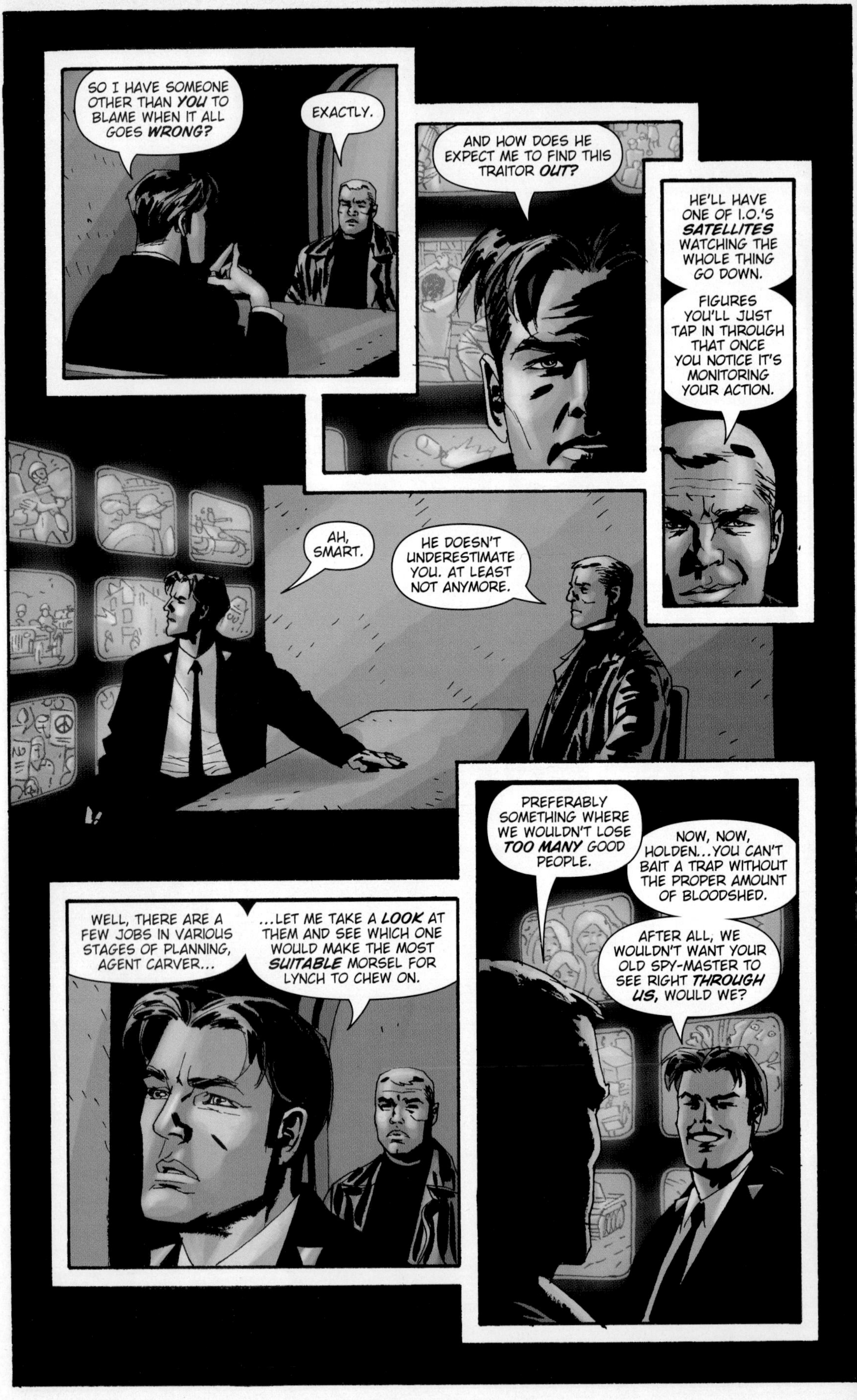
SO I HAVE SOMEONE OTHER THAN YOU TO BLAME WHEN IT ALL GOES WRONG?
EXACTLY.
AND HOW DOES HE EXPECT ME TO FIND THIS TRAITOR OUT?
HE'LL HAVE ONE OF I.O.'S SATELLITES WATCHING THE WHOLE THING GO DOWN.
FIGURES YOU'LL JUST TAP IN THROUGH THAT ONCE YOU NOTICE IT'S MONITORING YOUR ACTION.
AH, SMART.
HE DOESN'T UNDERESTIMATE YOU. AT LEAST NOT ANYMORE.
WELL, THERE ARE A FEW JOBS IN VARIOUS STAGES OF PLANNING, AGENT CARVER...
...LET ME TAKE A LOOK AT THEM AND SEE WHICH ONE WOULD MAKE THE MOST SUITABLE MORSEL FOR LYNCH TO CHEW ON.
PREFERABLY SOMETHING WHERE WE WOULDN'T LOSE TOO MANY GOOD PEOPLE.
NOW, NOW, HOLDEN...YOU CAN'T BAIT A TRAP WITHOUT THE PROPER AMOUNT OF BLOODSHED.
AFTER ALL, WE WOULDN'T WANT YOUR OLD SPY-MASTER TO SEE RIGHT THROUGH US, WOULD WE?

...that actually is ~~ hope--that Lynch ~~ Tao are spending ~~ much time looking ~~ each other...

...that I become invisible.

So, while I spend a few weeks setting up the big show--which is what it is, since the only people not ACTING will be the ones walking into a DEATHTRAP--

--I'm also mulling over MY OWN plan of action.

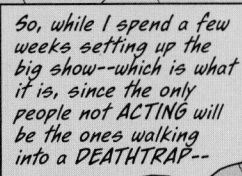

Because the way I see it, even after all I've been through, I'm still just a glorified PAWN at the mercy of two master gamesmen...

...and I've played enough chess to know that pawns rarely make it out alive.

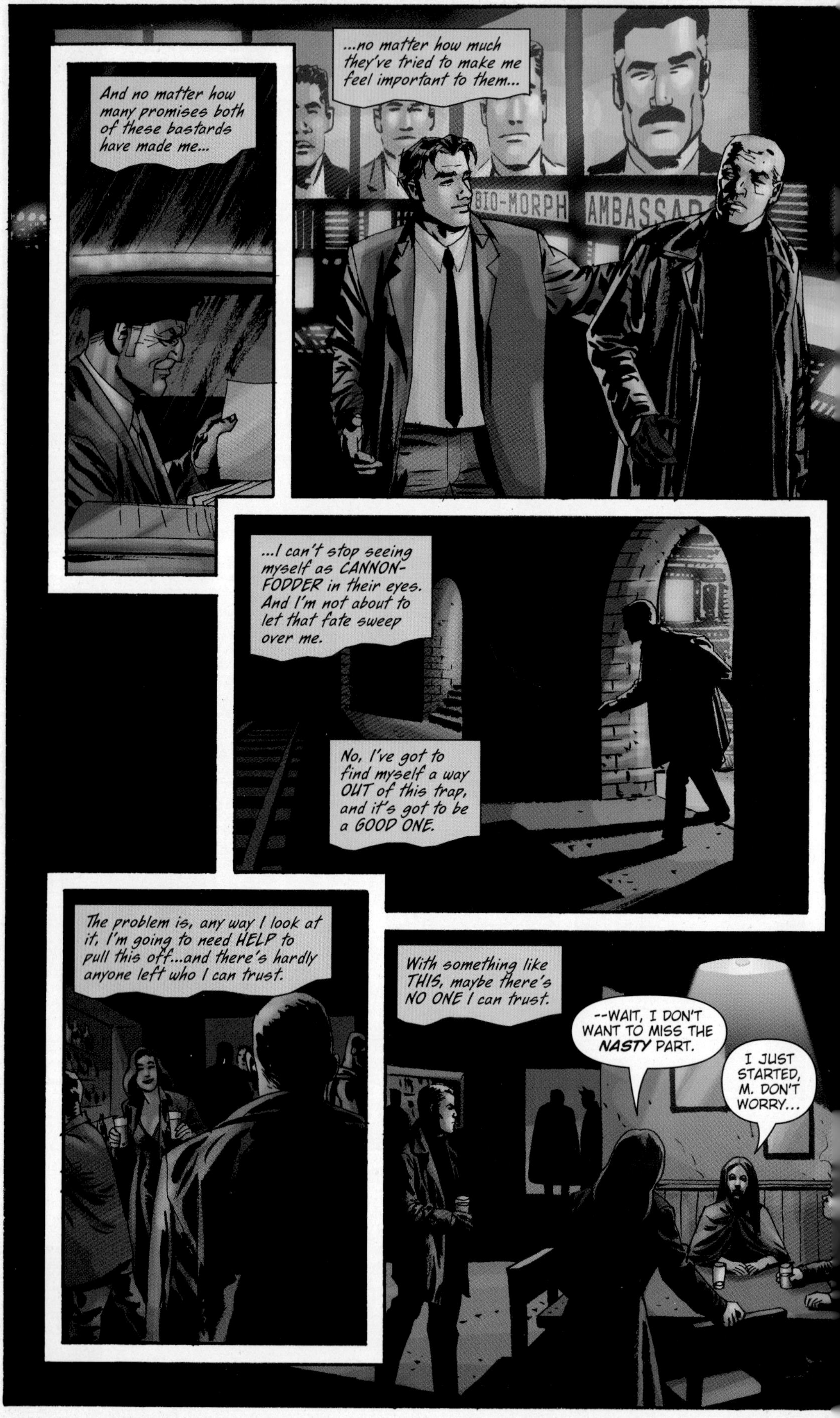

And no matter how many promises both of these bastards have made me...
...no matter how much they've tried to make me feel important to them...
BIO-MORPH
AMBASSAD
...I can't stop seeing myself as CANNON-FODDER in their eyes. And I'm not about to let that fate sweep over me.
No, I've got to find myself a way OUT of this trap, and it's got to be a GOOD ONE.
The problem is, any way I look at it, I'm going to need HELP to pull this off...and there's hardly anyone left who I can trust.
With something like THIS, maybe there's NO ONE I can trust.
--WAIT, I DON'T WANT TO MISS THE NASTY PART.
I JUST STARTED, M. DON'T WORRY...

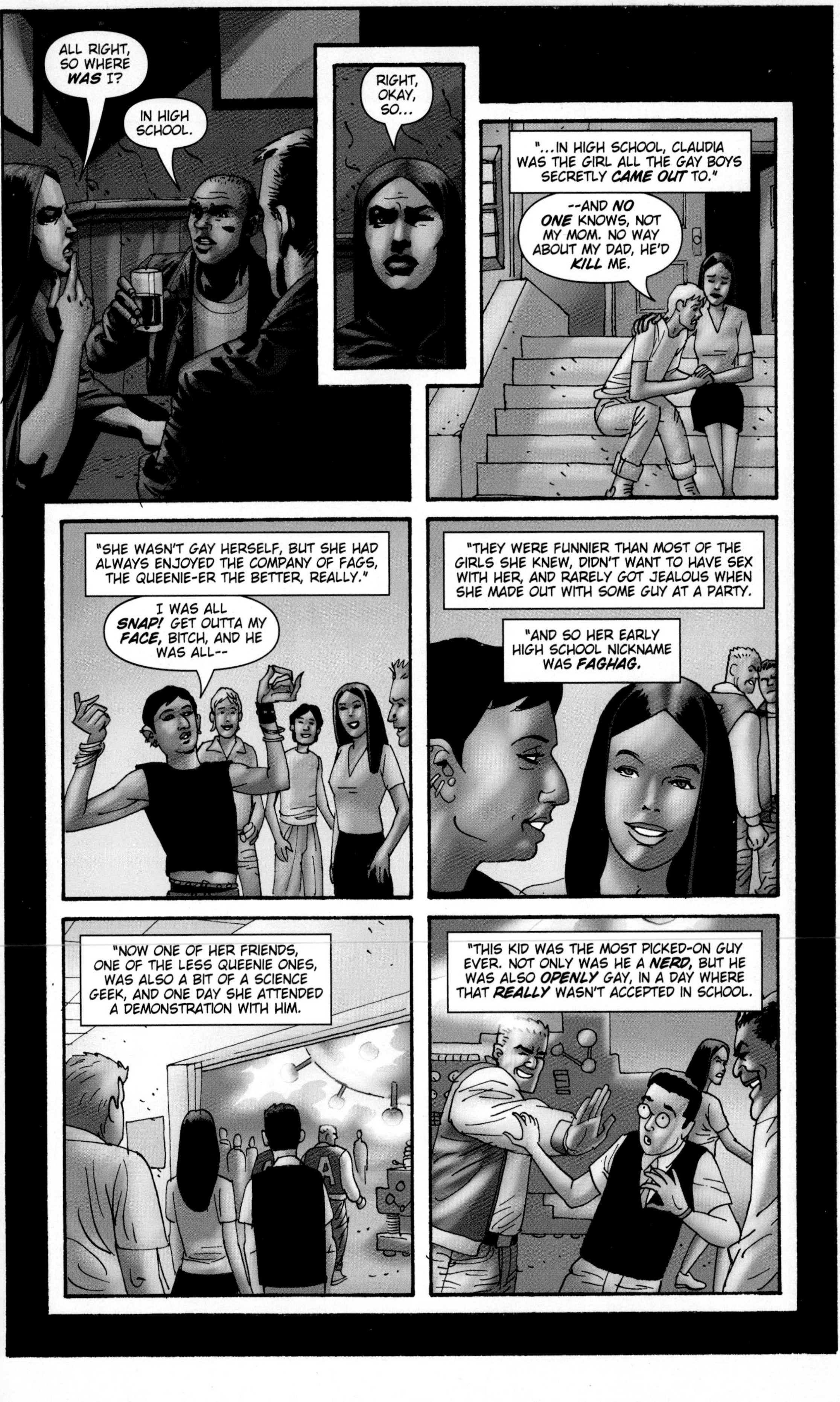

ALL RIGHT, SO WHERE WAS I?
IN HIGH SCHOOL.
RIGHT, OKAY, SO...
"...IN HIGH SCHOOL, CLAUDIA WAS THE GIRL ALL THE GAY BOYS SECRETLY CAME OUT TO."
--AND NO ONE KNOWS, NOT MY MOM. NO WAY ABOUT MY DAD, HE'D KILL ME.
"SHE WASN'T GAY HERSELF, BUT SHE HAD ALWAYS ENJOYED THE COMPANY OF FAGS, THE QUEENIE-ER THE BETTER, REALLY."
I WAS ALL SNAP! GET OUTTA MY FACE, BITCH, AND HE WAS ALL--
"THEY WERE FUNNIER THAN MOST OF THE GIRLS SHE KNEW, DIDN'T WANT TO HAVE SEX WITH HER, AND RARELY GOT JEALOUS WHEN SHE MADE OUT WITH SOME GUY AT A PARTY.
"AND SO HER EARLY HIGH SCHOOL NICKNAME WAS FAGHAG.
"NOW ONE OF HER FRIENDS, ONE OF THE LESS QUEENIE ONES, WAS ALSO A BIT OF A SCIENCE GEEK, AND ONE DAY SHE ATTENDED A DEMONSTRATION WITH HIM.
"THIS KID WAS THE MOST PICKED-ON GUY EVER. NOT ONLY WAS HE A NERD, BUT HE WAS ALSO OPENLY GAY, IN A DAY WHERE THAT REALLY WASN'T ACCEPTED IN SCHOOL.

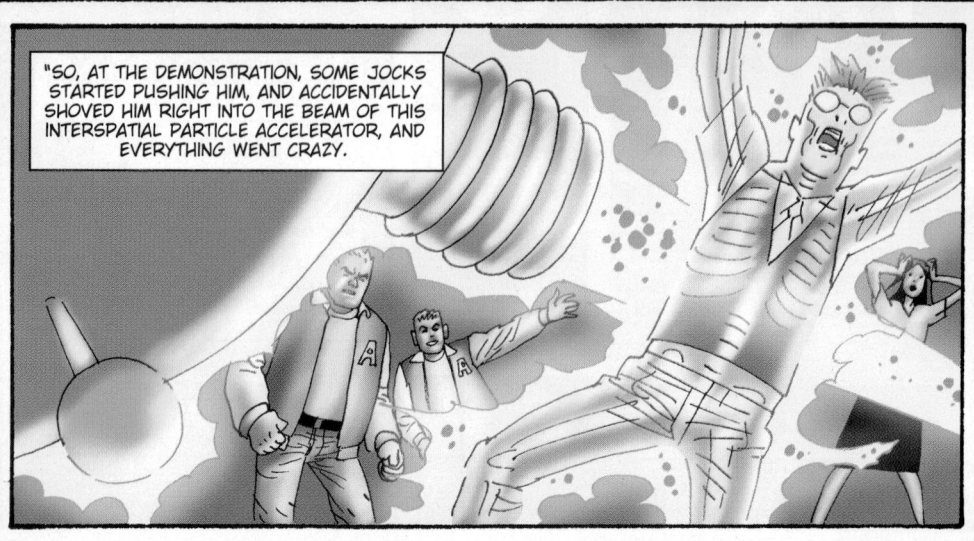

"SO, AT THE DEMONSTRATION, SOME JOCKS STARTED PUSHING HIM, AND ACCIDENTALLY SHOVED HIM RIGHT INTO THE BEAM OF THIS INTERSPATIAL PARTICLE ACCELERATOR, AND EVERYTHING WENT CRAZY.

"HER POOR FRIEND WAS *IRRADIATED* OR SOMETHING. SHE NEVER UNDER-STOOD EXACTLY WHAT HAPPENED.

"BUT IN HIS DYING MOMENT, AS HE FLAILED FOR LIFE, HIS *TEETH* RIPPED RIGHT INTO HER NECK."

WAIT. YOU WERE *BITTEN* BY AN *RADIOACTIVE HOMO*--?

CAN I PLEASE TELL THE STORY *MY* WAY?

OH, YOU *GO*, GIRL...

"AND SUDDENLY, SHE FELT ENERGY RUNNING THROUGH HER, AND *ANGER*. AT ALL THE BASTARDS SHE'D SEEN DUMP ALL OVER HER FRIENDS FOR YEARS.

"WHO'D NOW KILLED ONE OF THEM.

"BEFORE SHE KNEW WHAT WAS HAPPENING, SHE'D KILLED HALF THE FOOTBALL TEAM...

...AND WAS FORCING THE OTHER HALF (ON THREAT OF DEATH) TO *DO* EACH OTHER ON THE FLOOR OF THE LAB.

"CLAUDIA LAUGHED WITH THE RUSH OF POWER AND THE SUDDEN FEAR EVERYONE AROUND HER WAS IMMOBILIZED WITH...

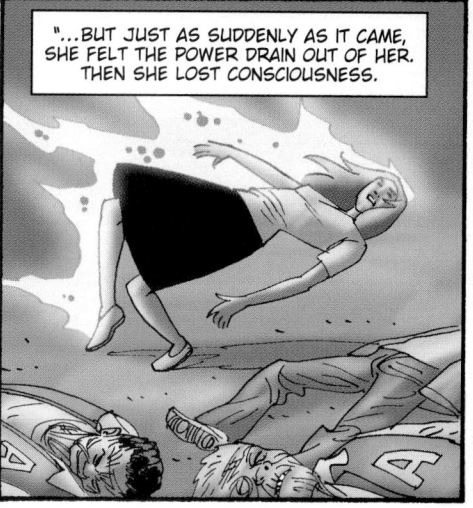

"...BUT JUST AS SUDDENLY AS IT CAME, SHE FELT THE POWER DRAIN OUT OF HER. THEN SHE LOST CONSCIOUSNESS.

"WHEN SHE WOKE UP, SHE WAS IN A LAB SOMEWHERE, STRAPPED TO A TABLE, AND A LOT OF MEN IN WHITE COATS WERE EXAMINING HER.

"SHE WAS TERRIFIED, BUT THEN SOME-THING IN THAT ROOM LEAPT OUT AT HER-- THE ORDERLY IN THE CORNER WAS *GAY*, SHE JUST *KNEW IT* SOMEHOW.

"AND WHEN THAT ORDERLY CAME NEAR HER, SHE REACHED OUT FOR HIM...TOUCHED HIM.

"AND SUDDENLY SHE FELT THE POWER RUSHING THROUGH HER AGAIN, AND SHE BROKE FREE OF HER BONDS.

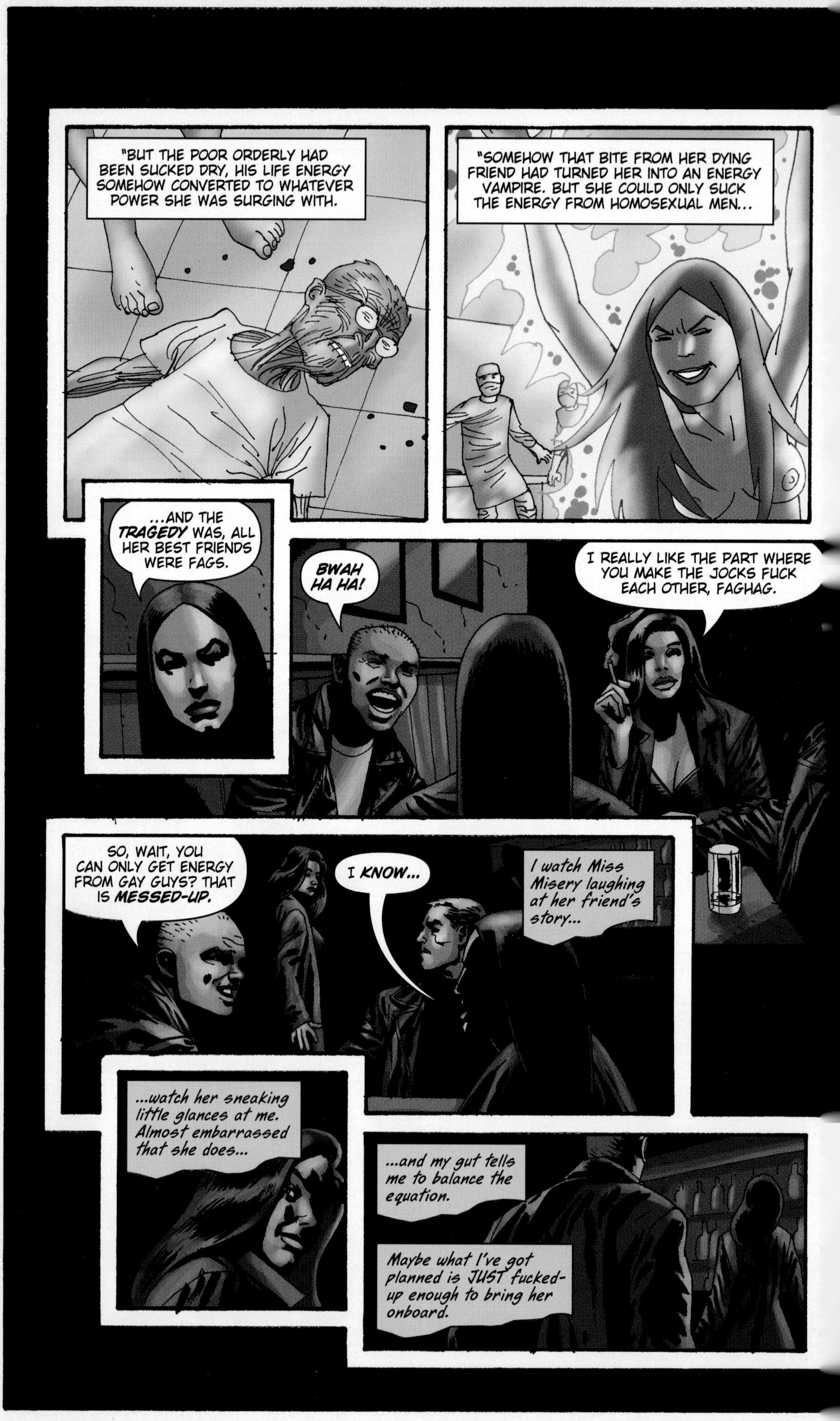
"BUT THE POOR ORDERLY HAD BEEN SUCKED DRY, HIS LIFE ENERGY SOMEHOW CONVERTED TO WHATEVER POWER SHE WAS SURGING WITH.
"SOMEHOW THAT BITE FROM HER DYING FRIEND HAD TURNED HER INTO AN ENERGY VAMPIRE. BUT SHE COULD ONLY SUCK THE ENERGY FROM HOMOSEXUAL MEN...
...AND THE TRAGEDY WAS, ALL HER BEST FRIENDS WERE FAGS.
BWAH HA HA!
I REALLY LIKE THE PART WHERE YOU MAKE THE JOCKS FUCK EACH OTHER, FAGHAG.
SO, WAIT, YOU CAN ONLY GET ENERGY FROM GAY GUYS? THAT IS MESSED-UP.
I KNOW...
I watch Miss Misery laughing at her friend's story...
...watch her sneaking little glances at me. Almost embarrassed that she does...
...and my gut tells me to balance the equation.
Maybe what I've got planned is JUST fucked-up enough to bring her onboard.

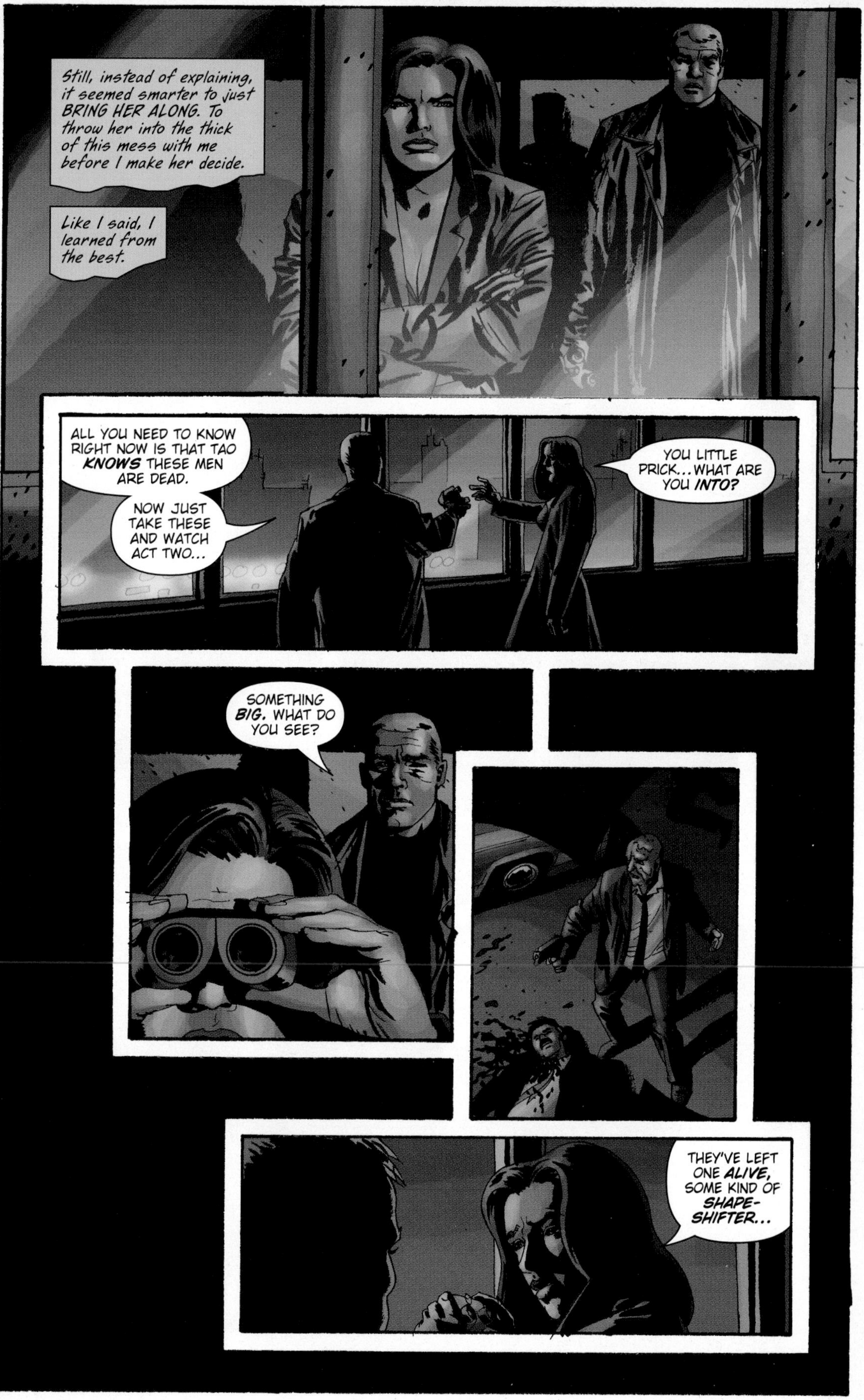
Still, instead of explaining, it seemed smarter to just BRING HER ALONG. To throw her into the thick of this mess with me before I make her decide.
Like I said, I learned from the best.
ALL YOU NEED TO KNOW RIGHT NOW IS THAT TAO KNOWS THESE MEN ARE DEAD.
NOW JUST TAKE THESE AND WATCH ACT TWO...
YOU LITTLE PRICK... WHAT ARE YOU INTO?
SOMETHING BIG. WHAT DO YOU SEE?
THEY'VE LEFT ONE ALIVE, SOME KIND OF SHAPE-SHIFTER...

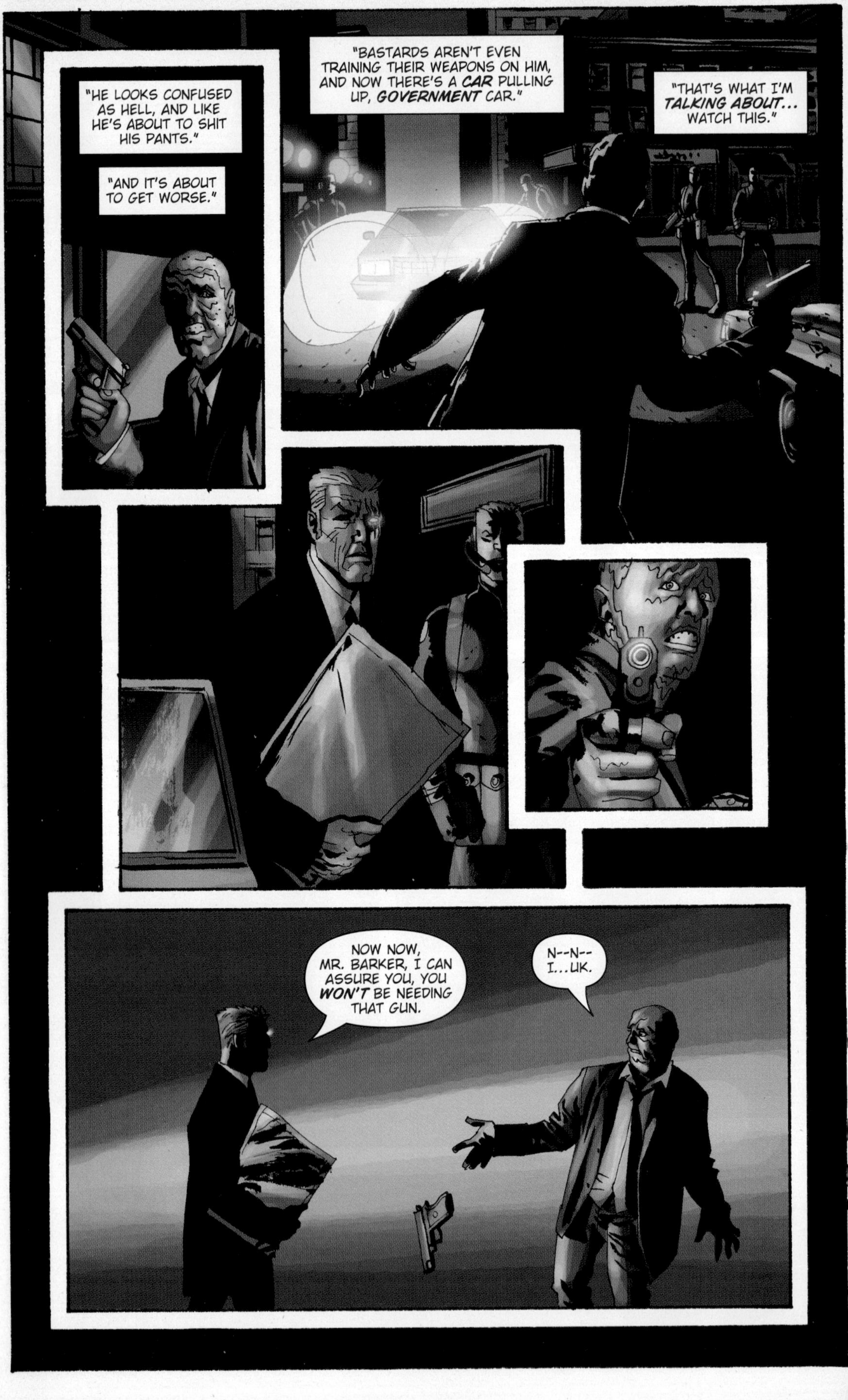
"HE LOOKS CONFUSED AS HELL, AND LIKE HE'S ABOUT TO SHIT HIS PANTS."
"AND IT'S ABOUT TO GET WORSE."
"BASTARDS AREN'T EVEN TRAINING THEIR WEAPONS ON HIM, AND NOW THERE'S A CAR PULLING UP, GOVERNMENT CAR."
"THAT'S WHAT I'M TALKING ABOUT... WATCH THIS."
NOW NOW, MR. BARKER, I CAN ASSURE YOU, YOU WON'T BE NEEDING THAT GUN.
N--N-- I...UK.

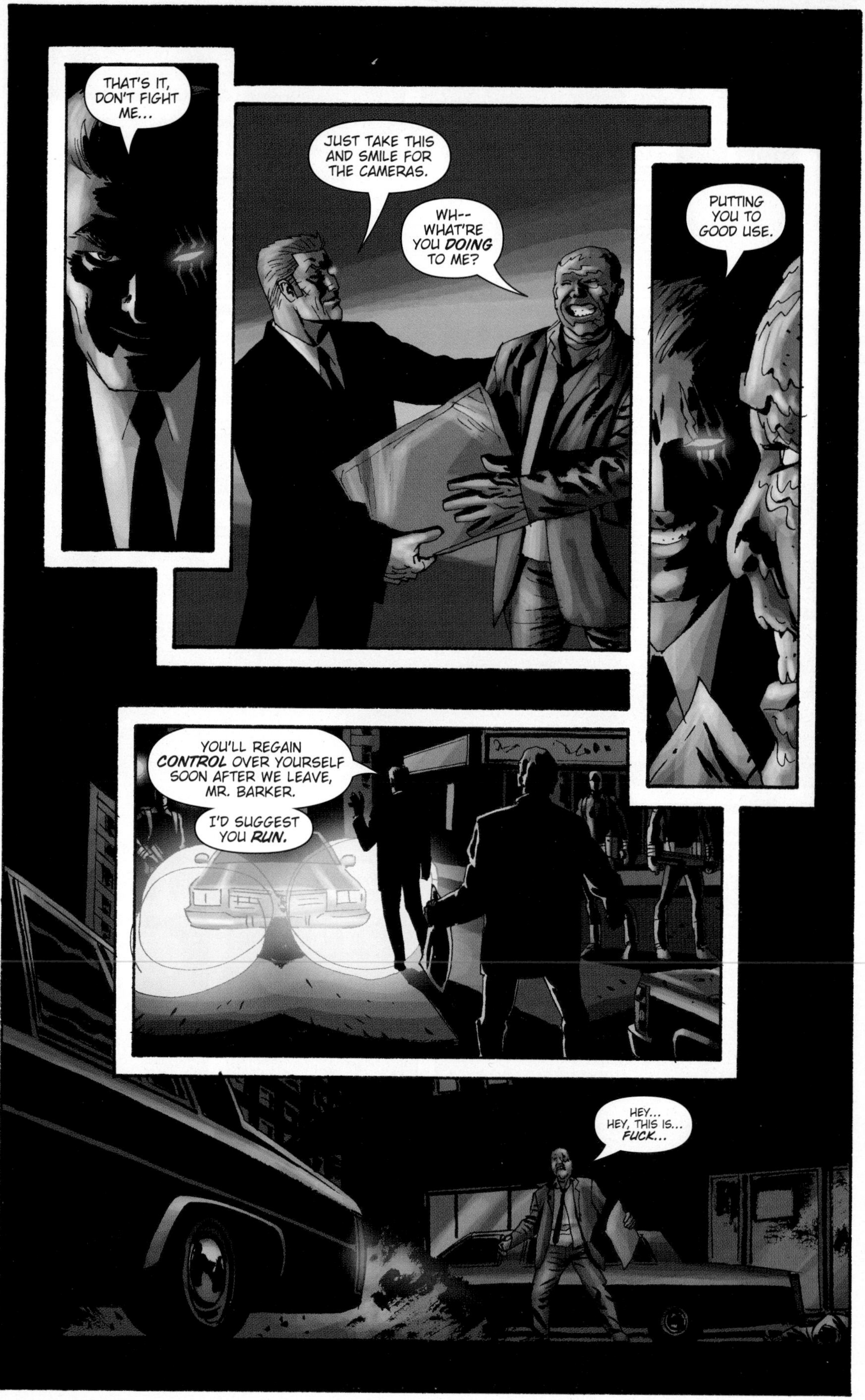
THAT'S IT, DON'T FIGHT ME...
JUST TAKE THIS AND SMILE FOR THE CAMERAS.
WH-- WHAT'RE YOU DOING TO ME?
PUTTING YOU TO GOOD USE.
YOU'LL REGAIN CONTROL OVER YOURSELF SOON AFTER WE LEAVE, MR. BARKER.
I'D SUGGEST YOU RUN.
HEY... HEY, THIS IS... FUCK...

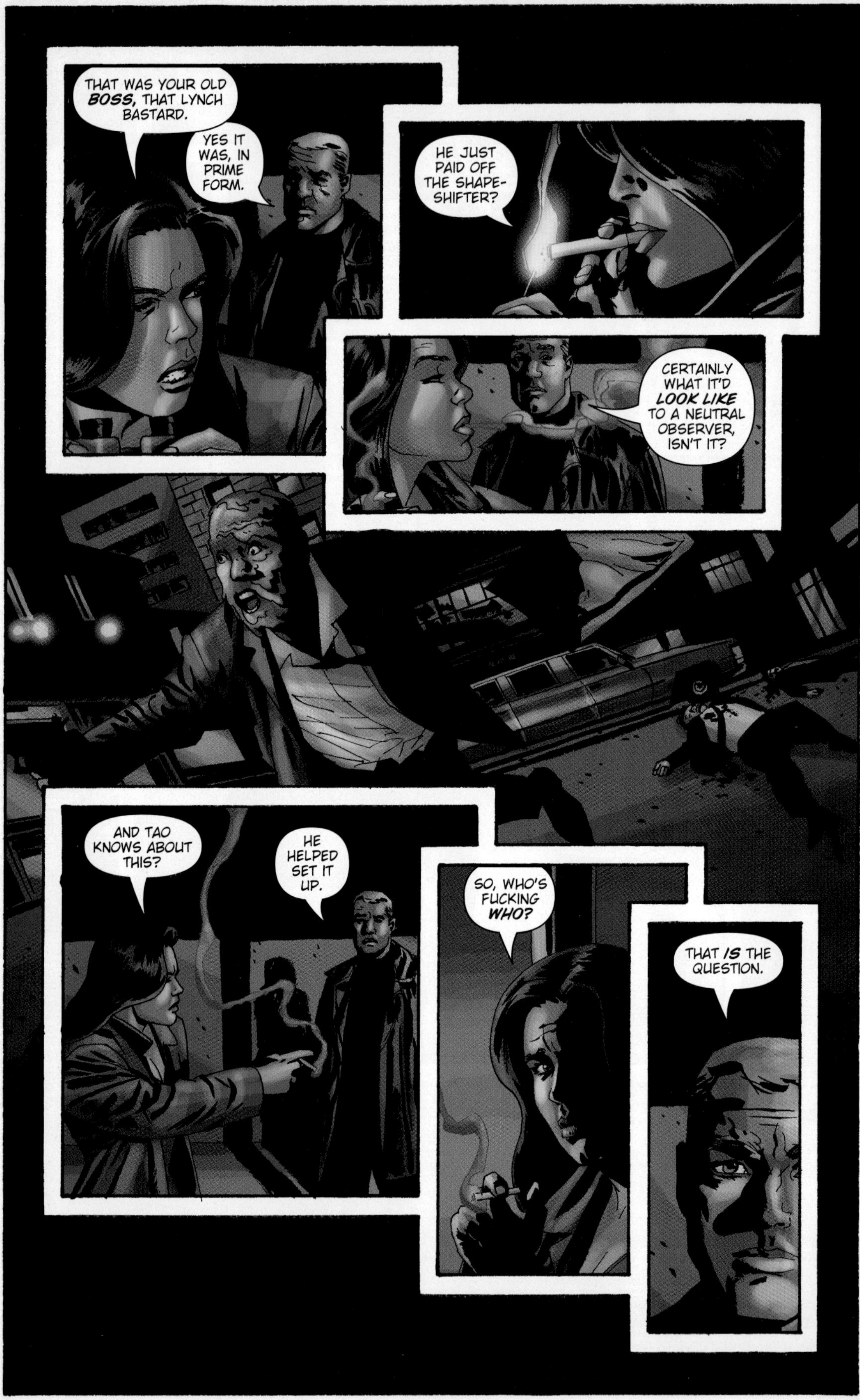
THAT WAS YOUR OLD BOSS, THAT LYNCH BASTARD.
YES IT WAS, IN PRIME FORM.
HE JUST PAID OFF THE SHAPE-SHIFTER?
CERTAINLY WHAT IT'D LOOK LIKE TO A NEUTRAL OBSERVER, ISN'T IT?
AND TAO KNOWS ABOUT THIS?
HE HELPED SET IT UP.
SO, WHO'S FUCKING WHO?
THAT IS THE QUESTION.

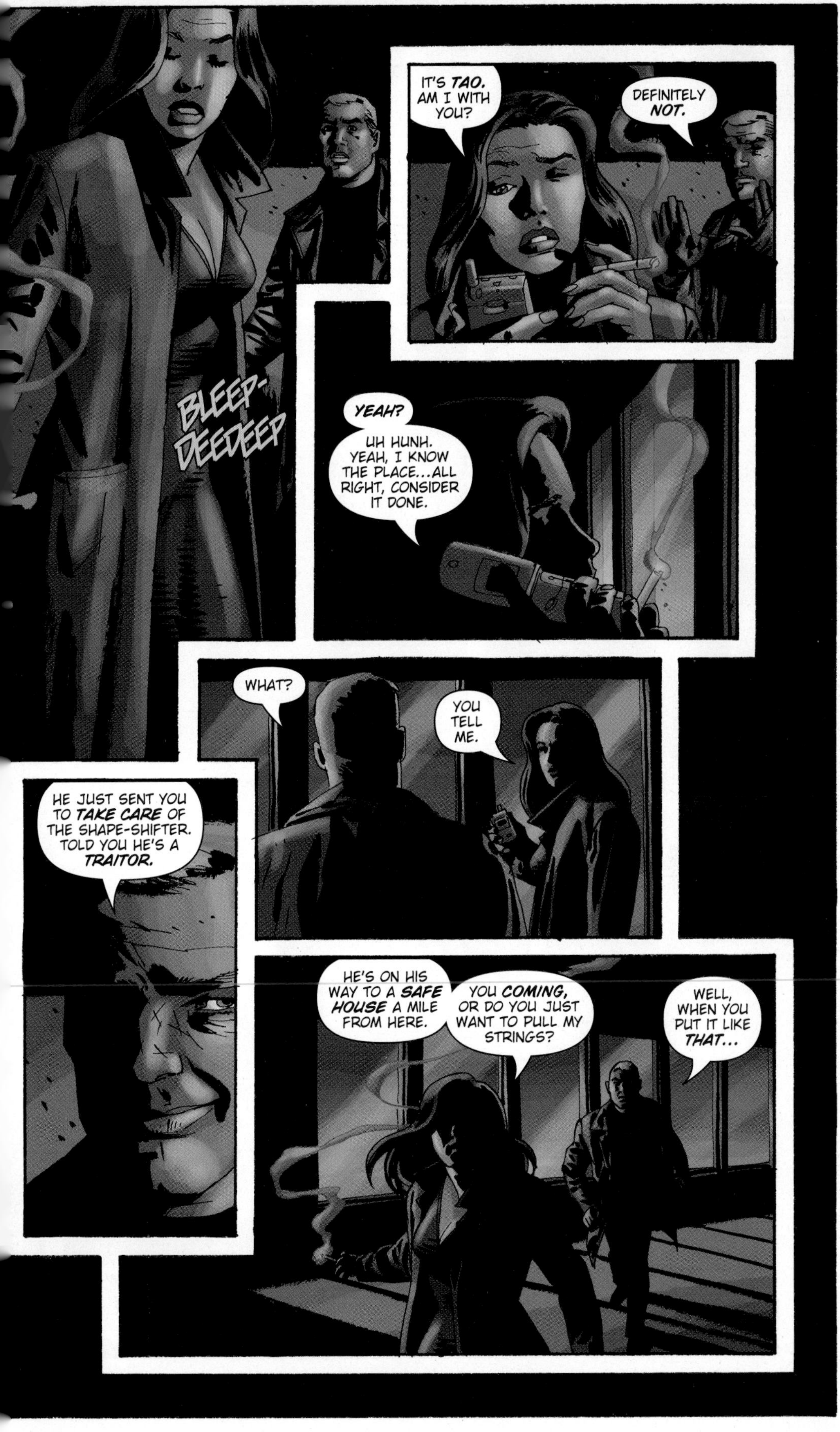
BLEEP-DEEDEEP
IT'S TAO. AM I WITH YOU?
DEFINITELY NOT.
YEAH?
UH HUNH. YEAH, I KNOW THE PLACE...ALL RIGHT, CONSIDER IT DONE.
WHAT?
YOU TELL ME.
HE JUST SENT YOU TO TAKE CARE OF THE SHAPE-SHIFTER. TOLD YOU HE'S A TRAITOR.
HE'S ON HIS WAY TO A SAFE HOUSE A MILE FROM HERE.
YOU COMING, OR DO YOU JUST WANT TO PULL MY STRINGS?
WELL, WHEN YOU PUT IT LIKE THAT...

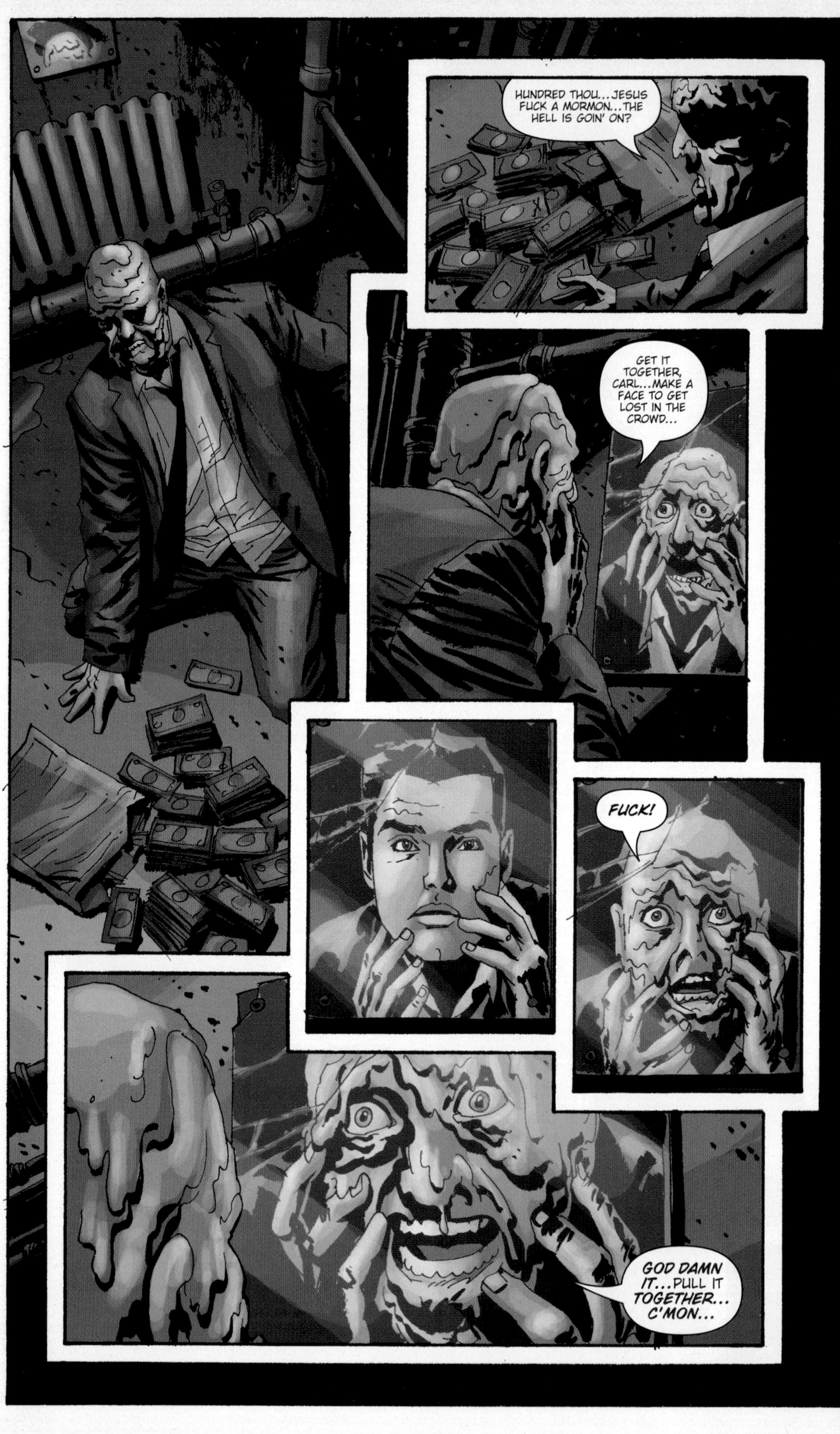
HUNDRED THOU...JESUS FUCK A MORMON...THE HELL IS GOIN' ON?
GET IT TOGETHER, CARL...MAKE A FACE TO GET LOST IN THE CROWD...
FUCK!
GOD DAMN IT...PULL IT TOGETHER... C'MON...

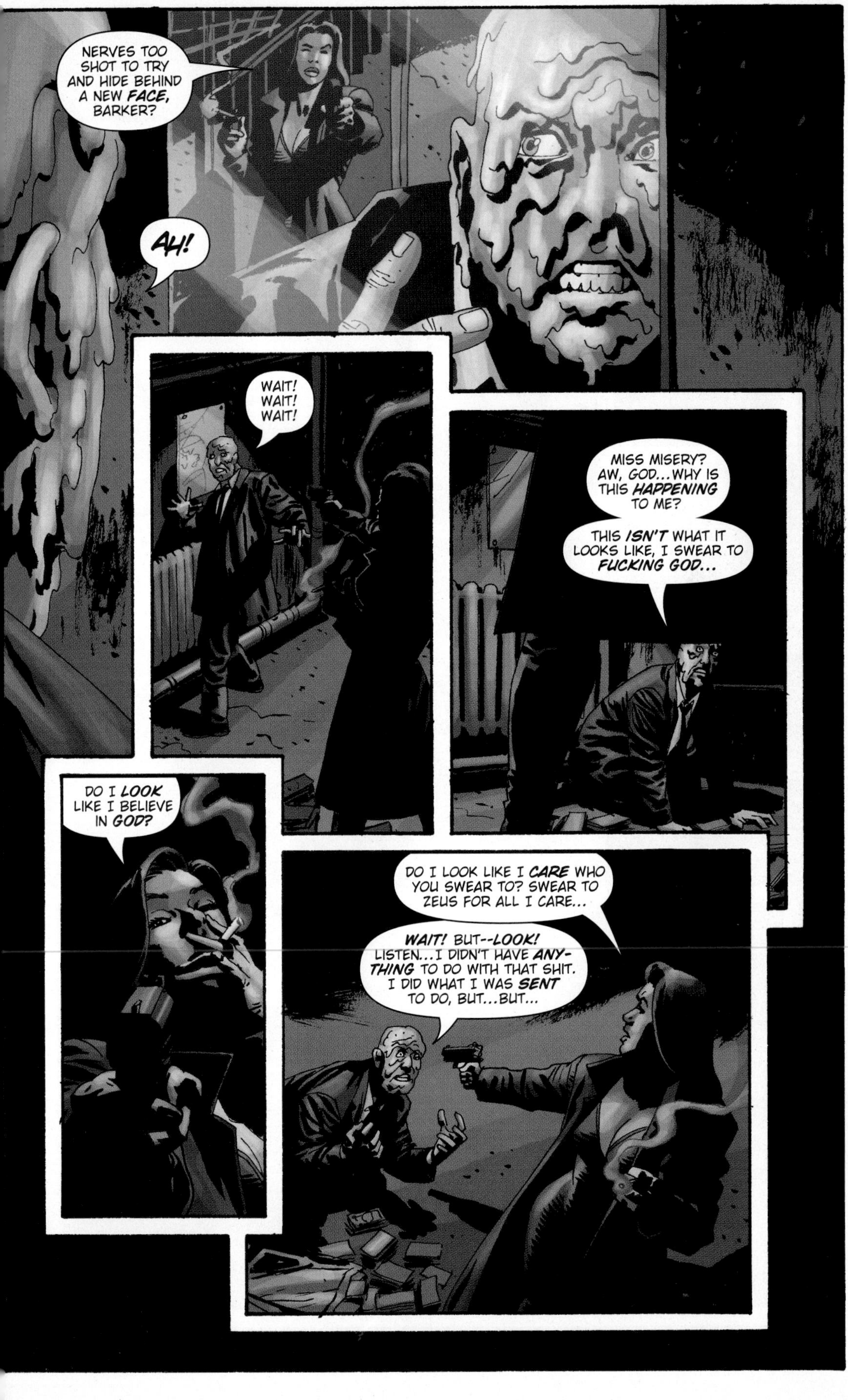
NERVES TOO SHOT TO TRY AND HIDE BEHIND A NEW FACE, BARKER?
AH!
WAIT! WAIT! WAIT!
MISS MISERY? AW, GOD...WHY IS THIS HAPPENING TO ME?
THIS ISN'T WHAT IT LOOKS LIKE, I SWEAR TO FUCKING GOD...
DO I LOOK LIKE I BELIEVE IN GOD?
DO I LOOK LIKE I CARE WHO YOU SWEAR TO? SWEAR TO ZEUS FOR ALL I CARE...
WAIT! BUT--LOOK! LISTEN...I DIDN'T HAVE ANYTHING TO DO WITH THAT SHIT. I DID WHAT I WAS SENT TO DO, BUT...BUT...

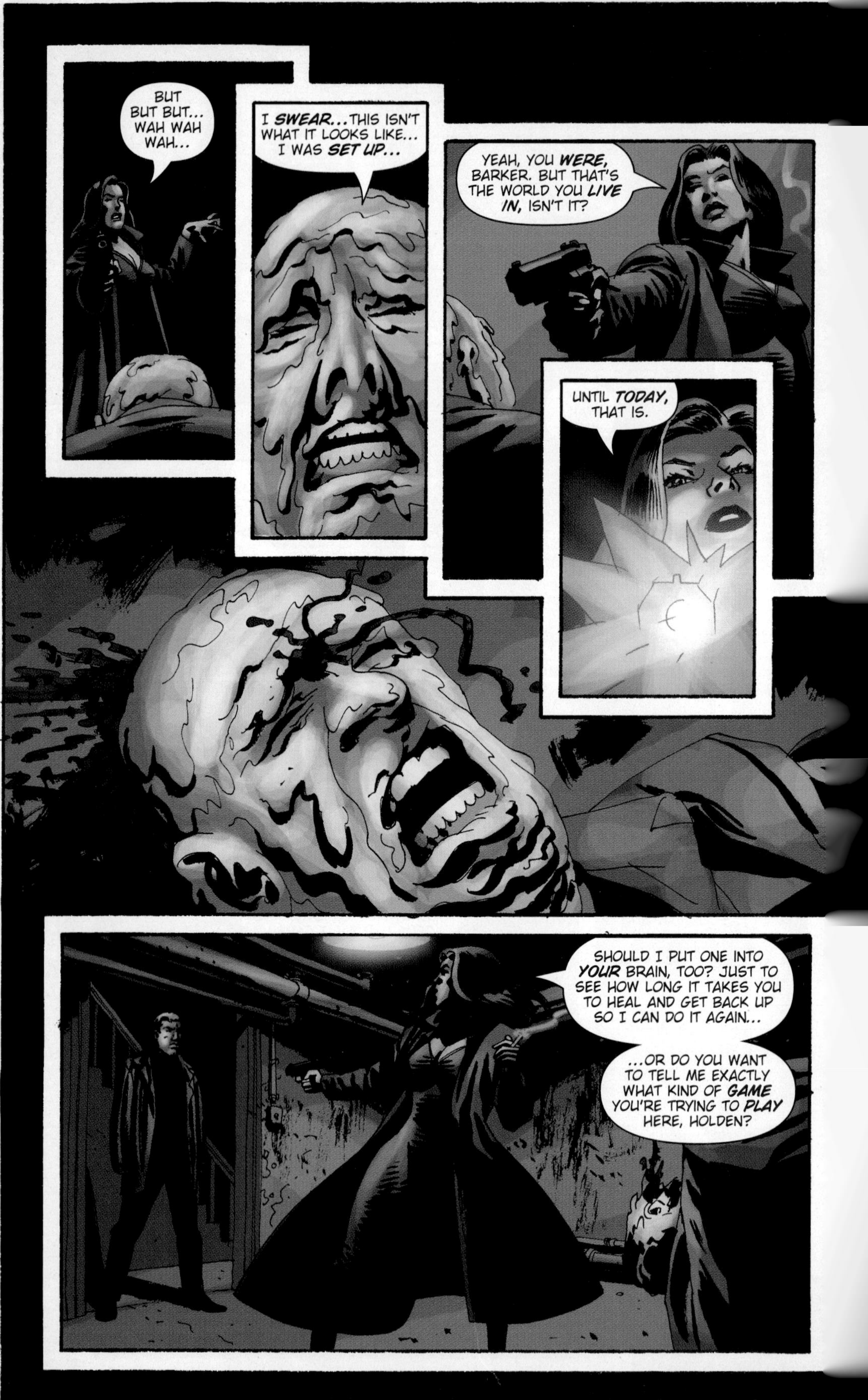
BUT BUT BUT... WAH WAH WAH...
I SWEAR...THIS ISN'T WHAT IT LOOKS LIKE... I WAS SET UP...
YEAH, YOU WERE, BARKER. BUT THAT'S THE WORLD YOU LIVE IN, ISN'T IT?
UNTIL TODAY, THAT IS.
SHOULD I PUT ONE INTO YOUR BRAIN, TOO? JUST TO SEE HOW LONG IT TAKES YOU TO HEAL AND GET BACK UP SO I CAN DO IT AGAIN...
...OR DO YOU WANT TO TELL ME EXACTLY WHAT KIND OF GAME YOU'RE TRYING TO PLAY HERE, HOLDEN?

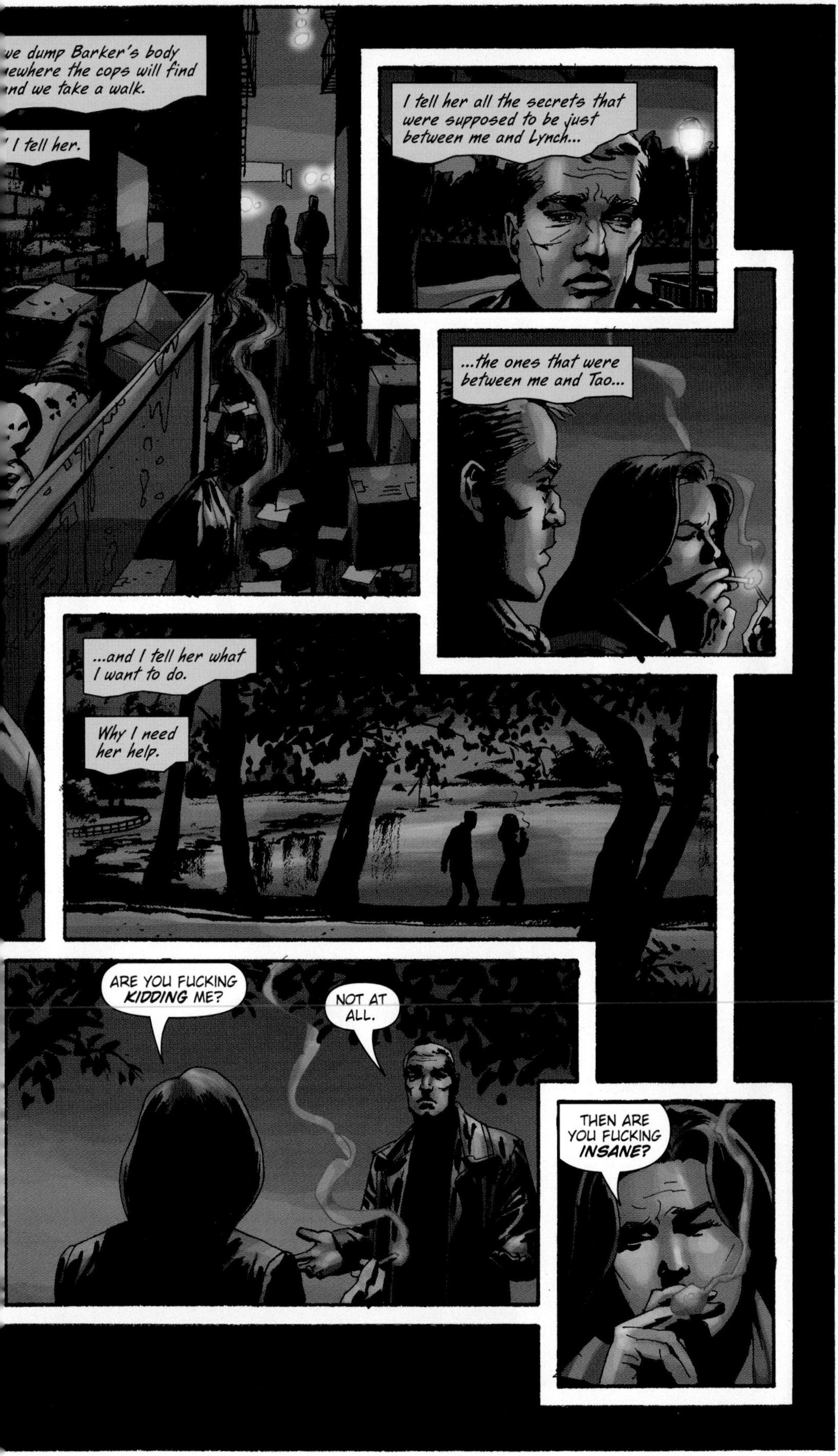
we dump Barker's body
ewhere the cops will find
nd we take a walk.
I tell her.
I tell her all the secrets that were supposed to be just between me and Lynch...
...the ones that were between me and Tao...
...and I tell her what I want to do.
Why I need her help.
ARE YOU FUCKING *KIDDING* ME?
NOT AT ALL.
THEN ARE YOU FUCKING *INSANE?*

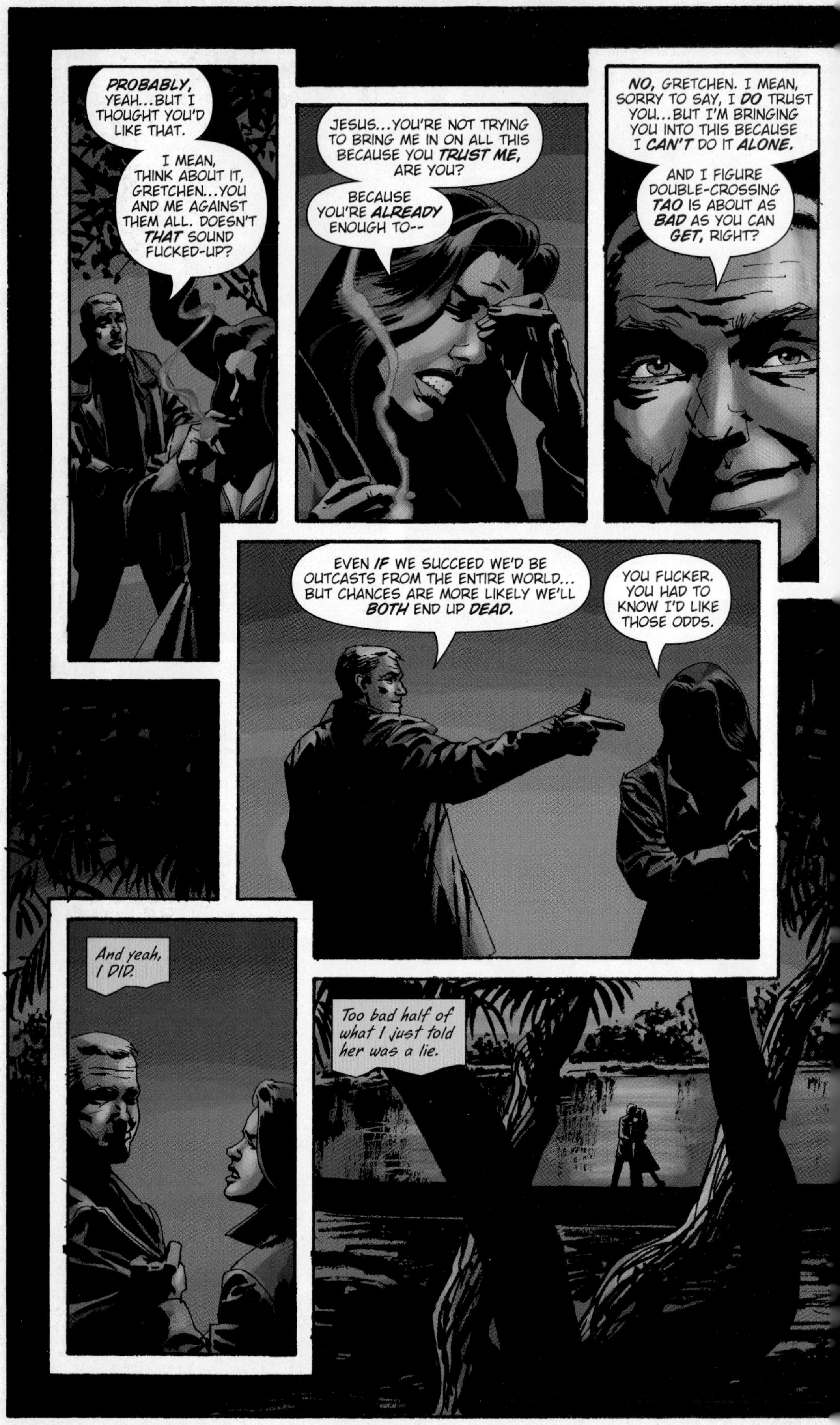
PROBABLY, YEAH...BUT I THOUGHT YOU'D LIKE THAT.
I MEAN, THINK ABOUT IT, GRETCHEN...YOU AND ME AGAINST THEM ALL. DOESN'T THAT SOUND FUCKED-UP?
JESUS...YOU'RE NOT TRYING TO BRING ME IN ON ALL THIS BECAUSE YOU TRUST ME, ARE YOU?
BECAUSE YOU'RE ALREADY ENOUGH TO--
NO, GRETCHEN. I MEAN, SORRY TO SAY, I DO TRUST YOU...BUT I'M BRINGING YOU INTO THIS BECAUSE I CAN'T DO IT ALONE.
AND I FIGURE DOUBLE-CROSSING TAO IS ABOUT AS BAD AS YOU CAN GET, RIGHT?
EVEN IF WE SUCCEED WE'D BE OUTCASTS FROM THE ENTIRE WORLD... BUT CHANCES ARE MORE LIKELY WE'LL BOTH END UP DEAD.
YOU FUCKER. YOU HAD TO KNOW I'D LIKE THOSE ODDS.
And yeah, I DID.
Too bad half of what I just told her was a lie.

sleeper

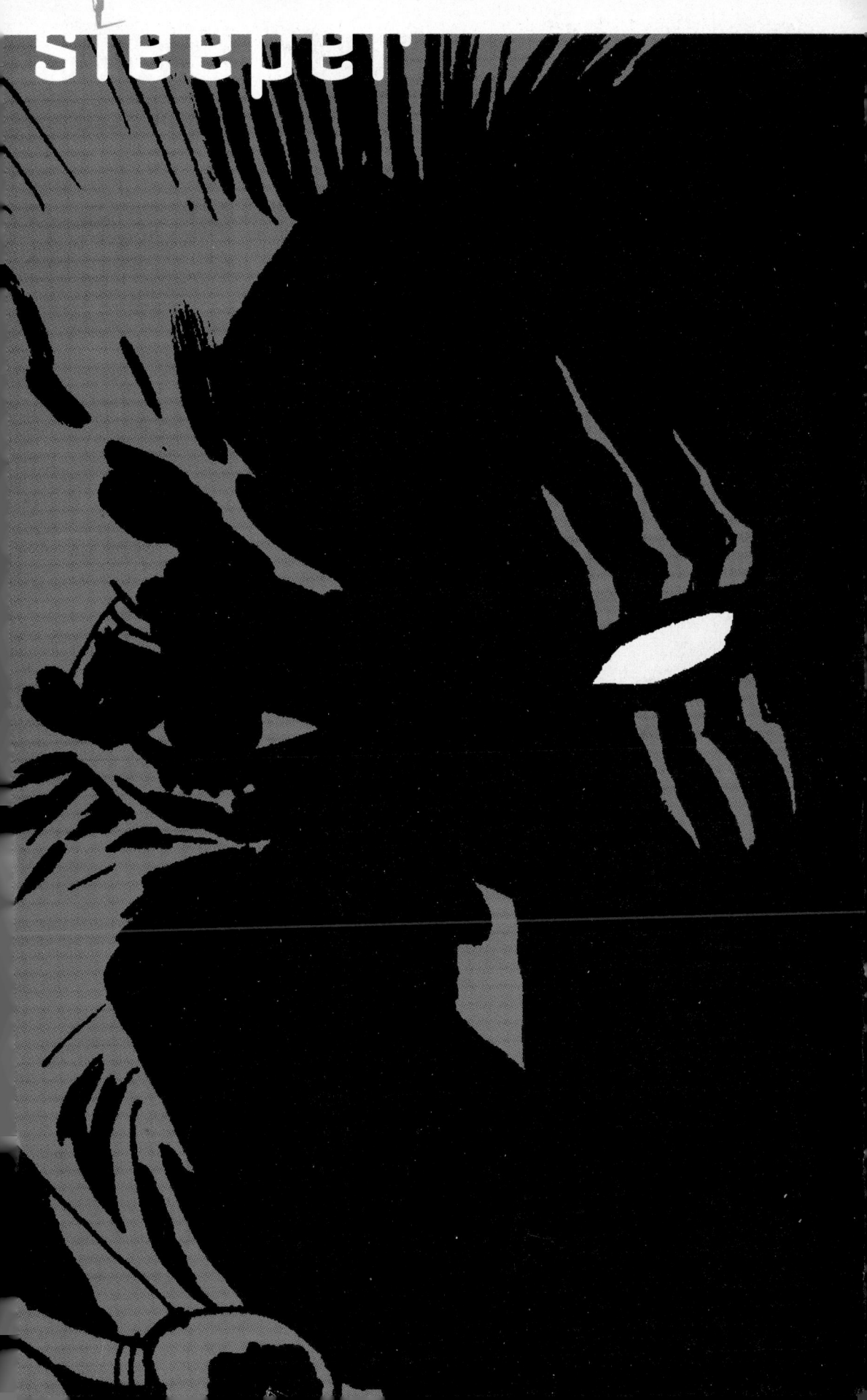

sleeper
out in the cold
Ed Brubaker Sean Phillips

SLEEPER BOOKS 1 & 2
Brubaker * Phillips

COLE CASH IS THE GRIFTER
STARRING IN
POINT BLANK
ED BRUBAKER COLIN WILSON

POINT BLANK
Brubaker * Wilson

WILDCATS
VICIOUS CIRCLES
JOE CASEY • SEAN PHILLIPS

WILDCATS V2 BOOKS 1-4
Casey * Phillips

THE AUTHORITY
JOHN RIDLEY BEN OLIVER
HUMAN ON THE INSIDE

THE AUTHORITY:
HUMAN ON THE INSIDE
Ridley * Oliver

COUP D'ETAT
ED BRUBAKER JOE CASEY ROBBIE MORRISON MICAH WRIGHT
JIM LEE CARLOS D'ANDA ALÉ GARZA WHILCE PORTACIO

COUP D'ETAT
Various Writers and Artists

backlist

WARREN ELLIS
GLOBAL FREQUENCY
DETONATION RADIO

GLOBAL FREQUENCY Books 1 & 2
Ellis * Various

Search the Graphic Novels section of wildstorm.com for art and info on every one of our hundreds of books!

To find more collected editions and monthly comic books from WildStorm and DC Comics, call 1-888-comic book for the nearest comic shop or go to your local bookstore.